# The Hypercontemporary Novel in Portugal

# The Hypercontemporary Novel in Portugal

*Fictional Aesthetics and Memory after Postmodernism*

Edited by Paulo de Medeiros and
Ana Paula Arnaut

BLOOMSBURY ACADEMIC
NEW YORK • LONDON • OXFORD • NEW DELHI • SYDNEY

BLOOMSBURY ACADEMIC
Bloomsbury Publishing Inc, 1359 Broadway, New York, NY 10018, USA
Bloomsbury Publishing Plc, 50 Bedford Square, London, WC1B 3DP, UK
Bloomsbury Publishing Ireland, 29 Earlsfort Terrace, Dublin 2, D02 AY28, Ireland

BLOOMSBURY, BLOOMSBURY ACADEMIC and the Diana logo
are trademarks of Bloomsbury Publishing Plc

First published in the United States of America 2024
Paperback edition published 2025

Copyright © Paulo de Medeiros and Ana Paula Arnaut, 2024

Each chapter © of Contributors

For legal purposes the Acknowledgements on p. xi constitute
an extension of this copyright page.

Cover design by Eleanor Rose
Cover image: Lisboa, Portugal © Artur Carvalho / Getty Images

All rights reserved. No part of this publication may be: i) reproduced or transmitted in any
form, electronic or mechanical, including photocopying, recording or by means of any
information storage or retrieval system without prior permission in writing from the publishers;
or ii) used or reproduced in any way for the training, development or operation of artificial
intelligence (AI) technologies, including generative AI technologies. The rights holders expressly
reserve this publication from the text and data mining exception as per Article 4(3) of the
Digital Single Market Directive (EU) 2019/790.

Bloomsbury Publishing Inc does not have any control over, or responsibility for,
any third-party websites referred to or in this book. All internet addresses given in
this book were correct at the time of going to press. The author and publisher regret
any inconvenience caused if addresses have changed or sites have ceased
to exist, but can accept no responsibility for any such changes.

Library of Congress Cataloging-in-Publication Data
Names: Medeiros, Paulo de, 1958- editor. | Arnaut, Ana Paula, editor.
Title: The hypercontemporary novel in Portugal : fictional aesthetics and
memory after postmodernism / edited by Paulo de Medeiros and Ana Paula Arnaut.
Description: New York : Bloomsbury Academic, 2024. | Includes bibliographical references. |
Summary: "The first volume of critical essays on the contemporary
Portuguese novel in English, this book theorizes the concept of
the hypercontemporary as a way of reading the novel after
its postmodern period"– Provided by publisher.
Identifiers: LCCN 2023030946 (print) | LCCN 2023030947 (ebook) |
ISBN 9798765100318 (hardback) | ISBN 9798765100356 (paperback) |
ISBN 9798765100325 (epub) | ISBN 9798765100332 (pdf) | ISBN 9798765100349
Subjects: LCSH: Portuguese fiction–21st century–History and criticism. |
Postmodernism (Literature)–Portugal.
Classification: LCC PQ9108.2 .H97 2024 (print) | LCC PQ9108.2 (ebook) |
DDC 869.3/509–dc23/eng/20231019
LC record available at https://lccn.loc.gov/2023030946
LC ebook record available at https://lccn.loc.gov/2023030947

| ISBN: | HB: | 979-8-7651-0031-8 |
|---|---|---|
| | PB: | 979-8-7651-0035-6 |
| | ePDF: | 979-8-7651-0033-2 |
| | eBook: | 979-8-7651-0032-5 |

Typeset by Integra Software Services Pvt. Ltd.

For product safety related questions contact productsafety@bloomsbury.com.

To find out more about our authors and books visit www.bloomsbury.com
and sign up for our newsletters.

# Contents

List of Contributors   vii
Acknowledgements   xi

Introduction   Ana Paula Arnaut and Paulo de Medeiros   1

Part One   Intermediality, Intertextuality, and Self-Reflexivity in the Hypercontemporary Novel

1. The Page as a Hyperfictional Hypothesis in New Portuguese Literature: Patrícia Portela and Joana Bértholo, a Case Study   *Sofia Madalena G. Escourido*   9
2. *Astronomia* by Mário Cláudio: Memory, Intermediality, and the Cosmic Imagination   *João Faustino*   23
3. Sketching *Gnaisse*: The Process of Reading a Metamorphic Novel   *Daniela Côrtes Maduro*   41
4. Representations of *elsewhere* and New Forms of Dystopia in Hypercontemporary Portuguese Literature   *Silvia Amorim*   57
5. *Charon Awaits*: Do All Things Come to Those Who Wait?   *Ana Isabel Martins*   71

Part Two   Memory and Post-Memory in the Hypercontemporary Novel

6. 'What's in a Name?' Reading the Hypercontemporary   *Isabel Cristina Rodrigues*   87
7. Paulo Faria's Wars: Owning Experience, Violence, and Postmemory   *Felipe Cammaert*   101
8. The Attraction of Autofiction in *Contra mim*: Paths and Chasms of Memory   *José Vieira*   115
9. The Shattered Narrative of Mafalda Ivo Cruz   *Paulo Ricardo Kralik Angelini and Samla Borges Canilha*   127

10  Of Technology and Lost Connections: A Decolonial
    Approach to *As Telefones* by Djaimilia Pereira de Almeida as a
    Hypercontemporary Novel  *Emanuelle Santos*                         141
11  Through a Glass Darkly: Violence, Intimacy, and Memory in Dulce
    Maria Cardoso  *Paulo de Medeiros*                                  157

Index                                                                   173

# Contributors

**Silvia Amorim** is Lecturer at Bordeaux Montaigne University in the Portuguese-Speaking Studies Department. As a specialist of the Portuguese writer José Saramago, much of his research focuses on the work of the Nobel Prize. More broadly, she works on contemporary Portuguese literature, in an approach that is at the same time literary, narratological, and linguistic. She is interested in the Literatures of Portuguese-speaking African countries and, more recently, in Portuguese Post-Colonial Studies. Her publications include *José Saramago. Art, théorie et éthique du roman*, Paris: L'Harmattan, 2010; 'Levantado do chão: anacronismos e novos compromissos literários', in *Revista de Estudos Saramaguianos*, n. 12.1 (2020): 49–66; and, co-organized with Martine Bovo and Ilana Heineberg, *Visions décentrées des Études Culturelles*, (Ravenna: Giorgio Pozzi Editore, Gallica-Italica 6, 2019).

**Ana Paula Arnaut** is a full Professor at the Faculty of Arts and Humanities of the University of Coimbra. She has been Vice-President of the Faculty, Director of the Department of Languages, Literatures and Cultures, and Course Director, among other positions. She teaches Contemporary Portuguese Literature at the same university and is a researcher at the Center for Portuguese Literature, where she is a member of the group 'Figures of Fiction'. Her main interests are post-modernist and Hypercontemporary literature, areas in which she has published several books and articles. Among others, *Memorial do Convento. History, Fiction and Ideology* (1996); *Post-Modernism in the Contemporary Portuguese Novel: Fios de Ariadne-Máscaras de Proteu* (2002); *José Saramago* (2008); *António Lobo Antunes* (2009); *As mulheres na ficção de António Lobo Antunes. (In)variantes do Feminino* (2012); *O Ano da Morte de Ricardo Reis de José Saramago* (2017); and *As Palavras Justas. Ensaios sobre Literatura e Direito* (ed.) (2020).

**Samla Borges Canilha** is a PhD student in Literature Theory at the Pontifical Catholic University of Rio Grande do Sul (PUCRS) and holds a Bachelor in Portuguese and Portuguese Language Literatures from the Federal University of Santa Maria (UFSM), and an MSc in Literature Theory from the PUCRS, with a thesis titled *Sangue e sombras: a memória familiar em Vermelho, de Mafalda*

*Ivo Cruz*. Her research interests cover contemporary Portuguese literature, especially those texts that break with traditional writing forms. She integrates the research group *Cartografias narrativas em língua portuguesa: redes e enredos de subjetividade*.

**Felipe Cammaert** is a researcher at the Languages, Literatures and Cultures Centre (CLLC/DLC), University of Aveiro (CLLC/DLC). He holds a PhD in Romance Studies and Comparative Literature from Paris Nanterre University, with a thesis on memory representations in António Lobo Antunes and Claude Simon's works. He was a postdoctoral fellow at the Centre for Social Studies, University of Coimbra (CES/UC), on the project MEMOIRS – Children of Empires and European Postmemories, and at the National Library of Colombia, amongst other institutions. He has lectured at the University of Picardie (France), University of Lisbon and University of Aveiro (Portugal), and Los Andes University (Colombia). He has translated French and Portuguese contemporary authors into Spanish for Latin America. In 2021, he received a mobility grant for literary translators from i-Portunus (Creative Europe-European Commission).

**Daniela Côrtes Maduro** holds a master's degree in Anglo-American Studies and a PhD in Materialities of Literature from the University of Coimbra (Portugal). As a researcher, she collaborates with several digital archives and projects focused on the study of narrative, digital media, multimodality, experimental literature, and electronic literature. She was a postdoctoral fellow at the University of Bremen (Germany), where she completed a project about electronic literature, and currently works at the Centre for Portuguese Literature (group 'Digital Mediation and Materialities of Literature') hosted by the University of Coimbra.

**João Faustino** completed a degree in Modern Languages and Literature, specializing in English and Portuguese Studies, at the University of Lisbon, where he also completed a degree in Language and Literature teaching. He is currently Teaching Fellow at the University of Warwick, from which he received his PhD. His research focuses on the intersection of issues of late-modernity, memory (individual, familial, national, and transnational) and expression in the work of Portuguese contemporary novelist Mário Cláudio. His recent publications include 'The Point of View of the Animal: An Ontology and Ethics of Alterity in Emma Geen's The Many Selves of Katherine North.' In *Colloquy: Text, Theory,*

*Critique* 35/36 (2018): 54–81 and '(Mis)Understanding Bach: Fiction, Art and Resistance.' Portuguese Studies, 33.2 (2017), 185–201.

**Paulo Ricardo Kralik Angelini** holds a PhD in Literature and Portuguese Language from the Federal University of Rio Grande do Sul, with post-doctoral research at Lisbon University. He is Professor of literature at the Humanities School of Pontifical Catholic University of Rio Grande do Sul (PUCRS), and Languages/Literature undergraduate coordinator at the same institution. He also coordinates the research group *Cartografias narrativas em língua portuguesa: redes e enredos de subjetividade* and has published widely on contemporary Portuguese literature.

**Sofia Madalena G. Escourido** cherishes a great affection for words, especially those which take refuge within books, but also those that inhabit people. After undergrad studies in Portuguese and Lusophone Studies and a master's degree in Text Edition (both at FCSH, New University of Lisbon), she realized that she wanted to help making books, props that allow the reading of the world – so she is an editorial assistant since 2008, and currently works in the New Portuguese Authors Department of the LeYa group. And in parallel to that, to better understand books, she completed a post-graduate degree in the Arts of Writing (also at FCSH) and received her PhD in Materialities of Literature from the University of Coimbra with the thesis 'A Página como Possibilidade: Patrícia Portela, Joana Bértholo e Afonso Cruz' (2020).

**Ana Isabel Martins** was Maître de Langue at University of Rennes 2 (2018–22). Her PhD was awarded by the University of Coimbra where she remains as researcher. Her research and teaching focus on Portuguese Literature, Portuguese as foreign Language, Reception of Classical Antiquity, Rhetoric, and Humanism in the Renaissance. She has published widely in international journals.

**Paulo de Medeiros** is Professor of Modern and Contemporary World Literature, and Head of the English and Comparative Literary Studies Department at the University of Warwick. He was Associate Professor at Bryant College (the United States) and Professor at Utrecht University (the Netherlands). During 2011–12 he was Keeley Fellow at Wadham College, Oxford, and in 2013 and 2014 President of the American Portuguese Studies Association. Recent publications include a volume, co-edited with Livia Apa, on *Contemporary Lusophone African*

*Film: Transnational Communities and Alternative Modernities* (Routledge, 2021). Current projects include a study on Postimperial Europe.

**Isabel Cristina Rodrigues** is Assistant Professor at the University of Aveiro (Portugal), where she teaches and does her research since 1991. She received a PhD in 2006, with a thesis on Vergílio Ferreira's literary work (*A Palavra Submersa. Silêncio e Produção de Sentido em Vergílio Ferreira*). Her thesis was published in 2016 by the National Press of Portugal and was awarded the National Prize for Essay 'Eduardo Prado Coelho' in 2017. She has two more books on Vergílio Ferreira's work – *A Poética do Romance em Vergílio Ferreira* (Lisboa, Colibri, 2000) and *A vocação do lume. Ensaios sobre Vergílio Ferreira* (Coimbra, Angelus Novus, 2009). Her research and teaching focus on Portuguese Contemporary Literature and Literary Theory, and she has published widely in national and international journals.

**Emanuelle Santos** is Associate Professor in Modern Languages at the University of Birmingham where she coordinates the Portuguese Studies programme and the Instituto Camões' Cátedra Gil Vicente. Her research focuses on the intersections between the cultures of the Portuguese-speaking world, postcolonial studies, and theories of world literature, drawing attention to the global-local dialectics in epistemology and literary and critical theory. Her work also addresses representations of race, gender and sexuality, memory studies, world-systems theory, and decolonial critique especially with regards to structures of inequality, oppression, and hegemony.

**José Vieira** holds a PhD in Portuguese Literature (April 2019) from the University of Coimbra, with the thesis entitled 'A Escrita do Outro. Mentiras de Realidade e Verdades de Papel', supervised by Ana Paula Arnaut. He is a member of a research Project on Figuras da Ficção, at the Portuguese Literature Center, University of Coimbra, and is also a collaborating member of the project 'Roots and Horizons of Philosophy and Culture in Portugal' at the University of Porto. He co-organized, with Celeste Natário, *Trilogia do Belo* (Dom Quixote, 2020), celebrating Mário Cláudio's fifty years of literary life.

# Acknowledgements

Preparing this volume has been a rich experience of dialogue and exchange. In a sense, it goes back to a symposium held at King's College, London, on 'Saramago: From the Land of Sin to the Fields of Blood', organized by João Silvestre and Ana de Medeiros on 30 and 31 October. We both had been invited speakers. Ana Paula Arnaut's paper, in particular, already addressed the topic of the Hypercontemporary, and this led to a series of discussions among us concerning the need to explore the concept further and more inclusively. From those initial discussions came the idea of contacting a number of colleagues, all working variously on related issues and that led to the preparation of the current volume. As such we would like to thank the organizers of that symposium as well as the institutions supporting it, King's College, London, and the Instituto Camões. We also have special thanks for all of the contributors, for their enthusiasm and ready willingness to join us in exploring the various ways in which we can, and need to, think the present.

Ana Paula Arnaut and Paulo de Medeiros would also like to thank the Faculty of Arts and Humanities of the University of Coimbra and the Centro de Literatura Portuguesa (CLP) for their financial support, as well as Mark Weeks for his rigorous reviewing of the articles. Special thanks are also due to the Department of English & Comparative Literary Studies at Warwick and to the editorial team at Bloomsbury, Amy Martin and Hali Han, who have been indefatigable all along and whose good cheer and patience steered us through any difficulties to a successful completion of this project.

# Introduction

Ana Paula Arnaut and Paulo de Medeiros

[Period concepts] *will be combined with different traits, survivals from the past, anticipations of the future and quite individual peculiarities.*

(Wellek 1963: 252)

*Il faut être absolument moderne.*

(Rimbaud 1979: 116)

The contemporary, as Giorgio Agamben among others suggests, is above all a temporal condition (Agamben 2009: 39–54). Yet, the very notion of what it means to be contemporary is far from reducible to a question of time and much less to one of chronological or linear time. Alain Badiou makes that clear when he enjoins us to become contemporaries of the great modernist Fernando Pessoa (Badiou 2005: 36–45). Similarly, the 'Hypercontemporary' only is a temporal condition on a primary level. As impossible as it may be to define without any precision the nature of the ever-shifting contemporary, so is it even more difficult to seize on any one version of the Hypercontemporary agreeable even to the relatively small group of those who, often unwittingly, engage in its practice or try to think it. For doing so, in a very real sense, would amount to a negation of the very urgency and flow of the Hypercontemporary. Yet, as urgent and fluid as the Hypercontemporary might be, it is not as fleeting as some would have it, nor is it simply an intensification of the temporal aspects of the contemporary. Rather, if the Hypercontemporary can be said to intensify the contemporary condition, then, we would suggest, what it intensifies is that capacity already diagnosed by Agamben of those who are contemporary to 'perceiv[e] the darkness of the present, [and] grasp[s] a light that can never reach its destiny'. The contemporary 'is also the one who, dividing and interpolating time, is capable of transforming it and putting it in relation with other times' (Agamben 2009: 53).

In the dark times we traverse that capacity to see a light through the darkness of the present has neither been scarcer nor more necessary.

We then take the liberty of adding a double 'post' prefix to Rimbaud's formula in our epigraph, which thus reads that, at present times, *Il faut être absolument [post-post]moderne* (One must be absolutely post-postmodern), emphasizing the fact that this (not quite) new word is open to the possibility of a close relationship with another concept: that of the Hypercontemporary. For common to both the contemporary and the Hypercontemporary is the ability, the need even, to hold a broken mirror to the present and see the archaic in the modern as Walter Benjamin (2002: 462) and Giorgio Agamben (2009) already had alerted us to, but without any trace of nostalgia. This was adumbrated in the writing of the three of the most significant Portuguese novelists of the latter quarter of the twentieth century, José Saramago, Lídia Jorge, and António Lobo Antunes. In the last two decades this tendency has only become more accentuated in an expanding number of younger novelists whose work both inherits that of the three writers just named, continues it, and in some cases could be said to radically accelerate and intensify both the deep affection and the intense rage at the present condition of Portugal and the world. One feature in common that connects the different generations is the unabating confrontation with the violence that permeates the present as well as the intense dedication to form and its use as a registration of that same violence that also provides readers with some possibility for resistance.

Therefore, the concept of Hypercontemporary seems to stem from both the more systematic cultivation of this variant and from the need for a terminology shift which may correspond to the development of historic-social dynamics and, consequently, to the need to include new themes and new scenarios mirroring the (inter)individual and (inter)social behaviour changes resulting from a new, globalized world in constant transformation (the case of Mário Cláudio and Dulce Maria Cardoso), which is becoming increasingly violent.

Regarding the identifying traits of the new paradigm, it should be borne in mind that the concept of intertextuality is now fully rescued from the 1970s and 1980s, when it had caught the attention of many narratologists, but of few writers, and is revitalized and developed through practices that often make it visually present. The overt or covert use of inter-artistic practices may, therefore, justify the creation of a new genre (that of intermedial novels).

The articles included in the first part of this book clearly exemplify and illustrate this trend. Based on works by Patrícia Portela and Joana Bértholo,

Sofia Escourido both explores the significance of hybrid fictional narratives and their possibilities on the printed page and the combining, transforming, and subverting of the conventions of literary genre, thus illustrating the inter-artistic capacities of the Hypercontemporary novel. The subversion of literary genres and the important role of intermediality on the construction of meaning are also approached by Daniela Maduro, who describes *Gnaisse* by João Carmelo as a work capable of modifying and extending itself by recombining pieces of a shattered reality, as well as by taking the shape of an intermedial artefact. João Faustino follows a similar path on his reading of *Astronomia* by Mário Cláudio, seeking to understand the role which intermediality and intertextuality play in the processes of construction of individual and collective memory. Ana Isabel Martins also recognizes the importance of intertextuality and in her approach to Cláudia Andrade's work *Charon Waiting* she acknowledges that the act of weaving together ideas makes a text a rich tapestry of potential meanings that dialogues with various influences and has a host of resonances. Through the analysis of the novels by Ricardo Adolfo and Rui Zink, that question the uncertain borders between here and elsewhere, and at the same time the links between identity and otherness, Sílvia Amorim reflects on Hypercontemporary Portuguese society and portrays a globalized world inclined to precariousness, in which geography seems doomed to disappear, and violence becomes commonplace.

Following this line, it does not seem difficult to also include in this sort of neo-naturalist drive the books of Mafalda Ivo Cruz, Paulo Faria, Ana Margarida de Carvalho, Dulce Maria Cardoso, Rui Zink, Ricardo Adolfo, or Cláudia Andrade.

The second part of the volume then focuses on the role of violence as a key component of the Hypercontemporary novel, as we read in Isabel Cristina Rodrigues's text, that also displays the post-modernist literary inheritance of Ana Margarida de Carvalho's work and the link between Hypercontemporary practices and the ones of the epigonic generation of Realism-Naturalism. Felipe Cammaert and José Vieira take up again the topic of violence. The former analyses the narrative techniques used in its representation in the works of Paulo Faria, which he compares with war narratives such as Lobo Antunes's in order to show the increased awareness of postmemorial literature in reappropriating someone else's memory; the latter shows the tension between fiction and reality in a novel by Valter Hugo Mãe which portrays a time of violence against the slowness of critical thinking and the solidity of the ideas that find in writing a form of resistance and, at the same time, reflecting a celebratory manifestation of our liquid and fragmented times.

Paulo Kralik and Samla Borges Canilha pay particular attention to the inscriptions that overflow, break, and contradict the classical narrative paradigms, using as examples two novels by Mafalda Ivo Cruz, a novelist whose works are marked by deconstruction, fragmentation, and disruption, thus demanding new views, new approaches, and new responses. Emanuelle Santos reads Djaimilia Pereira de Almeida's sixth novel *As Telefones* against the wider backdrop of the relationship between technology and modernity that marks the Hypercontemporary novel, arguing for a view of the book that situates it in a tradition of the European semi-peripheral novel that sheds light on technology's entanglement with capitalism and international division of labour expressed in economic migration. Paulo de Medeiros, on the other hand, focuses on tracing and exploring the imbrications of violence and intimacy and their significance in six of Dulce Maria Cardoso's novels and briefly compares *The Return* with J. M. Coetzee's *Foe*.

In this day and age, when the novel genre is said to no longer be what it used to be (and it indeed is not, and could not be, although, obviously, books are still being published which comply with traditional narrative rules), some, or, in certain cases, all canonical narrative categories dissolve away. Narrator, plot, time, space, and character implode at different levels and in varying degrees, generating a text for fruition to the detriment of a traditionally appealing text for pleasure. As a result, and also definitively, because our 'poetic faith' is transformed, Coleridge's willing suspension of disbelief becomes a willing suspension of belief. And perhaps, together with Antunes's fictional work, one of the best examples of this dissolution-subversion at all possible levels may well be Luís Carmelo's novel *Gnaisse*, published in 2015. Simultaneously reviving the neo-naturalistic strand mentioned above, the protagonist (the teacher), as readers learn, or confirm, in the second part, is an apt illustration of pathological abnormalism (in his case, stemming from his somewhat defective capacity for thinking), which is very much evident in Abel Botelho's novels. As regards the subversion of form, in the last fourteen pages (corresponding to thirteen numbered blocks), a diegetically apparent metafictional practice, which may be described as dual or mirror-like because it provides an insight into the metafictionality of the first part (which is linguistically both overt and covert), elucidates (explains or justifies) the narrative that was initially told, again with some variants.

However, more important than the aspects mentioned, we believe that the protagonist in *Gnaisse* illustrates one of the most interesting characteristics of this new tendency (certainly a reflection of the fluidity of the world we live in and the way how the *I* stages itself and how it stages the *other*). By this we mean the fact that its composition as a character no longer follows a canonical technique where the physical and psychological portrait of the beings that populate the fictional word is drawn in its entirety, that is, densely, with clear-cut outlines (through direct or indirect characterization processes). Sometimes, as it is the case of Patrícia Portela or Joana Bértholo, in order to fully know characters and environments the reader needs to activate his encyclopaedia and search for a relation between what is said and the image-drawing-painting-sculpture that is directly or indirectly inserted in the materiality of the words.

In sum, what are we readers to make of this newest fiction whose permanent relationship with other art forms may justify a new classification, that of intermedial novels? We do not think that the answer to this question entails claiming that the novel is dead, or taking a more general and fundamentalist approach, suggesting that it be excluded from the realm of literature. Maybe the solution is to calmly accept its 'vagabond morphology', as Luís Carmelo puts it in *Gnaisse*, and admit that overlapping imagination and fantasy do not invalidate its genially literary dimension. In order to achieve this, we must recognize that, in Carmelo's own words, 'fantasy is but a form of memory emancipated from the order of space and time which receives its material ready-made through the law of mental association', whereas imagination does indeed correspond to 'true creative power', the mother of all 'inspiration' and an exclusive quality of 'geniuses'.

# References

Agamben, G. (2009), 'What Is the Contemporary?', in David Kishik and Stefan Pedatella (trans.), *What Is an Apparatus? and Other Essays*, 39–54, Stanford: Stanford University Press.
Badiou, A. (2005), *Handbook of Inaesthetics*, Trans. Alberto Toscano, Stanford: Stanford University Press.
Benjamin, Walter (2002). 'Awakening', in Rolf Tiedemann (ed.), *The Arcades Project*, 462, Cambridge, Mass.: Harvard University Press; n2a, 3.
Rimbaud, A. (1979), *Une saison en enfer, Oeuvres Complètes*, Paris: Gallimard, Bibliothèque de la Pléiade.
Wellek, R. (1963), *Concepts of Criticism*, New Haven and London: Yale University Press.

# Part One

# Intermediality, Intertextuality, and Self-Reflexivity in the Hypercontemporary Novel

# 1

# The Page as a Hyperfictional Hypothesis in New Portuguese Literature: Patrícia Portela and Joana Bértholo, a Case Study

Sofia Madalena G. Escourido

If the main aim of literature is to tell stories, then the narrative exists to be understood in its many different forms, and it is up to the readers – in the broadest sense – to activate it. In Hypercontemporary Portuguese fiction, the mechanisms that the reader must manipulate to access the story seem mainly to involve intermedial elements and a certain self-reflexivity of the narrative; and if authors resort to multimodal narration to make their stories more engaging, then readers draw on this creative method to understand its different implications on the reading.

A significant number of authors look on the printed page today not as a neutral space, but rather as a surface on which to inscribe a narrative made up of letters and graphic arrangements that can be manipulated creatively as complete fictional devices, and thus are calling attention to the hybrid nature – visual and verbal – of the printed page. Looking at these narrative pages as renewed fictional possibilities means admitting that the entire page can tell a story, even the blanks. There are many pictographic and typographic devices that can be used to show expressiveness on a page: punctuation, footnotes, headings, typography, cover design, blank spaces (printed area, margins, line spacing), pictures, etc. When these are intentionally manipulated, they become a substantial part of the literary form of a text, non-neutral devices in terms of meaning.

In the Hypercontemporary fictional environment, there is thus a clear intensification of the metamedial and hybrid dimension of the typographic page, accompanied by a creative attitude of exploring its boundaries, both visually and textually. Therefore, the experiences of reading Patrícia Portela and Joana

Bértholo cannot have a merely textual dimension: visual elements intertwined with the typography and scattered around the page have become rhetorical tools for these authors, and their dynamics and function are now correlated with the narrative complexities of the text. In the works of these the visual devices are part of the printed page, in a symbiotic and necessary relationship with the text. And although these books are generically labelled as hybrid or metamedial narratives, they combine, transform, and overturn the conventions of literary genre, encouraging reflection on the presence of the book's materiality and its expressive manipulation.

## Patrícia Portela: The Book as a Performance

The constant ability to overturn and reinvent is evident in the majority of Patrícia Portela's books. If this is, potentially, true for most authors, Portela's case is notable and paradigmatic of an incessant, consistent, and challenging quest to explore how fiction is produced today, which results in a work marked mainly by its intermedial nature, but also by self-reflection. This author, by using the text in a place – in the case of books, on the page – reflects on the space of the novels and stories in the world today, marking a substantial literary difference in the publishing universe (particularly the Portuguese one), mainly because of her patently intermedial books.

The performative nature of her works has two senses: it comes from the printed pages in the books and expands from there; or from the impulse of the stage imprisoned in the printed format. Moving between the page and the stage, the narratives tend to escape conventional boundaries, resulting in hybrid literary experiences. The merging of the literary with theatrical language is evident in each book, as well as the fusion of visual semantics that are hybridized with the text to create a new form of narration. This simultaneous impulse for critical thought on the bibliographic nature of books and for drama on the page means that the book is constantly acting as a performance. Designed to be read in a performative way, as if the page were a stage, these books also contain dramatic devices working for the narrative – such as footnotes and other stage directions – to complement reading, as if each novel contains within it the key to its full and autonomous access.

Patrícia Portela's story can start being told with *Odília ou a História das Musas Confusas no Cérebro de* (Odília or the History of the Confused Muses in the Brain of), published in 2007, a journey through ideas, a maze of thought printed on the page. In the ball of thread that this book is, stability resides in the repetition that marks the narrative, the textual and visual repetition that provides the structure for the circular nature of the story. The metaphor of the ball of thread is taken from the pages of the book itself, with a thread running through it – the thread of the story and a graphic design thread.

*Para Cima e Não Para Norte* (Up, Not North) (2008) is a peculiar book, not only for its profuse inclusion of visual devices, but also because of how the author interacts with its visual dimension, thus establishing a relationship between the text and the page. The main character – for instance, the Flat Man – takes on another dimension when he is understood by others (readers, viewers), without ever gaining a body of his own, constituting a metafictional representation of how the book only exists when it is read.

The relationship between *O Banquete* (The Banquet) (2012) and Greek mythology is already clear from the title; after all, it would be almost impossible not to think of *The Banquet* by Plato. What binds the two banquets together seems to be a dialogue with several voices taking part and ideas running through the pages, occupying them in different ways. As it is not a static book, readers share the same existential, graphical, and verbal banquet.

*Wasteband*[1] (2014) is a paradigmatic example of analogue and digital interaction in Hypercontemporary Portuguese literature, a proposal for an interactive game the reader takes part in, embarking on a voyage to a space of loss, as if they were handling a computer and not a book. By using the language of videogames to narrate what could be a story of love and loss about two characters through the visual simulation of a mechanism, there is the creative assumption that the page is a mechanical and material device made up of graphic and typographic ideas that generate meanings.

*A Coleção Privada de Acácio Nobre* (The Private Collection of Acácio Nobre) (2016) is an inventory novel of objects in catalogue form, all belonging to a diffuse figure, Acácio Nobre. The unforeseen, the ambivalent, stimulus and obstacle prevail in this printed compilation of a variety of materials. This book embodies the impulses of the modern day, Hypercontemporary novel by exploring a certain blurring in the portrait of the characters, such as a disfigured anti-hero with no identity of his own, conceived using narrative techniques that presuppose the erasure of any form of direct characterization. This figure becomes a character whose journey is subverted, commented on in footnotes – given clues, pictures, and gestures – mixing fiction and historical reality.

---

[1] Title originally written in English, as an untranslatable expression.

## Joana Bértholo: Metafictional Intensity

Joana Bértholo has written inventive books, both from an aesthetic and a literary standpoint. They show in-depth reflection and study of words and the place they occupy, whether on the page or in the mind. Coming from a generation in which many writers are creators of multimodal narratives, by incorporating resources of different forms or hybrid narratives – which, despite being very diverse, come together on the page in order to give rise to a new narrative structure that is sufficiently stable, regardless of the particular form, but rather how they intertwine; even so, the specific nature of the experimentation in Bértholo's books and the way she looks at the challenges and the possibilities of the page stand out.

This author often uses multimodal and hybrid strategies to intensify metafictionality, given that her texts seem to think for themselves, as she uses many textual forms of self-reflexivity; there is even a narrative contained inside or beyond the actual narrative, which uses typography to intensify its nature, questioning the means of literary production and the circumstances of its creation. Thus, the book works as a unit that is conceived and materialized as a metafictional mechanism.

Joana Bértholo's literary career begins in 2012, with *Havia – Histórias de coisas que havia e de outras que vai havendo* (There were – Stories of things that used to be and others that will be). It's an experimental book where all the texts begin with 'havia', grouped in dyads – an extended version and, on another page, a condensed version, of the same subject. Making each text move from a kind of short, adulterated version of itself enriches its reading, offering different possibilities for the same idea.

Also made up of short texts organized into one volume, *Inventário do Pó – estudos para a makina de produzir desertos* (Dust inventory – studies for a desert-producing machine) (2015) presents itself as a game between the Portuguese writer Joana Bértholo and her distant relative, the artist René Bertholo. This figure, whom the author digresses about in this book, is used as a creative counterpoint and a theme for the textual production of her stories or studies.

*Diálogos para o Fim do Mundo* (Dialogues for the End of the World) (2010), Joana Bértholo's first novel, is a formal innovative work. At the beginning the author asks herself if this is the best way to tell stories and if the printed page is the most appropriate device. The future will respond affirmatively, and her fictions will largely involve working creatively on this narrative format, using mechanisms and textual forms to problematize its nature.

Her second novel, *O Lago Avesso – Uma hipótese biográfica* (The Upside-Down Lake – A biographical hypothesis) (2013), is effectively a visual book whose story is read and seen, but it is also a literary work built to ask questions about the idea of a book, of a novel, and even of a biography. More than a multiple and fragmentary narrative about the well-known choreographer Ella Bouhart, the apparent disconnection and the *staged* inconsistency of the narration are exactly what make the novel interesting since this logic not only questions a certain narrative regularity, in order to introduce a new (renewed?) way of narrating, but it also reflects the nature of life itself, a major subject of literature.

*Ecologia* (Ecology) (2018) is a book about language(s), with a special focus on writing, which tends to be visually more 'discreet'. This powerful, singular novel presents the reader with the premise that soon people will have to pay to speak, using an increasingly more complex and effective system to charge for a resource which today is believed to be inexhaustible. There is clearly a balance of forces in this novel, which allows to consider it one of the best examples in the Hypercontemporary literary environment, given the profusion and the balance of intermedial elements that the reader is faced with on its pages and the narrative self-reflection that emanates from it.

## Portela-Bértholo

There are some curious points of contact between these two authors, showing not only the existence of common ground or areas they tend towards, but also reflecting an ambition to develop narrative possibilities. Of note, for example, are the conceptual connections between René Bertholo (catalogued in *Inventário do Pó*), Acácio Nobre (and his *Coleção Privada*), and Ella Bouhart (the choreographer in *O Lago Avesso*), all outlines of other empirical or imagined figures. There is also the coincidence of the dialogues established with other works, such as in *O Banquete,* which is as much Plato as it is Patrícia Portela; in *Inventário do Pó,* where Joana Bértholo reinterprets the musician René Bertholo through writing; or in *Para Cima e Não Para Norte,* where Patrícia Portela brings the theories of Edwin Abbot to the present.

The attempt to creatively distort conventional literary genres is another of the points of contact between them. Bértholo attempts to distort the novel in several ways, from the experimental to the provocative: a novel can be full of footnotes as if it were an essay *(Diálogos para o Fim do Mundo)*; or an apparent essay turns out to be a collection of short stories *(Inventário do Pó)*; or even a somewhat inside-out biography, which is actually a novel *(O Lago Avesso)*.

Portela in turn promotes the bibliographic renovation of the genre with her inventory novel, *A Coleção Privada de Acácio Nobre*, and writes *Wasteband*, which is like a videogame played on the printed page. The notion of games in literary texts is nothing new; however, this attraction for constantly revising and subverting literary rules now results in a type of hybridism in which the interruptions by visual devices combine in an underlining of the textual materiality. As the novel is conceived as a hybrid space that tends to be interactive, this hypothesis is tested on every page, trying to generate the desire to lose: of the reader becoming lost in the game, of the printed book losing the fixed, structured form it is more or less used to.

The two authors use structures from other literary genres to make clear the creative tensions between genres that do not conventionally belong to fiction, and the actual fiction arising from this game. They do not only explore the novel genre, but also the cataloguing of a collection – even if the subject of the collection does not exist – or an inventory – where the identity of the catalogues is not more important than how it is done – all fictional possibilities on the printed page in this Hypercontemporary literary context that bring a certain singularity to Portuguese literature.

It is also important to look at the paratextual devices of the page: that set of textual or graphic elements which are also elements of fiction and creativity for these authors. The book covers, headings, and tables of contents all contribute actively and intentionally to the narrative. These mechanisms function on the different planes of fictional construction as markers of space and time, as a way of describing the characters, as notations for voices and thoughts, as emulators of different discursive genres. The intensification of the printed experience through manipulation of its graphic conventions will always be significant to the experience of reading these authors.

Sometimes Portela and Bértholo play with bibliographic conventions, such as tables of contents. This apparently paratextual element of the books should be looked at as part of the literary game whenever the narrative strategy and its sequencing diverge from what is their usual function, questioning their location and/or conventional positioning. A minor or additional element in most books, Bértholo almost always gives them a lot of care and attention, turning them into significant fictional elements. In *Inventário do Pó*, for example, when you consult the table of contents – which the author entitles 'Machine for producing deserts/instructions for use' (2015: 11–12) – it soon becomes clear that this is a reinforcement of the René-Joana connection this book is made up of, and it is the table of contents that holds this reading key, this emphasis. In *O Lago Avesso* too, it is the table of contents (2013: 9–11) that shows the fundamental parameters for accessing the novel: the different types of fonts on these pages – round, italic, bold, small caps, fonts with and without serifs, numerical digits, capital letters, and small letters – provide the reading key for this novel, as each different graphical format will correspond in the narrative to a different type of chapter or subchapter. But it is in *Diálogos para o Fim do Mundo* that Joana Bértholo further distorts the functionality of the paratextual element table of contents. It is strange not to find this device as soon as you open the book. It is there, but 'lost' among the different chapters (more than halfway through the book, from page 181 to 186). What is a table of contents for if not to guide the reader? If the author questions the most conventional of literary structures, the table of contents cannot escape her hand; in this case, she not only transforms it into a chapter discreetly arranged among the others – it has the same graphic layout – but she also moves it from its conventional location at the beginning or the end of the book.

In some books, Patrícia Portela also looks at the table of contents as a bibliographic device that can be structured unconventionally, taking on the role of a participant in the narrative. In *Wasteband* (23–6), although it is a conventional paratextual device made up of a methodical list that gives the page numbers of the different items in it, it is not tightly bound to alphabetic or other layouts, but rather according to the general dynamics of the narrative, which gives a good first idea of the book, like a map, so that the reader won't get lost while reading/playing. In *A Coleção Privada ...*, almost at the end of the book, there is the collection index (2016: 213–15) and the general table of contents of the book (2016: 217), very common paratextual elements in catalogue-type books that exist here in the most conventional way possible. These devices are very similar to those that can be found in a catalogue, but this book is a novel – its redefinition is done precisely through incorporation of the paratextual devices.

The use, also, of the paratextual element 'footnote' in narratives that use the entire space of the page as a fictional device is neither innocent nor innocuous. It is one of the preferred fictional elements, subverting the function of being complementary to the text that it would conventionally refer to and being used as a favourably positioned reference device which certain Hypercontemporary authors also like to use to tell stories. Particularly with Patrícia Portela, footnotes are a notable fictional device. Conventionally used to explain, comment on, or provide references to the main text, these annotations isolated at the bottom of the page in small print are usually used to provide clarification or to insert complementary considerations into the narrative, and their inclusion in the main text would interrupt the reading sequence. However, a look at the use and function of this typographic device on the printed page in Portela reveals other aspects arising from her creative distortion.

The footnotes are sometimes ironic and invert the actual meaning of the device; they are no longer an addition to the text, rather becoming actual text, even the entire book – as is the case with *Wasteband*, through the mention that all of 'this book is a footnote' (2014: 23). In *A Coleção Privada …*, the text contained in footnotes presents a narrative that is essential for understanding the book, with comments, corrections, or complementary information by the organizer of the collection that either contradict or elucidate understanding of the elements of the collection that are on the pages without which the reader would be unable to understand the fictional game that makes this inventory a novel. In *Odília*, there are footnotes that are attributed to a translator (in a book that is not translated), to a publisher …, which consist of an entertaining game, one more redundant, but one that has relative metafictional value.

In the works of Joana Bértholo, footnotes are not so commonplace, but there are certain significant cases, particularly in her first novel, *Diálogos …* The footnotes that are distributed throughout the book end up being an independent chapter of that book – the ones that have already appeared, up to page 130, and the ones that are yet to come – and, when aligned into a single chapter, have sequential narration, which is thus inserted into a metafictional game that uses its conventional location on the page to call the reader's attention to the materiality and nature of the book.

Almost empty pages are another similarity between the works of Portela and Bértholo, particularly the last virtually blank pages in *Diálogos Para o Fim do Mundo* and the last pages in *Para Cima e Não Para Norte* and *Wasteband*, where the *problem* of the empty page is resolved by intensifying its paratextual or material characteristics. In *Diálogos …*, there are still a few blank pages before you actually get to the end of the book, but they're not completely empty; they have page numbers – which could mean that if all the elements of the book are important, then they should all be treated the same way, numbered as constituent parts of this novel. In *Para Cima …*, so that the last pages of the book aren't left blank/empty, only the essential is written: 'a page turns and is heard' (2008: 235), 'did you hear it?' (2008: 237), because the sound made by the page when it is turned is all that exists there, a fact that Patrícia Portela puts in writing, asking the reader if they have really heard this sound, in one of the many moments of interactivity with them.

About page numbering, it should be noted that this graphic strategy is quite widely used in *Wasteband* (2014). It might well have gone unnoticed if page 187 did not happen to be followed by 188.5, or if the last page of the book were not numbered 208.5, or if the numbering from pages 197 to 199 were not just an 'undo' arrow at the bottom of the page, in the centre, where the page numbers should actually be and even using their normal typographic formatting. Authors like Patrícia Portela are always using typographic pages as fictional devices and, as such, distort what would be expected from the narrative, because numbering also tells stories: for example, the 'undo' arrow comes after the 'delete' page (2014: 197), when the story of *Wasteband* is over; somebody has pressed 'delete' and now they want to go back, like in a digital environment, which will only be possible by turning the pages, something the book allows, if the reader so wishes. In turn, decimal numbering appears on transition pages. In other words, the pages where nothing happens in narrative terms, the author can play an entertaining game with the typographic devices. In *O Banquete* – a distinguished example – the numbering is always regular, but an unusual notation system is used: Roman instead of Arabic numerals, which results in more characters used for the numbering and, consequently, a visual underlining of the paratextual device.

As to the nature of the typographic page, the distortion of the expected page of white paper with black lettering also needs some attention, as it is not a rule in itself, but is the most common, regular form. Differences in this regularity can be looked at as creative variations whenever the change in the actual method encourages narrative differentiation. This aspect is seen in Joana Bértholo's *Inventário do Pó*, where in fact the entire book is the colour of sand, of dust – the cover, the colour of the fonts throughout the book, even the pictures and photos it contains – with a constant colour and visual sense that sets the tone for the book: while René Bértholo composes his musical work 'An Argentine in the desert' using an arid place where what is necessary is to survive as an existential geographic space, Joana Bértholo uses the work of this artist, tracing it out and creating a book in sandy hues, incorporating art as a territory, cycle and, finally, dust. This *Inventário*, as it is a fluid, fragmentary text, in which each passage is an excerpt of movement, sound, image, and representation, is a particular expression of this exercise of fictionalizing by doing it on paper and using a dusty colour, a remnant of what has gone.

The recycled paper used in *Ecologia* by Joana Bértholo is also of note, making a correspondence between the content and form of the novel: from the point of view of physical materiality, the pages' paper is a result of reusing other paper, thus reflecting the notion of ecology, evident from the title, but also occurring inside the narrative. This citing or recovery of elements of the book through giving them a new meaning comes not only with the photo of the author on one of the flaps (which is part of the same sequence that later appears on pages 174–9 and 222, with a different fictional construction), in the excerpt selected for the back cover, and the graphic of the blank pages between chapters that takes advantage of the graphic layout of the cover (although now in black and white), but also in the headings, through which the work strangely cites itself, as if it were a structure contained and enclosed within its literary nature – almost like an ecological mechanism for reusing language and graphic structures, fictionally responding to the literary challenge of the book itself.

The paper used in *Wasteband* by Patrícia Portela is not white either, being rather more greyish in colour, and the words on the page are not black, but a darker shade of grey than the background, which could be an attempt to simulate something other than a paper page, something more like a screen. This visual simulation of a machine, of a mechanism – or the creative assumption that the page is a mechanical and material device made up of graphic and typographic ideas and components that generate meaning – has more variations throughout the book: on page 70, several lines punctuated with ellipses but no printed text are a visual simulation of a computer processing information; on the next page, the word 'Wait … ' is repeatedly distributed over the surface of the page with the uniformity of an automated mechanism. This obsessive typographic repetition recalls the use of computers, with information being processed by the machine. Then comes the 'Result' on the next page (2014: 72), as if you were handling a computer and not a book.

There are also pages in the works of Joana Bértholo that show the repercussions of the digital universe on the printed page. In one of the short stories in *Inventário*, 'The crickets' (2015: 153–2), the narrative uses the graphic structure of a Facebook feed, through pictures, shares, likes, and sound and video clips – obviously iconographic only – to speak of some significant events of the twentieth century, all related to oppression and war, which are thus transposed to the page. There is no narrative line that is not linked in this structure in this graphic mimicking of the social media interface on which users chirp like crickets. In several structures in *Ecologia*, as the story is set in the not-too-distant future, the use of new technologies, increasingly present in the world – and even in fiction – comes as no surprise, giving rise to the incorporation of so many elements from the digital and interactive universe – hyperlinks, QR codes, emoticons – on paper pages. For example, take the binary inscription 'zero' and 'one' in the body of the text (2018: 143), following the same graphic layout in the entire paragraph (the option for binary language is a result of the impossibility of reading this paragraph, but the exercise of showing the device is also proof of its occasional impossibility), or even a graphic representation of a computer error, which takes up several pages (2018: 148–51) and whose title is key to its interpretation. Although it is an analogue book, it has a post-digital metamedial logic, in which the printed book wants to subsume the current medial ecology and the novel wants to subsume the multiple genres and discursive forms.

For all these reasons, it is impossible to ignore the clear relationships between writing technologies and textual experience in the works of these authors. Multisemiotic texts built by different languages are part of Hypercontemporary writing methods. But the simulation/representation that is a page of a book has not disappeared, in fact it is where all the technological advances that have migrated to the literary environment are applied and have become narrative tools. In the works of Portela and Bértholo, conventional printed materials combine multimedia elements that conserve the structure and organization of the page, although they are constantly adapting to new formatting possibilities, which result in the intensification and transformation of how the book is experienced.

Apart from the ones already mentioned, also of note are the pictographic elements, which are spread throughout the works of these authors in a way that, while not very regular, is not sporadic either. These material differences coexist on the page, appearing harmoniously and providing for other means of narrating and reading; after all, they are a language too. They are not merely illustrative or dispensable at the expense of the typography, their presence is essential to the narration. They are complementary and not repetitive: the visual multimodal elements are not limited to illustrating the typographic elements; they contain new narrative information that does not appear anywhere else on the page.

The conceptual problem of visual devices – which, in a generic way, can be functionally grouped into 'photographs, illustrative elements, unconventional typesetting, ephemera and diagrams' (Sadokierski 2010: 28–54) – have particular expressions in the novels of these two authors because they challenge you to gauge to what point narrative strategies of page visuality work as a way of simplifying, or complicating, the reading, by adding one more element of unconventional legibility; as well as determining if this relationship with the illustration, the photograph, or other type of visual device provides keys to symbolically or allegorically reading the narratives or, on the contrary, contaminate and resist legibility; and these devices also complicate the questions of reading and the role of the reader, an essential element for activating all the complexity that exists on the page.

In *A Coleção Privada de Acácio Nobre*, the apparent uniformity on the page is constantly broken or destabilized by the inclusion of a wide variety of visual devices, although the layout of the book remains constant. Despite being fully numbered, captioned, and annotated, the volume is a set of multimodal documents that are so diverse in nature that following a chronological order becomes unimportant. The narrative progresses by topics: it is a narration made of ideas, of rhythmic transposition of subjects from one multimodal fragment to the next, united by a single character. The collection that Portela organizes from this existing collection – this gathering/assembling of objects of the same conceptual and even fictional nature, most graphic devices reproduced on the page – is the artistic act that resignifies these objects, giving context and life to the character.

In Portela's novels there are also self-reflective graphic elements on the page, such as the illustrations that are only captioned without graphic figures in *Wasteband*. In this novel, the 'images' are so discreet that they consist only of typography, very often decimal – 'Image 8.5' or 'Image 9.8' – or enumerating things that are absent – graphics that aren't there; colours that aren't there; and reproductions of tables, diagrams, or facsimiles that the reader never sees on the page except as a caption of absence. This emptiness challenges the reader to deal with the image mechanisms or to reflect on their nature, validating them and their many possibilities.

There are other noteworthy examples in the works of Portela, in *Odília* and in *Para Cima* … In the latter, by constantly intersecting the narrative and the graphic in a self-referencing fashion, the book presents itself as an exercise on the graphic dimension of the text as a constituent part of fiction. The fictional reality of events and characters depends on cognitive action and the actual reading of the page, which oscillates between the verbal plane and the graphic plane.

However, the most paradigmatic example seems to be *Ecologia*, by Joana Bértholo, in which visual devices are used differently for the narrative, establishing particular dynamics by becoming complete narrative elements: they are not with the text, they are narrative, and the function of telling parts of the story is delegated to them, in conjunction with other merely typographic elements on the page[2]. The book is therefore a commitment between these two aspects: the visual and the textual, which combined constitute a rather effective narrative unit. These pages thus become narrative units that depend on effective reading of the elements scattered over their surface.

## Confluences on The Printed Page

Patrícia Portela and Joana Bértholo accustom readers to a certain amount of theatricality, whereby all the elements of the book are incorporated into their works like narrative or metanarrative elements. They are therefore significant examples of this creative approach in Portuguese literature, clearly standing out from others of their generation because of their more explicit exploration of the multimodal function of the printed page – few books published in the last decade have gone so far in stretching the fictional possibilities of the page. For all these reasons, they are perhaps two of the most singular authors on the contemporary scene, because they manage to outdo themselves in each book through the narrative strategies they come up with.

If we take the book – and the page – as a significant unit, what sets Patrícia Portela apart is certainly the performative nature of her work. What this author imprisons in her books, all the performative strategies and tensions that are seen on the page, makes her books not only a language and narration laboratory, but also a prompt for reflection on the nature of fiction which is to tell a story using only paper pages. Joana Bértholo may well be a reference for any book lover. The plasticity of the pages, the self-awareness of the narrative devices and their places and functions in the act of telling a story result in a deep conceptual dive into the metafictionality that intensifies with each page. That is not only interesting from a critical point of view, but also beautiful to read. Her narratives are always an invitation to dive into a conceptual place, each page an experience not only of reading, but on reading.

Much more than a surface for the pragmatic and expressive use of language, the creative use of the page is already quite a highly materialized literary practice, with singular narrative effects that are clearly expand it, and, in the

---

[2] For an in-depth study and analysis of these devices in this novel, see Escourido 2020: 405–49.

Hypercontemporary literary environment that is now enlarging, this confirms the survival and renewal of a literary mechanism as old as the printed page. For all these reasons, the narrative forces that single out the way Portela and Bértholo tell stories must include looking at the pages as a possibility, as a place, and a vital support for their fictionality.

## References

Bértholo, J. (2010), *Diálogos Para o Fim do Mundo*, Alfragide: Caminho.
Bértholo, J. (2012), *Havia – Histórias de Coisas que Havia e de Outras que Vai Havendo*, Alfragide: Caminho.
Bértholo, J. (2013), *O Lago Avesso – Uma Hipótese Biográfica*, Alfragide: Caminho.
Bértholo, J. (2015), *Inventário do Pó*, Alfragide: Caminho.
Bértholo, J. (2018), *Ecologia*, Alfragide: Caminho.
Escourido, S. (2020), 'A Página como Possibilidade: Patrícia Portela, Joana Bértholo & Afonso Cruz', PhD diss., Coimbra University. Available online: http://hdl.handle.net/10316/94390.
Portela, P. (2007), *Odília ou a História das Musas Confusas no Cérebro*, Alfragide: Caminho.
Portela, P. (2008), *Para Cima e Não Para Norte*, Alfragide: Caminho.
Portela, P. (2013), *O Banquete*, Alfragide: Caminho.
Portela, P. (2014), *Wasteband*, Alfragide: Caminho.
Portela, P. (2016), *A Coleção Privada de Acácio Nobre*, Alfragide: Caminho.
Sadokierski, Z. (2010), 'Visual Writing: A Critique of Graphic Devices in Hybrid Novels from a Visual Communication Design Perspective', PhD diss., University of Technology Sydney. Available online: http://hdl.handle.net/10453/20267.

2

# *Astronomia* by Mário Cláudio: Memory, Intermediality, and the Cosmic Imagination

João Faustino

*Astronomia* (Cláudio 2015) is the fictional autobiography of author Mário Cláudio. In the work, which is formally classified as a novel, Cláudio's life trajectory is depicted against the backdrop of the social, economic, and political developments occurring in Portugal and beyond during the period portrayed. In tune with what has become customary in the author's works, which are often grouped into trilogies, *Astronomia* is divided into three sections: 'Nebulosa', 'Galáxia', and 'Cosmos'. These correspond respectively and in broad terms to the undefined potential associated with childhood, to the wandering explorations of adult life and, finally, to the desired order and harmony achieved in old age. In this chapter, I begin by exploring the structure of enunciation and representation evidenced in the novel, contextualizing it in relation to Cláudio's artistic practice and highlighting its interpretative consequences. I then progress to the analysis of the memory work enacted in *Astronomia*, focusing especially on the role which intermediality and intertextuality play in the novel. I argue that they are catalysts for the exercise of imaginative invention, which is fulfilled in an intensely intricate, personal and evidently fictional narrative pattern. Moreover, I clarify how the notions of reflective and prospective nostalgia, ruinophilia, and anamorphosis emerge in the work and are helpful for its interpretation. Complementarily, I propose to relate the engagement with memory evidenced in *Astronomia* with the challenges posed on individuals and communities by the current social, economic, and cultural conditions. Progressing from this discussion, I contend that the unresolved tensions relating to memory and understanding evidenced in the novel lead to the exploration of a cosmic imagery, which I examine. I clarify that said imagery is grounded on a reflection on the arts and especially on writing, and that it acquires a truly existential dimension.

In this respect, I further argue that the retrieval and use in *Astronomia* of a Pythagorean-Platonic conception of the cosmos is one of the responses to the challenges previously outlined, expressing the narrative subject's desire for indexation in time and space, as well as to achieve a harmonious rapport with his trajectory. I conclude this chapter with a reflection on what *Astronomia* tells us about the most recent novelistic production in Portuguese. In this regard, I discuss the distinctive traits of this production and I speculate on whether a new mode can be identified in these works which would justify a new categorization.

## Oneself as Another

In *Astronomia*, the narrator represents the experiences of Mário Cláudio in the third person. Throughout the work, the main character is successively referred to as *o velho* (the old man), *o rapaz* (the young man), and *o menino* (the little boy), in the first, second, and third sections of the novel, respectively. I shall deal with the reversed attribution of age in relation to chronology below; at this point, however, I would like to stress that the structure of enunciation selected institutes a break between the narrator and the main character, which in turn makes it possible for the process of reading oneself as another person to be achieved. To this general strategy, we must add the fact that in the novel the character of Cláudio is occasionally portrayed as being in the act of observing and interpreting himself as another *persona*, via his identification with various literary characters or with those represented in paintings. This en abyme devise has the effect of further highlighting the overall enunciative structure of the novel.

The first notable instance of this occurs in a passage in which the character of Cláudio identifies himself and his partner with the two historical figures depicted in the painting 'The Ambassadors', by Hans Holbein (Cláudio 2015: 239–41). Here, the impending separation of the two men is associated with the image of the globe, of travel, and of the measuring of time depicted in the painting, but most especially with the skull represented at the feet of Jean de Dinteville and Georges de Selve by means of anamorphosis. The reference to anamorphosis (a distorted projection requiring the viewer to occupy a specific vantage point and/or to use a special device to view an image) is relevant. First, because of the significance which the skull and the ideas of death and perishability have in the novel, and also because this device, which became increasingly popular in the Baroque period, is a manifestation of perspectivism and a signifier of ambiguity. It conveys the concurrent notions of presence and absence, and revelation and concealment. In this specific case, of the characters of Cláudio and his then partner, both present and absent in the painting, and of the empirical author-narrator himself, also ambiguously present and absent in the work. In addition, anamorphosis will prove instrumental for our reading of a novel which, through its cultivation of ruins that are given new life, addresses the presence and absence of the past, the ambiguity associated with its imaginative reinvention through memory.

The other clear example of an instance in which the main character is shown observing himself occurs in the third section of the novel, and again relates to painting. In a telling passage, Cláudio is seen going through his morning routine and finally taking on the *persona* of the aged writer who, having prepared himself appropriately, sits at his writing desk. It is at this point that he contemplates and assesses the paintings of himself produced throughout the years, which he proceeds to read in a detached and detailed manner, finally choosing to take on *a máscara de lama* (the mask of mud) that presents itself to him, a signifier of the transitory human condition (Cláudio 2015: 309–10).

What we witness in the two passages just mentioned, and likewise arguably in the novel in general, is therefore a game of multiple representations en abyme, which should not be mistaken for a hall of mirrors, by which a given subject seeks to understand his trajectory, both identifying and detaching from the person he imagines he was at different points in time. This process, which underlines the hermeneutic virtues of self-projection in art and narrative (a means to construct the narrative self, one could argue, precarious as it may be), is deeply ambiguous and involves both concealment and revelation, presence and absence, and affirmation and doubt.

Cláudio's approach to self-representation in *Astronomia* should furthermore be understood in relation to his specific artistic practice. To begin with, one should highlight the fact that Mário Cláudio is a pseudonym and that, following David Martens (2007: 44), the process by which an author adopts a pseudonym entails a fictionalization of the self. This means that by taking a pseudonym an author becomes a character, in fact a supposed author, a strategy of depersonalization which is similar to the one involved in the creation of a heteronym, that is to say, of an alter ego, with their own distinctive biography and artistic trajectory. In addition, Cláudio himself has on several occasions explained that he understands his creative process as partly depending on the adoption of masks of others, which at any given point may obliquely reveal his own concerns and character. This is a process which is fictionally depicted in the author's works, including *Astronomia* (Cláudio 2015: 135, 188). Finally, in reference to the subject at hand, we must mention the character of Tiago Veiga, who is regarded by many critics as a Claudian heteronym (Arnaut 2012; Machado 2018; Real 2011; Soares 2019). Whilst I would dispute the immediate identification of Tiago Veiga as a heteronym of Mário Cláudio in the same manner as, for instance, Álvaro de Campos is a heteronym of Fernando Pessoa, one must recognize the logic of the differential projection of Cláudio onto the figure of the poet from Minho (and from many other places), which, to use a concept proposed by Maria Irene Ramalho, firmly situates the pair Cláudio/Veiga within the constellation of Pessoa.

The constellation is an attempt on the part of Ramalho to break with the conditioning logic of the theory of influences and to think of engagements with others as offering the possibility for creative self-discovery (Santos 2021). Following this train of thought, I would argue that there is a notable conjunction between the artistic processes followed by Pessoa and Cláudio, but likewise a patent divergence, a fact which the Claudian creative processes described above help clarify. Be that as it may, Veiga enables Cláudio to fictionally explore a variety of concerns and aspects of his own *persona*, through differential self-projection. Moreover, it is in *Tiago Veiga – Uma Biografia* (Cláudio 2011), the monumental biography of the poet produced by Cláudio, that the trajectory of the character of Mário Cláudio, the author-narrator of this novel, is for the first time depicted at some length. So we can see the ways in which *Astronomia* fits into a broader artistic practice, and how it bears a special affinity with the *Biografia*, a work that not only constitutes an ambitious recreation of the social and cultural developments in Portugal and abroad in the course of the twentieth century, but in which memory (personal and collective) is itself one of the main subjects.

## Memory

I should like to examine at this point how the textualization of memory is fulfilled in *Astronomia*, and what role intermediality and intertextuality play in this process. This will enable me to delve into the motivations for this engagement with memory, interpreting it in relation to a specifically Portuguese and likewise to a broader context.

The process of recovery of the past is initially depicted in *Astronomia* as the reconstruction of the demolished family home, operated by the character of the author-narrator, who represents himself sitting at the desk of the office of this ruined home: 'À secretária do gabinete o velho, tendo esfregado os olhos, reedifica a casa demolida' (Cláudio 2015: 39). This image, which is recurrently present in the first section of the novel, equates writing with the reclamation of the ruins of a demolished home, and implicitly of the narrator's long lost family. Furthermore, it has the contradictory effect of conveying the elision of the passage of time whilst evidently acknowledging it. Finally, one can argue that these ruins stand for memories and for thought processes themselves, which constitute the very substance of the work.

The elements employed to fulfil the imaginative reconstruction of memory signalled here include for the most part biographical anecdotes and personal observations and reflections. These are crucially complemented by references to photographic portraits, objects, and places, some of which are graphically presented in the work. Likewise, excerpts of literary texts are frequently inserted into the novel. These excerpts and the other elements alluded to are carefully integrated into the text, thus adding layers of meaning to the account and contributing to its distinctive structure and rhythm. By focusing on exemplary passages from *Astronomia*, I now briefly examine how these strategies are put into place and what effects they have.

The first portrait referenced in the novel is that of Mariozinho, Cláudio's uncle deceased in infancy, whose name he adopted when defining his literary *persona*. The portrait, which is graphically reproduced in the novel, evidently elicits a sentiment of nostalgia, which is explored in the text (see figure 2.1 below).

But more importantly, the photograph is framed by a textual apparatus that allows for it to be meaningfully integrated into the structure of the narrative (Cláudio 2015: 26–7). This apparatus includes excerpts from the collection of short stories titled *Stella Matutina*, as well as the depiction of the behaviour of the protagonist's grandmother towards the photograph of her deceased son (she briefly and longingly contemplates the photograph, only to hide it from sight). Finally, we witness how the central character himself, inspired by the short stories and his grandmother's grief and behaviour, identifies Mariozinho with an angel, a phantasmatic and unpredictable companion who in this manner comes to life. The intricate structure summarily described here serves the purpose of representing the manner in which the protagonist processed not only the death of an infant relative, but his own near-death experience, which

**Figure 2.1** Photographic portrait of Mariozinho. In *Astronomia* (Cláudio 2015: 27).

is depicted in the following sequence. Here again intertextual memory plays a crucial role, as the illness and subsequent recovery of the main character is told in a narrative thread punctuated by excerpts of Charles Perrault's *Little Thumbling*, with whose narrow escapes he identifies.

The passage illustrates how portraits demand narrativization in order to become individually relevant (Stewart 1993: 125–6). The narrative structure is composite, defining a rhythmic pattern which has the effect of stressing the fictionality of the events depicted. This in turn allows for the subversion of what Marianne Hirsch described as familial gaze or a set way of remembering (arguably illustrated in the behaviour of the protagonist's grandmother) in view precisely of the configuration of personal memories (Hirsch 2012). Finally, we should note that these facts are made especially dramatic on account of the extreme use of creative concatenation that characterizes the first section of *Astronomia*, in which a child's thought processes are imagined.

In all the sections of *Astronomia*, memorial objects, whether they are represented graphically in the work or not, become the nucleus for imaginative appropriations, initiating narratives and reflections on the part of the narrator. In infancy, objects are recurrently represented as taking on a life of their own, whilst in later life they are still the point of departure for narrative creativity, although in this case the prevailing outlook may be either cynical or nostalgic. One fine example of the former case occurs in the passage in which the death of the protagonist's grandmother is obliquely told (Cláudio 2015: 93–105). The text again begins by staging the act of writing at the desk in the office of the demolished family home, from where the narrator, who identifies with the protagonist, observes his faithful memory of his grandmother's bedroom, onto which he slowly enters: 'À secretária do escritório da casa demolida, e observando a memória que não o atraiçoa, o velho entra pé ante pé ao fim da tarde no quarto da Avó' (Cláudio 2015: 93). The sequence is made up of a diverse range of elements, including for the most part anecdotes relating to the grandmother's habits: for instance, her expressed devotion to Mariozinho, which is compounded with her religious fervour, or the fact that she used to write in order to process her grief (an attitude which mirrors that of the narrator). These descriptions are in turn complemented by excerpts from religious texts, consistent with both the tone of the sequence and the grandmother's character. But certainly the most striking references are to the objects in the room, one of which, a figurine of our Lady of Lourdes, is presented graphically in the work (Cláudio 2015: 96). From the imagined perspective of a child, these objects acquire a life of their own and, animated by *uma energia mágica* (a kind of magical energy), they move and perform actions consistent with the character attributed to them. Clearly, objects are associated with the grandmother and bringing them to life dramatizes the actualization of the space and of the characters depicted in the text. Furthermore, like we saw earlier, objects too contribute towards the construction of a composite and harmonious patterned structure, ultimately designed to re-imagine the traumatic passing of a close relative. Once again, referentiality and material memory serve only to highlight the role played by imaginative recreation of memory in the work, of which the representation of the moving objects is the clearest signifier. As the young boy grows older, although memorial objects become static and return to their places, they remain the pretext for imaginative elaborations on the part of the protagonist (Cláudio 2015: 159–61).

Intermediality and intertextuality are therefore complementary in *Astronomia*. The photographs inserted into the novel include one sole image of a person (Mariozinho) and of a place (a ruined house), representing for the most part objects (a statuette, personal documents, medals, a coffee pot, an electric toothbrush, and soft toys) and book related items (mostly book covers and illustrations). The graphic materialization of memory present in the work creates meanings through intermedial border crossing, conveying ideas of nostalgia, playfulness, and self-deprecation. In spite of their referential nature, through their integration into the fabric of the text, the images contribute to stressing the fictionality and partiality of the narrative and the role which imagination plays therein; likewise, they enhance the ambiguity of the memory work enacted in the text, putting into relief the contradictory nature of the recollection of the past, inevitably gone and yet still present, patently derelict but perhaps still holding potential for the future.

How are we to interpret the memory work present in *Astronomia*, its cultivation of memorial objects and images, and its use of intertextuality and intermediality in order to create textual patterns that re-invent the past? How can we understand the novel's engagement with an imagery of ruins, which entails the exploration of the ambiguity between presence and absence, persistence and perishability, and life and decay? We can perhaps begin to unravel this thread by examining a passage located at the very end of the second section of *Astronomia*, which engages in a clear manner with all of these matters (Cláudio 2015: 306–7).

In the sequence, the protagonist tells of when he decided to acquire and rebuild a house in the countryside. The act of re-building the house, we are told, was meant to provide the main character with an *ilusão da perenidade* (illusion of perpetuity), proposed in the face of the destruction of all of his previous family homes, whose ruination the narrator proceeds to describe at some length. This new country home is populated with family heirlooms, which, it is said, *duram na obstinação da sua rebelião contra a morte* (last in the obstinacy of their rebellion against death). But if objects constitute a form of support for the protagonist ('Neles se ampara a cavalgada dos dias'), they are at the same time reminders of death and perishability, whose imagery is in many ways alluded to: the clock whose pendulum was immobilized at the time of the death of a family member, the Brussels lace brought by an uncle from the battle of La Lys, the ragged clothes from days gone by which the protagonist imagines to be wearing, and the crumbling manuscript on which he writes his novel.

Certainly, following Marianne Hirsh and Leo Spitzer, the testimonial objects referenced in the passage and in the novel in general can be regarded as 'points of memory – points of intersection between past and present, memory and postmemory, personal and cultural recollection' (Hirsch and Spitzer 2006: 353). Moreover, as the passage clarifies, the insistence in *Astronomia* on objects and

**Figure 2.2** Photograph of ruined country home. In *Astronomia* (Cláudio 2015: 306).

technologies that allow for the materialization of memory is linked with a deep-seeded sense of loss deriving from the awareness of the passage of time and consequent break in continuity.

We can argue that the acceleration of the pace of change is part and parcel of the modern technological, economic, and cultural landscape, causing memory crises and corresponding coping strategies, including, for instance, the development of instruments and technologies for the materialization of memory, as well as the artistic exploration of individual appropriations of the past, or even the idealization of rural life (Terdiman 1993: 3–4). In *Astronomia* a connection is established between the current social and cultural arrangements and the memory crisis depicted in the work. In this respect, the novel gives special attention to the current modes of communication, which by their speed of circulation on local and global scales, impose the logic of the ephemeral on the subject's life and undermine his possibilities for understanding his own trajectory and the world he lives in. In 'Cosmos' the aged protagonist is shown zapping through television channels, whose constant flow of disconnected images is sarcastically depicted, anxiously and blindingly longing to retain them and thus to achieve a semblance of redemption: 'cego por essa ânsia de redenção a que nenhum invento humano alcança dar resposta' (Cláudio 2015: 414).

One of the ways of coping with this pervading sense of precariousness is the recourse to memory. And so, immediately after the sequence above, the protagonist is portrayed having lunch by himself. The scene is an opportunity to elaborate on the frailty of the human body and condition, a recurrent theme in the final section of the novel, in which the daily routine and ailments of the aged author are at times intricately (almost voyeuristically) described (Cláudio 2015: 332–40). But it also offers some of the clearest examples of the process of transposition between present and past in *Astronomia*. The main character is here both an old man and a little boy, who recalls the past family meals as if they were taking place at the moment of description, a sort of complete moment in which, partly aided by the effects of wine, past and future become amalgamated as if into one single cloud: 'E recorre portanto à garrafa pousada no soalho a seu lado … para produzir o suave obnubilamento, expresso na nuvem em que se amalgam passado e futuro' (Cláudio 2015: 417). Two important ideas emerge in the passage. The first is that of a totalizing present, in which the past, present, and future are merged. Second, the fact that the novel explicitly connects past and future is significant for what it reveals in terms of how the relationship between memory and the future is conceived in the work. Memory is regarded here not only as retrospective, nor as being merely convocated and made present at any given point in time: it contains a prospective dimension and is valuable in view of the future.

Still, another matter is at work here, one which is hinted at above through the allusions to the general precariousness of human life and to the notion of redemption. It refers to an existential, arguably religious longing, which would enable the main character to overcome the feelings of loneliness and frailty just mentioned. As we saw, the modern mechanisms that ensure the flow of information are often the pretext for these reflections. Indeed, the protagonist's contact with the digital world, including the meanderings of Facebook, elicits in him a sentiment of profound dissatisfaction with *uma era em que tudo se abraça, mas em que nada afinal se integra* (an age in which all things are embraced but nothing is ultimately integrated) (Cláudio 2015: 449). Moreover, it is stated, of the universal machine (a signifier for information technology which is at the same time evocative of past representations of the cosmos) the main character asks something more: *a sumária revelação do rosto único de Deus* (the revelation of the face of God) (Cláudio 2015: 447). I return to this matter shortly, but I would like now to zoom in again on the memory work evidenced in *Astronomia* and to read it in relation to contemporary cultural trends in Portugal and beyond.

Certainly, a critical approach to memory has been one of the central concerns in the Portuguese arts since the end of the dictatorship in 1974 and the ensuing democratic transition of the 1970s and 1980s. During this period, Portuguese artists engaged with the country's post-colonial, post-imperial, and semi-peripheral status, as well as with its contradictory integration into the European Union and the global economic and cultural system, which among many things imposed a media- and market-oriented culture that often brushes over diversity and complexity. In literature, one of the facets of this engagement was the cultivation of the nineteenth-century family novel, which allowed for social developments in the fabric of Portuguese society to be assessed via the portrayal of the trajectories of families. As João Barrento argued, the family, the clan, and the family home became frequently explored literary *topoi* during this time. These were often represented as being in the process of decaying, a fact which conveyed both the notion of the end of a certain way of living, and likewise the ambiguities of history, all of which are mirrored in the complex structure of the works (Barrento 2016: 36–47). This being said, *Astronomia* is a much more recent work which, although being informed by the trend above, is arguably related to a recent renewal of interest in history in Portuguese culture. In fact, the events leading to the sovereign debt crisis of 2008 and its immediate aftermath brought to the fore concerns relating to the trajectory followed by Portuguese society since the democratic transition, including the flaws of its institutions, its difficult integration into the capitalist World-System, and its deeply problematic understanding of its colonial history and respective consequences.

Moreover, as we plainly saw above, Cláudio's approach to memory is motivated and informed to a great degree by global developments which affect specific places in particular ways. The resurgence of memory in many societies in the 1980s and 1990s was associated by Andreas Huyssen with time-space compression, cultural acceleration, and the informational and perceptual overload, which individuals are not well equipped to handle (Huyssen 2000: 35). He further stressed that the attention given to memory has both political and cultural motivations: 'Politically, many memory practices today counteract the triumphalism of modernization theory in its latest guise of "globalization". Culturally, they express the growing need for spatial and temporal anchoring in a world of increasing flux in ever denser networks of compressed time and space' (Huyssen 2000: 36). In this sense, what he called the present pasts trend recovers the high modernist dream of a better past, which consisted of living 'in a securely circumscribed place, with a sense of stable boundaries and a place-bound culture with its regular flow of time and a core of permanent relations' (Huyssen 2000: 34). However, Huyssen also argued, the question was no longer that of recovering a golden mythical past, but simply, as he put it, 'the attempt, as we face the very real processes of time-space compression, to secure some continuity within time, to provide some extension of lived space within which we can breathe and move' (Huyssen 2000: 34). This entails contesting the denial of time, space, and place proposed by cybercapitalism and globalization, and finding a permeable place and time from which to speak and act. Somehow memory, individual, familial, regional, and inevitably national, was found to provide the coordinates for this exercise of resistance. But memory, Huyssen alerted, is transitory and unreliable, and its uses multiple; moreover, he stressed, we should not forget to remember the future (Huyssen 2018).

*Astronomia* expresses precisely the need to articulate in the present links between the past and the future, established in the face of the awareness of cultural acceleration, informational overload, and of a pervading sense of individual and collective breakage. At any rate, it is important to stress that this attempt is materialized in what I would like to characterize, following Svetlana Boym, as a brand of reflective nostalgia (Boym 2001: 41–9). For Boym, the latter is a product of times of accelerated social and cultural change and conveys an ironic stance regarding the possibility of retrieving and understanding the past, which explains its obsession with the imagery of ruins. Ruins express exactly the ambiguity associated with the retrieval of the past, regarded as still present and yet as manifestly gone. But I would like to go further and to read *Astronomia* in reference to another concept proposed by Boym, that of prospective nostalgia (Boym 2017: 39–49). With this notion, Boym stresses the productive nature of nostalgia, the idea that in the past (critically understood) may lie alternatives for the future. Boym identifies this trend in contemporary art, in works that in her view tap into a Baroque vein, evidenced, for instance, in the activation of the figure of anamorphosis, with its play between presence and absence, and its mode of operation grounded on the awareness of the effects of varying perspectives. As we saw above, through its imaginative re-invention of characters and social landscapes, and likewise via its activation of intermedial and intertextual memory, and its reflection on memorial objects, *Astronomia* proposes a creative, future-oriented engagement with the past, in the context of which both ruins and anamorphosis play a relevant role. However, as we also saw, the Baroque inspired musings on permanence and impermanence, life and death, and the precariousness of the human condition lead in turn to a broader sense of being lost and to existential angst. These are tentatively resolved through the activation of a cosmic imagery, which I argue has religious undertones and on which I shall now focus.

## Cosmos

In *Astronomia*, the arts and especially writing are regarded as a means to understand and confer meaning to an individual's journey, and likewise in this manner to overcome the feeling of frailty, loneliness, and loss of purpose that sets in as life progresses towards its end. The work expresses the belief that through the representation and re-ordering of the facts of life one may become harmonized with one's trajectory and with the world. In an attitude clearly evocative of the modernists, the narrator, aware of the difficulties inherent in artistic expression, still believes he can find the elusive word that shall redeem him.

In the novel, writing entails the exercise of an almost childish imagination: it is akin to drawing, a process that is both conscious and unconscious, and intuitive and rational. In addition, it involves a long process of revision on the part of the writer, which is meant to achieve *uma escrita fluente, posto que não correcta, e poderosa bastante para que ele pressinta a recôndita harmonia que resulta da coincidência do arrazoado que debita com esse que platonicamente corresponde a uma ideia guardada na mente dos deuses* (a fluent account, not necessarily correct, but powerful enough for him to perceive the hidden harmony that results from the coincidence between the speech he produces and that which platonically corresponds to an idea kept in the mind of the gods) (Cláudio 2015: 349). According to this view, writing should exist in accordance with the rhythm of the world, it should be in tune with the music of the Pythagorean spheres and give access to a dimension of pre-existing words: *no princípio não era o verbo* (in the beginning it was not the word) is the title of the image on the cover of the book.

The passage clearly references the Ancient Greek concept of cosmos. For Ancient Greeks, cosmos stood for order, and it was associated with ideas of harmony and beauty. In Pythagorean-Platonic philosophy, the order and beauty of the universe consisted of mathematical ratios and proportions, which were expressed in the music of the spheres. The cosmos was therefore conceived as an ontological *logos* which the rational subject should strive to perceive via contemplation. If in the end one achieved this, then order would rule the soul, and desire and chaos would be replaced with inner order and harmony. In Platonic philosophy, the subject is therefore not conceived as opposed to the world; on the contrary, human beings must strive to be in tune with the cosmos so as to achieve a state of inner harmony. Modernity brought an entirely different understanding of the universe and subjectivity, which would decisively contribute to the development of a secular culture: the idea of a subject as a disengaged rational being, who constructs and manipulates a world that is in itself devoid of meaning. By the nineteenth century, Charles Taylor argued, the notion of *cosmos* was eventually replaced by the idea of the *universe*: an infinite, timeless, anonymous, and meaningless space (Taylor 2007: 326). Yet, under different guises the idea of cosmos enjoyed a long life in Western cultures, evidenced, for instance, in the retrieval of the Pythagorean-Platonic archetype during the Renaissance, or later in the Romantic period. I would like to argue that *Astronomia* recovers the notion of cosmos in order to posit a subjective indexation in time and space that goes beyond human limitations. This is made clear in the final passage of the novel.

Here, the aged author (referred to as 'o menino') prepares to go to bed, every detail of his routine and condition being described in order to underline his human frailty. It is in a state of limbo between vigil and sleep that the character imagines himself drifting into the cosmos, the separation between the subject and the universe collapsing, as do the oppositions between outside and inside, past and future, and beginning and ending:

> E rompem-se num relâmpago as fronteiras do espaço, absorvido pela cristalina amplidão de um firmamento que não se estrutura em norte e sul, nem em este e oeste, e onde não se aponta um cima, nem um em baixo, um aqui, nem um além, um ontem, nem um amanhã. No seu solitário trajecto, limpo de ponto de partida, e liberto de lugar de chegada, o menino estende os dedos para os corpos celestes que se lhe disseminam à volta, ele próprio transformado em corpo astral, e atado por um imperceptível cordão à substância do mundo, mas lançado no voo em que o nada se agrega à totalidade, e em que a luz se desenvolve em luz, a energia se multiplica em energia, e a vaga imensa se derrama na escuridão.
>
> (Cláudio 2015: 453–4)

And in a flash the frontiers of space are broken, absorbed by the crystalline vastness of a firmament not structured between north and south, and east and west, and in which there is neither an up or down, here or there, nor yesterday or tomorrow. In his solitary route, clear from a point of departure, and free from a place of arrival, the boy stretches his fingers towards the celestial bodies that surround him, himself transformed into an astral body, and connected by a barely perceptible cord to the substance of the world, launched in the flight in which nothingness is aggregated to totality, and light develops into light, energy is multiplied into energy, and the immense wave pours into darkness.

The text is at the same time evocative of one of the great modernist texts, Hermann Broch's *The Death of Virgil*, and of Dante's luminous neo-platonic *Paradiso*. It proposes the integration of the protagonist into a diffuse mass, also figured in *Astronomia* as an amniotic fluid, accessed via sleep and dreams. In this space, a coincidence of opposites (*coincidentia oppositorum*) occurs, which prompts a more radical explanation for the coincidence of present and past evident from the very beginning of the novel. Finally, this passage invites us to revise the interpretation of the composite fabric of the work, and to propose reading it as a textual cosmos, made up of connections between different elements, subjectively determined constellations which have a distinctively rhythmic or musical dimension and are designed to achieve a state of harmony between the subject and his known references of time and space. Thus the predicaments depicted throughout the work (associated with the disordered non-indexed space of the galaxy) are fleetingly overcome.

## Conclusion

What does *Astronomia* tell us about the contemporary Portuguese novel? Certainly, the novel inherits a postmodern outlook regarding representation, a fact which is evidenced in its very structure. But there is no radical hermeneutics of doubt at play here: we are not lost in a labyrinthine structure designed to question representation, nor do we witness a revision of received discourses, traits which would also be identified as postmodern, or at least with a given interpretation of postmodernist aesthetics and worldview. What comes across from the work is a predominant notion that words matter and that they can be successfully used to engage with individual and collective predicaments.

Researchers have tried to determine the traits that characterize the cultural trend which followed postmodernism. A return to historicity is among them, manifested in an engagement with current issues and likewise in the recovery of realism (which now includes multimodality). The resurgence of an interest in affect and relationality is another of the features identified, coming as a response to a prevailing sense of fragmentation in our modes of living, as well as arising from the desire for connection stimulated by the threats to our common existence. But perhaps one of the most interesting contributions to this discussion was made by Van den Akker, Gibbons, and Vermeulen. Besides mentioning historicity and affect, they refer to oscillation (rather than synthesis) as one of the characteristics of the current artistic landscape, which they dub metamodern – oscillation between the artistic practices and outlooks associated with postmodernism, realism, and earlier movements, such as Modernism. Oscillation 'between irony and enthusiasm, between sarcasm and sincerity, between eclecticism and purity, between deconstruction and construction', which in their view point to a new sensibility 'situated beyond the postmodern, one that is related to recent metamorphoses or qualitative changes in Western capitalist societies' (Van den Akker, Gibbons, and Vermeulen 2017: 11).

Adopting a contemporary standpoint and addressing current challenges, *Astronomia* fits this description in peculiar fashion: it engages with history and memory in a subjective and affectual way, and it delves in mythical meaning making, even entering the realm of the existential and religious. In doing so, it displays affinities with modernism and earlier trends (the Baroque and Romanticism), and it reveals an oscillation between affirmation and doubt, and scepticism and sincerity, which ultimately and in its own manner strikes a final hopeful note.

# References

Arnaut, A. P. (2012), 'Tiago Veiga: Uma Biografia (Mário Cláudio): a invenção da verdade', in C. Reis, J. A. C. Bernardes, and M. H. Santana (eds.), *Uma Coisa na Ordem das Coisas: Estudos para Ofélia Paiva Monteiro*, 59–76, Coimbra: Imprensa da Universidade de Coimbra. Available online: https://doi.org/10.14195/978-989-26-1164-8_3.

Barrento, J. (2016), *A Chama e as Cinzas: Um Quarto de Século de Literatura Portuguesa: 1974–2000*, Lisboa: Bertrand Editora.

Boym, S. (2001), *The Future of Nostalgia*, New York: Basic Books.

Boym, S. (2017), *The Off-Modern*, New York, London: Bloomsbury Academic.

Cláudio, M. (2011), *Tiago Veiga: Uma Biografia*, Alfragide: D. Quixote.

Cláudio, M. (2015), *Astronomia*, Alfragide: Dom Quixote.

Hirsch, M. (2012), *Family Frames: Photography, Narrative, and Postmemory*, Cambridge, Mass.: Harvard University Press.

Hirsch, M. and Spitzer, L. (2006), 'Testimonial Objects: Memory, Gender, and Transmission', *Poetics Today* 27: 353.

Huyssen, A. (2000), 'Present Pasts: Media, Politics, Amnesia', *Public Culture* 12 (1): 21–38.

Huyssen, A. (2018), 'State of the Art in Memory Studies'. Available online: https://www.politika.io/en/notice/state-of-the-art-in-memory-studies-an-interview-with-andreas-huyssen.

Machado, Á. M. (2018), 'Culto Do Lúdico, Heteronímia e Espírito Do Lugar Em Mário Cláudio', *Revista Do Centro de Estudos Portugueses* 38 (59): 11. Available online: https://doi.org/10.17851/2359-0076.38.59.11-21.

Martens, D. (2007), *L'invention de Blaise Cendrars: une poétique de la pseudonymie*, Leuven: UCL.

Rajewsky, I. O. (2011), 'Intermediality, Intertextuality, and Remediation: A Literary Perspective on Intermediality', *Intermédialités* 6 (August): 43–64. Available online: https://doi.org/10.7202/1005505ar.

Real, M. (2011), 'Nova Teoria Da Heteronímia', *Jornal de Letras, Artes e Ideias* 1062 15 June 2011: 10.

Santos, M. I. R. (2021), *Fernando Pessoa e outros fingidores*, Ensaios sobre Pessoa, Lisboa: Tinta-da-China.

Soares, M. (2019), *O Essencial sobre Mário Cláudio*, Lisboa: Imprensa Nacional.

Stewart, S. (1993), *On Longing: Narratives of the Miniature, the Gigantic, the Souvenir and the Collection*, Durham: Duke University Press.

Taylor, C. (2007), *A Secular Age*, Cambridge, Mass.: Belknap Press of Harvard University Press.

Terdiman, R. (1993), *Present Past: Modernity and the Memory Crisis*, Ithaca: Cornell University Press.

Van den Akker, R., Gibbons, A., and Vermeulen, T. (eds.) (2017), *Metamodernism: Historicity, Affect and Depth after Post-Modernism*, London; New York: Rowman & Littlefield International.

# Sketching *Gnaisse*: The Process of Reading a Metamorphic Novel

Daniela Côrtes Maduro

## Entering the Labyrinth

*Gnaisse*, a novel written by Luís Carmelo, is a sinister and complex book designed to prevent the reader from completely deciphering its content. This 17.8-centimetre-high and 13-centimetre-wide book, published in 2015, contains a rapidly shifting fictional world, much like the fast-paced world inhabited by its readers. Prior to purchasing this 124-page book, the reader is warned about the subversive tone of its narrative. On the website of the Portuguese publisher Abysmo, the work's blurb seems determined to erode the readers' interest in the narrative (or to discourage buyers from acquiring this object). This fragmented text, mostly comprised of short and straightforward sentences, describes *Gnaisse* as a superposition of events. As a matter of fact, the blurb itself resembles a geological sample which allows the reader to observe the narrative sedimentation of *Gnaisse*:[1]

> A Professor is in love with a student that likes Nietzsche, bonsais, and butane canisters. This girl suddenly disappears. The Professor enters a religious temple, makes promises, is invaded by dreams that warn him about the dangers that he might be facing. One day, he starts smoking again and moves to another house. In this new house, there is a neighbour that screams at certain hours in the night. The Professor misses the student.
>
> (Carmelo 2015a)[2]

---

The research conducted to write this essay falls within the scope of the project UIDP/00759/2020, FCT – Foundation for Science and Technology, I.P.

[1] *Gnaisse* (in English, *Gneiss*) is the name of a sedimentary rock that changes in response to physical and chemical conditions (metamorphism).

[2] All quotations from *Gnaisse* (2015) were translated by the author of this essay.

This self-undermining blurb also portrays Carmelo's book as a 'novel where each mystery bestows the responsibility onto the next mystery, as in the strata of metamorphic rocks' (Carmelo 2015a). *Gnaisse* is comprised of two parts and six sections (A–F) further divided into thirteen subsections. Each one of these subsections complements and recombines the previous one, which means that the narrative is being permanently reinscribed during the reading process. Even though an alternative perspective on the events is introduced in each subsection, and therefore new information is added, *Gnaisse* does not offer a stable and complete account of events. To understand the narrative, readers need to diligently collect and fit together pieces of an intricate jigsaw puzzle, whose intertextuality and constrained writing resemble George Perec's *La Vie mode d'emploi* (1978).

No other voice besides that of the omniscient narrator is heard. Therefore, only he can help the reader decipher the enigma of the text. Unfortunately for those readers seeking coherence and precision, this narrator (we are ultimately informed that his name is Leonel or LC) displays clear signs of unstable behaviour. Readers learn that there is someone missing in his life (a mysterious woman who used to attend his classes) and come to understand that the disappearance of this female character has sentenced this man to a dark journey into his mind, during which he will obsessively replay memories of the time he spent with her. Devastated by pain, and struggling to overcome his sense of loss, LC is trapped in his own mind, and becomes unable to keep a clear division between fact and fiction. Readers soon learn that the novel's sinister tone and disintegration into loosely connected parts are motivated by LC's meltdown. Besides the feeling of uncertainty propagated by the narrator's mental state, we are told that the mysterious woman enjoys lying (Carmelo 2015: 94). Therefore, the readers of *Gnaisse* are continuously presented with inaccurate information that they cannot verify.

Since the account of events is presented as the result of intoxication, depression, and lying, a connection between deception and fiction is repeatedly emphasized. LC's interpretation of events is untrustworthy, which means that readers face unchartered territory that they must explore on their own. *Gnaisse* is a 'text without lines that evolves along the thickness of space in the same way that the land unmarked by trails and paths creates its infinite marks and orientations' (Carmelo 2015: 119). *Gnaisse*'s protagonist often refers to Coleridge's theories of imagination and fantasy. He states that it is possible to fantasize about nearly everything. However, as imagination allows the creation of anything from nothing, only imagination can reveal 'the disruptive side' of a human being (Carmelo 2015: 44). *Gnaisse* is therefore a novel about fiction's unlimited power to recombine and expand reality into alternate worlds.³

According to Matthias Stephan, postmodernism has been associated with 'intertextuality, metafiction, pastiche, playfulness, and the mixing of genres' (Stephan 2019: 6). The same author relates postmodernist thought with a 'rhizomatic labyrinth' that cannot be fully described (2019: 58). Due to the obsessive recapitulation of events, readers are continuously redirected to the same starting point: their ability to 'savour the fruit of slowness' (Carmelo 2015: 8) will be painstakingly tested in this meandering and cryptic novel based on 'rumours' (Carmelo 2015: 93). The following depiction of a bonsai (a multibranched and human-made plant that can last for a human lifetime) might well be an accurate description of this short, yet the size of a lifetime, novel: 'The Bonsai is a miniature that displays its roots developing from recurved trunks and a reduced number of branches' (Carmelo 2015: 7).

Ana Paula Arnaut claims that the first steps towards postmodernism in Portugal were taken in the pages of José Cardoso Pires's *Delfim* (1968). Thematically, Ana Paula Arnaut believes that there are two types of '(dis)orientation' in a postmodernist novel: a 'moderate' (dis)orientation that still fosters a connection with the real, despite the subversion of literary genres or narrative categories, and a 'celebratory' (dis)orientation which Arnaut relates to 'hypercontemporary fiction' created after 2000 (Arnaut 2018: 27). The term 'hypercontemporary' represents a new world order where technology and globalization (Arnaut 2018: 22) perform a central role. Though maintaining weak ties with reality, this second type of '(dis)orientation' overtly promotes multilinearity, evasiveness, and entropy, thus requiring the reader to act as an investigator (Arnaut 2018: 21). Carmelo's novel displays a 'vagrant morphology' (Carmelo 2015: 15), and, like the bougainvillea he often mentions, it can be equated with a 'labyrinth of branches' (Carmelo 2015: 15) that the reader must traverse. *Gnaisse*'s readers may try to disentangle the many links between events and, just like detectives, they may even try to gather information to unravel the mystery of the text. However, *Gnaisse* is an entropic narrative (Arnaut 2018, 42) that prevents readers from achieving their goals or reaching instant

---

³ In this essay, this term refers to the existence of distinct parallel worlds in *Gnaisse*. The term 'alternate' was extracted from the theory of possible worlds which contends that several distinct worlds may exist beyond the 'actual' or 'real' world. For more information on this subject, see Ryan n.d. and Ryan 1991.

gratification. Instead of reading the text to know more, readers are introduced to a plot that repeats the narration of the same events, recombining bits and pieces of reality, and relentlessly postponing a definite closure.

Citing Pareyson, Carmelo describes art as the process of 'creating radically new objects, i.e., pieces of reality added to the already existent reality ... with the same strength felt when initiating a new love affair' (2015: 21). According to *Gnaisse*'s narrator, Pareyson saw shapes as 'living organisms completely autonomous and independent' (Carmelo 2015: 22). As for works of art, these are described by the same author as 'forms of life and references to themselves, that are meant to be read, interpreted, and even modified, in a dynamic manner' (Carmelo 2015: 22). In section F, he explains to his students that Pareyson, once Umberto Eco's teacher, defined art as a process that permanently opens possibilities 'without walking towards the end or without ever reaching a summit' (Carmelo 2015: 91). As he explains Pareyson's theory, he claims that he felt that this theory was part of his body. His disorientation and undecidability mirror *Gnaisse*'s rhizomatic structure and cryptic tone.

After coming to terms with the narrative's indeterminacy, the reader accepts this novel as an unsolvable puzzle and as an endless treasure hunt. As Arnaut rightly remarks, in some postmodernist novels 'the Coleridgean voluntary suspension of disbelief is turned into a voluntary suspension of belief' (Arnaut 2018: 34). The reader of *Gnaisse* soon discovers that this labyrinthine book, careless of its readers' expectations, thrives on uncertainty and speculation.

## Recursive Memories[4]

As readers begin to engage with the different layers of *Gnaisse*, they plunge ever deeper into LC's mind. Carmelo describes memory as 'a chromatic game similar to a rainbow suspended on the brink of the ocean, from which everything, absolutely everything, can be explored' (Carmelo 2015: 8). LC obsessively reshuffles and reconstructs his own memories to tell an unfortunate love story. As a result, the reading process is turned into an archaeological venture during which objects or places trigger memories, and, consequently new retellings of the

---

[4] The term 'recursive' is used in different fields, namely computer science, biology, and literature. In this essay, this term is associated with works that, in order to evolve, repeatedly reconstruct previously narrated events, or that repeatedly describe the same events, though in an entirely different way. This is the case of *Gnaisse*.

same story. According to LC: 'When we lose someone important, some rituals and objects[5] emerge to supress that loss' (Carmelo 2015: 41). In the meantime, readers' expectations about a unifying closure are continuously frustrated.

The unfolding of events begins and ends when a point is drawn on a classroom's chalkboard. LC's first words are 'I had barely enough time to pull myself together, when', which indicates that the novel begins when he supposedly regained[6] his consciousness after becoming absentminded during an explanation of Kandinsky's circles and Pareyson's theories. However, instead of being back on track, the protagonist starts (or relapses into) his obsessive journey into the abyss: 'Nothing I said seemed clear … I felt I had become a runaway train' (Carmelo 2015: 9). Similar to a Möbius strip folding back on itself, the narrative is portrayed as nothing more than a series of reframed daydreams or a device scheduled to reboot at a certain point in time. The literary experiments created by Raymond Queneau in *Exercices de style* (1947), where the reader can read ninety-nine retellings of the same story, may come to mind while reading this novel. Indeed, the 'felt hat' around which Queneau's book gravitates is mentioned in *Gnaisse* more than once (page 68, 'felt beret', or page 75, 'felt hat'). In *Gnaisse*, the felt hat worn by the missing woman is described as the point 'around which reality revolved' (Carmelo 2015: 91–2).

The story that LC and the missing woman lived together is retold in each subsection. Even though some of these subsections may be transferred to other parts (for instance, in section F the name 'Nietzsche' is mentioned in Part 2, not in Part 3), they resurface in almost every section as described in Table 3.1. Unpredictability and mutation pervade the structure of the novel, rendering readers' attempt to rigorously schematize this gneissic novel impossible, and allowing nothing more than a vague sketch. In the already cited blurb, it is claimed that '[A]ll of the sudden, everything changes, as if the reported reality was nothing but a prestidigitation trick after all' (Carmelo 2015a). LC speaks about a 'conjuror that rearranges fragments' (Carmelo 2015: 8), surreptitiously referring to the role of the author in this story. Its self-reflexivity and exploration of narrative possibilities remind us of the rhizomatic book written by Italo Calvino, *Il castello dei destini incrociati* (1969), where a pack of cards is reshuffled

---

[5] Objects left behind by the vanishing woman are listed by L.C.: a pink lighter, a package with a rosemary bouquet that looked like marijuana and was always carried with her diligently wrapped with a ribbon (Carmelo 2015: 84).

[6] In section C, the protagonist will refer to this moment of awakening as the moment 'when he was still reasonably lucid' (Carmelo 2015: 43).

**Table 3.1** *Gnaisse*'s subsections

| Subsection | Elements |
|---|---|
| 1. | LC is in a classroom teaching and drawing on the blackboard. |
| 2. | Rape scene. Man with three hands. Blue tiles. |
| 3. | Nietzsche. Coffee factory. |
| 4. | Back to the classroom. |
| 5. | Memories from the missing woman. |
| 6. | Inability to describe the missing woman. |
| 7. | Encounter with transsexuals in the tram or reference to a documentary. |
| 8. | New house and screaming lady. Smoking in the balcony and reference to climbing plants. |
| 9. | Pastry shop and glass door. |
| 10. | Playground and description of the screaming lady. |
| 11. | Train station. Waking from a dream. |
| 12. | Encounter with a lady in the temple. |
| 13. | Pastry lady falls. |

to tell a story. However, in the final section of *Gnaisse*, the narrator declares that the entire story might not have been a product of an author but of LC's mind (Carmelo 2015: 114). Contrary to a conventional omniscient narrator who witnesses every action taking place, *Gnaisse*'s narrator is not omniscient in the sense that he sees, hears, or experiences everything, but because events are being obsessively reconstructed as fuzzy memories.

As the novel is mostly comprised of misleading clues that yield no concrete findings, together with possible paths that generally culminate in dead-ends, the process of filling in the gaps, as described by Wolfgang Iser (1980: 166), is taken to an extreme: those gaps that need to be filled in by the reader are deviously turned by Carmelo into bottomless black pits. An illustration of this vital part of the reading process is shared with the reader when LC refers to the empty spaces left by missing cobblestones in a Portuguese sidewalk (Carmelo 2015: 14).

LC claims that the work of art evolves from one point to the next in a manner that vastly exceeds its creator (Carmelo 2015: 6). This insubordination of the work of art is mirrored by LC's ineptitude at describing the mysterious female character around which the novel is built.[7] According to the overwhelmed narrator, she was supposed to be 'the first point of a set of points' he should have traversed (Carmelo 2015: 12) to reach 'the most desired of destinies' but, as much as he tries, she escapes 'the certainty of lines' (Carmelo 2015: 10). The narrator wishes he could tell a straightforward love story 'with no compass or rudder in his hand' (Carmelo 2015: 12), a story with a clear beginning, middle, and end, but all he can do is share a fragmented story that persistently alternates between unclear and conflicting impressions of reality.[8]

Like 'water running through his fingers' (Carmelo 2015: 10), the woman is portrayed as a fleeting and ungraspable moment.[9] LC names this character 'signal-woman' (Carmelo 2015: 16) and claims that she was a 'floating person' (Carmelo 2015: 11), reminding us of Lévi-Strauss's 'floating signifiers' (Lévi-Strauss 1980: 63). Devoid of meaning, these signifiers have the ability to disclose all possible (and even discordant) meanings.[10] Portrayed as the matrix of the fictional world, this woman's description is enmeshed within the novel's self-reference. In *Gnaisse*, people are described as 'labyrinths that go forward with two feet on the ground and two feet instigating the storm' (Carmelo 2015: 40), and therefore, they are also portrayed as volatile and undecipherable entities whose existence is determined by fate. Here is the information LC was able to recollect about the woman:

> Sometimes she was a brunette, at other times she was a blonde. Some days she would stutter, other days she would speak with the accent of sailors.[11] Her lips

---

[7] LC claims that, even though he repeated her name to exhaustion for months, he was never able to pronounce it (Carmelo 2015: 11). The portrayal of the woman as a stutterer further emphasizes the repetitive character of the novel (Carmelo 2015: 5).
[8] At a certain point, LC starts missing classes and appears unable to take control of his life.
[9] Here, we may identify a close link between the woman and the novel as part of a self-reflexive transgression.
[10] Luís Carmelo is a professor of semiotics and published abundantly about this field of research. This partly explains why the processes of signification and interpretation seem to hold substantial weight in this enigmatic novel. *Gnaisse* may reveal further autobiographical data whose presence was not explored in this essay.
[11] Carmelo uses the word 'nautas', also used as a suffix in words such as 'astronauts', 'argonauts', and 'cybernauts'. As the novel often refers to 'sailors', we opted for this translation.

were sometimes wide like a bay, or they would sometimes allow themselves to take the shape of a dike ... Some may find it strange, but I can assert that her name was always unpronounceable to me.

(Carmelo 2015: 10–11)[12]

According to Arnaut, postmodernist characters are no longer expected to have a name and are often identified by their attributes (Arnaut 2016: 16). These characters are introduced by sparse and limited (even cryptic or misleading) descriptions. As demonstrated before, this happens in *Gnaisse* due to the disintegrating state of the character. Arnaut claims that

> [T]he broken soul, the crooked and agonizing lives, the pain caused by different types of violence but also the fear and internal lacerations, are not described in a precise and unquestionable way, but must be guessed, or better, decodified through transferring images and figures/icons into characters.

(Arnaut 2016: 19)

Unable to describe events and characters[13] accurately, the troubled narrator introduces a collapsing fictional world that needs to be thoroughly reconstructed by the reader. Since nothing is presented as definite, this fictional world is permanently (re)generated. As already observed, the shattering of reality is caused by LC's neurotic revisitation of memories, which is triggered by his reiterated attempts to cope with suffering. Fragmentation of the self, a theme frequently addressed in postmodernist novels, is also explored in *Gnaisse*. As LC reveals: 'there are several Is, some teaching in the classroom, some navigating over the amphitheatre, others traversing her skin' (Carmelo 2015: 91). Instead of characters that disseminate Enlightenment's notion of a unified self, *Gnaisse* introduces irrational, troubled and ill-defined characters that are unable to guide readers through the fictional world.

In the already mentioned blurb, this novel is described as a 'metaphor of repetition and a metaphor of the ephemeral that portrays life in progress' (Carmelo 2015a). Although printed on changeless pages, this book uses

---

[12] Later, we are told that her father killed himself and that her mother lives in Angola. She worked in a bookstore that sold second-hand books, she took drugs and attended clubs *des bas-fonds*. The woman was also an obsessed reader, a kleptomaniac, a liar, and a wicked person (Carmelo 2015: 80–1). However, this information is shared by a character (her photographer friend) whom LC seems to distrust (Carmelo 2015: 62).

[13] LC is also unable to describe his own appearance and resorts to a comparison, made by the photographer, between himself and Matthew Brady's portrait of Edgar Allan Poe (Carmelo 2015: 46).

repetition to keep the narrative engine running. LC claims that he occasionally 'has the feeling that the time [he is] living is always the same' (Carmelo 2015a: 31). Besides LC's compulsive recollection of the time spent with the mysterious woman, the recursive movement of the novel is also created through the monotonous repetition of daily chores or, in LC's words, 'the day-to-day staging' (Carmelo 2015: 23). The pastry shop lady, the woman reading a magazine and Mr Correia are characters taken from everyday life. During the reading of *Gnaisse*, this group of characters seems to remain in an alternate universe, waiting until they are summoned to reinitiate the narrative once again.

The compulsive repetition of events (in LC's words, 'repetitions also have their own free forms that escape us', Carmelo 2015: 22) gives the work an open-ended character. In fact, the refusal to commit to a single ending, or to conclude the 'adventure of meaning' (Carmelo 2015: 34) is frequently highlighted by this novel. According to LC, the space he inhabits is made of letters and propagates an 'infinite curvature' (Carmelo 2015: 34). In Part B, he refers to a 'world that devours itself' and describes several self-cannibalistic processes that take place in the animal kingdom (Carmelo 2015: 27–8). Like the lemmings that feed on themselves and the scorpion that stings itself, Carmelo's novel consumes (or recombines) itself to ensure its survival. This multilayered and ouroboric[14] novel is the result of 'crossed alphabets' (Carmelo 2015: 119) that extend beyond the surface of paper sheets.

In one of the narrative's reconstructions, LC dreams he is climbing a bougainvillea and, as if gaining awareness of his own fictional existence, asks himself why he must climb all the way to the end of the journey, challenging the idea of a narrative as a path to closure (Carmelo 2015: 87–8). Characters that disrupt the barrier between fiction and reality, thus revealing the strings of their puppeteer, are common in postmodernist works and are part of a long tradition of metalepsis. An often-cited example of this metaleptic jump is Luigi Pirandello's *Sei personaggi in cerca d'autore* (1921), where a group of characters ask a director to finish their incomplete play. LC often declares that he feels lost and without purpose, like a sleepwalker (Carmelo 2015: 14). When he first meets the woman, he declares that 'it was like this moment was already inscribed on the mouth of some oracle' (Carmelo 2015: 23). However, contrary to Pirandello's characters, LC believes that his life is not ruled by an author, but, like all human beings,

---

[14] Carmelo's novel permanently refers to itself and, just like the Ouroboros eating its own tail, *Gnaisse* consumes itself to survive.

by indeterminacy and chance. In *Gnaisse*, randomness and metamorphism are mobilized to represent life.

According to LC, in *The Open Work* cited right at the beginning of section F, Eco describes art as a 'process that reopens possibilities, without making a work move along towards the end or the top' (Carmelo 2015: 91). In *Gnaisse*, circularity and self-reflexivity are used to postpone closure and, just like the Phoenix often mentioned in *Gnaisse*, to ensure this novel's continual reconstruction.

## Recursive Intermediations

According to Ana Paula Arnaut, postmodernist novels cultivate a 'mixture of genres' that is 'almost always subversive' (2016: 12). Arnaut also suggests the emergence of a new kind of novel, the 'intermedial novel', whose presence in Portugal becomes clearer after the year 2000 (Arnaut 2018: 23). The figure of the hermaphrodite, that 'intersects all potentialities and solutions' (Carmelo 2015: 47), is frequently invoked by Carmelo and expresses the hybridity and undecidability of this novel. Because it resorts to enigmatic illustrations and invokes several cinematic works, poems, seminal theoretical texts, paintings, and songs, *Gnaisse* can be described as an intermedial artefact that weaves together features associated with different media. Behaving like a living creature, *Gnaisse* exudes smells, makes noises, and breathes. *Gnaisse* also appeals, though metaphorically, to multiple senses, by painting pictures, talking, playing music, and immersing readers in an alternate world.

The four pictures created by Daniel Lima accentuate the surrealist and deranged nature of this novel. These illustrations, inserted at the beginning of the book, introduce the reader to the demanding narrative that follows. One of those pictures displays a naked woman inside a cocoon. Not only does this picture portray the metamorphic property of this novel, it also mirrors the inversion of order and logic promoted by LC's unbalanced psychological state. The straight plumb line located by the side of the cocoon proves that everything in this fictional world is coherent and symmetrical. Yet, if these pictures are read in the same order as the rest of the book, one may notice that North and East have been misplaced. Besides declaring the subversive nature of the novel, the shift of cardinal directions demonstrates that this fictional universe, like all fictional universes, will only obey its own rules.

A ripped graph sheet is added to the cover and drawings of this book. The disruption of this sheet's rigid and compartmentalized space visually epitomizes the disruptive nature of *Gnaisse*. Since LC is unable to explain what led to the deterioration of the relationship with his student, order and causality are dismissed as unessential to read the novel. As *Gnaisse*'s blurb suggests, the novel is not going to be offered in a 'literary package, wrapped up in a bow' (Carmelo 2015a). The action of connecting invisible dots mentioned right at beginning of the novel, and the desperate attempt to make sense of a crumbling world, mirrors the readers' effort to decipher a narrative based on fleeting memories. The reader is thus, at least initially, welcomed to the loop.

While unpacking in his new home, LC claimed that his life had remained 'inside the boxes and packages or covered by white sheets' (Carmelo 2015: 13). He tells the reader that he is storing his books on shelves in an orderly manner, as if he were trying to tie a 'lost thread'[15] (Carmelo 2015: 12–13). In the second part of *Gnaisse* we are told that, as a teenager, LC used to store his books in boxes and, in a similar way to the instructions added by Julio Cortázar to the book *Rayuela* (1963), he invented a method to read his library[16] made of 'crossed narratives' (Carmelo 2015: 119). Alberto Manguel, a well-known book lover and owner of a migrating library,[17] believes that libraries can contain our life story:

> I've often felt that my library explained who I was, gave me a shifting self that transformed itself constantly throughout the years ... When I'm in a library, any library, I have the sense of being translated into a purely verbal dimension by a conjuring trick I've never quite understood. I know that my full, true story is there, somewhere on the shelves, and all I need is time and the chance to find it.
>
> (Manguel 2018: 5)

However, libraries are vast and expanding universes. Manguel describes libraries as ever-changing entities, connecting them with his 'shifting self' whose story can never be told. Much like LC's life story, Manguel knows that his story 'remains elusive because it is never the definitive story' (Manguel 2018: 5). Feeling alone and shattered, LC recalls the image of his old bookshelf, emptied of books and 'reduced to a skeleton', and refuses to accept a 'treacherous invitation to memory' (Carmelo 2015: 13). Memory is equated with pain, and thus, LC avoids tracing

---

[15] The Portuguese word 'reatar' can be translated as 'to tie again'. However, it can also mean to 'recover', 'resume', or 'restart'.
[16] When he was twenty-two years old, besides numbers, he started adding rocks' names to his complex classification method. Work number 222 was named 'gneiss' (Carmelo 2015: 118).
[17] Manguel's library, comprising 40,000 books, is now located in Portugal.

back the steps to the moments he shared with the missing woman. The reader loses, once again, an opportunity to know more about LC.

*Gnaisse* persistently uses intertextuality[18] to challenge the reader at yet another level: readers' knowledge of the cited works and their ability to play literary games is persistently sought along the way. Kandinsky, a pioneering artist of abstract art frequently mentioned by Carmelo, believed that the circle was the expression of the fourth dimension (Rudenstine 1976: 310) located beyond our reality.[19] Challenging three-dimensionality, Carmelo frequently mixes myths, mundane scenes, and reveries. In one description of an encounter with the vanishing woman, he tells the reader that they sometimes inhaled butane gas to the point where they almost became unconscious (Carmelo 2015: 27). They would also take pink pills to numb themselves into oblivion (Carmelo 2015: 60). In fact, LC's recollections of the events are generally fuzzy, as if he were intoxicated or feverish, and trying to make sense of the world around him. The circular movement depicted in Kandinsky's paintings is transferred into the narrative and readers are enveloped in a whirlwind of memories and dreams from which, just like LC, they cannot escape. As observed by Carmelo (2015a), the unexpected arrival of the protagonist's sister (Carmelo 2015: 49) seems to be the way out of the continuous replay of memories that creep into LC's mind. However, the reader is redirected to the same classroom where it all began.

We are told that the woman was never enrolled in the university (Carmelo 2015: 79). In Portuguese, the word 'inscrita' means both 'inscribed' and 'enrolled'. This word's double-meaning seems to refer to both the deceitful and immaterial nature of this woman. As LC recalls, she considered matter as 'variable' and her verbal existence as a character is associated (let's not forget the affinity between the woman and *Gnaisse*) with an alphabet made of wind (Carmelo 2015: 58). The woman's illusory and shifting character is enabled by the inexhaustible language combinatoriality[20], which allows Carmelo (or LC) to describe her features and actions in a diverse number of ways.

---

[18] In fact, intermediality and intertextuality are closely connected. Klaus Bruhn Jensen observes that the 'aesthetic and broadly discursive approach to the media is the legacy of the humanities' and 'the idea of intermediality was preceded by an idea of 'intertextuality'' (2016: 1–2).

[19] Moreover, number four seems to have a particular meaning in this novel. The vanishing female character used to sit in the fourth row of the classroom. Since the novel adopts a self-reflexive and metafictional stance, as well as an intermedial character, the 'fourth wall' (a theatre-related expression) between the reader and the fictional world is consistently put at risk.

[20] Verbal language allows us to describe reality and create fictional events through the combination of syllables into words and words into sentences. Language's combinatoriality is at the basis of literary creation and is used in *Gnaisse* to introduce several perspectives over the same event, and therefore, to ensure this novel's expansion.

Besides repetition and narrative reconstruction, the novel also feeds on reference to several works that rely on different semiotic channels. For instance, Arnold Schoenberg's *Verklärte Nacht* (1899), Don DeLillo's *Point Omega* (2010), Krzysztof Kieslowski's *Blue* (1993), and Alfredo Marceneiro's Fado music. In *Gnaisse*, several media are cited to weave the narrative, producing a text that appeals to different senses:[21] a BASF tape created to 'die together' (Carmelo 2015: 93), the instant photos taken in the subway in order to record his transformation into Poe (Carmelo 2015: 97), blue tiles depicted as an intimate cinematograph (59), and the tri-dimensional daguerreotype into which LC is transformed (Carmelo 2015: 46). In fact, vocabulary associated with photography, cinema, and painting is used to weave the narrative and, though imprecisely, describe some of the characters. For instance, Mathew B. Brady's photo of Edgar Alan Poe is invoked to portray LC.[22] In the final strata of this novel, LC describes the missing woman's appearance in a documentary by resorting to terms used in painting. LC claims that her 'contour' could be seen twice: the first moment is too quick to be grasped, and the second moment only allows a few 'strokes' to be perceived by the retina (Carmelo 2015: 83). When LC plays a music box, instead of music he hears her voice repeating the love song authored by the Galician-Portuguese troubadour Bernal de Bonaval (Carmelo 2015: 83–4). In Part E, life is compared to a loose film tape that, separated from its reel, is merely able to project disjointed images (Carmelo 2015: 79).

## Leaving the Labyrinth

Close to the end of the first part of the novel, *Gnaisse*'s fictional universe expands: 'balcony's tiles were gradually cracking – slits were propagating as the result of some type of dilatation, creating a labyrinth that resembles the silk threads of a spider's web' (Carmelo 2015: 96). LC's body parts begin to vanish and, 'the moment when the message was about to stop being cryptic and become legible to everyone' (Carmelo 2015: 103), he finally disappears. As the novel nears its end, its different pieces become detached, as if the readers' anxiety to reach the end has sentenced the novel to its disintegration.

---

[21] *Gnaisse* refers to pleasant smells like incense, lavender, violets, and coffee, as well as smells that indicate decay, for instance, urine, mold, sewage, and dead mice.

[22] Later, LC described himself as an imitation of a 'mortified Poe' whose several layers of make-up have started melting (Carmelo 2015: 82).

In the second part of this book, the reader enters a house where LC and his sister (Eleonora) live. The novel's construction process running in the background is crudely revealed: the gas canisters, the rubber ball, Kandinsky's paintings, a magazine containing a photo of Edgar Allan Poe, and all the items around which Carmelo has built his narrative are displayed in a single room (Carmelo 2015: 109–110). LC is not a professor, but a proofreader who rarely leaves his room. He is currently proofreading a book about Pareyson and Duchamp (Carmelo 2015: 111). The narrator (now using the third person) tells the reader that LC transformed the landscape into a globe divided into countries and cities fully imagined by him (Carmelo 2015: 114). We are also told that his sister wishes to sell the family house but, to LC, this would mean 'amputating the many lives that he lived and listened' (Carmelo 2015: 114) and, as a result, the end of the fictional world. However, once the mechanism of the novel is revealed, and the glitch in the machine is fixed, the narrative is set to automatically refocus on the relationship between the main character and the mysterious woman once again. To lovers, time has no beginning or end (Carmelo 2015: 60), and therefore, LC and the woman's relationship is compared to an ever-expanding narrative. In order to continue its rebirth, the novel constantly describes its own decadence, playing 'the game of life falling inside death' (Carmelo 2015: 60). As readers recall the many references to putrefaction and sewage right at the beginning of the book (for instance, in page 6), they realize that signs of decadence and entropy were there all along. This happens because *Gnaisse* seems to be designed as a metaleptic loop.

In *Gnaisse*, fate is described as an 'account of the unattainable' or something that humans pursue as if trying to reach an 'extremely violent light – a torch – that lives in several hands … in several versions, each one of them collecting the possible facts' (Carmelo 2015: 68). Therefore, Carmelo's novel is described as a prospective itinerary, an oracle that points to different directions and a game of chance that, like life itself, the reader will not be able to win. We cannot avoid the impression that LC is aware that readers' voracity, fuelled by the hope to tie up any loose ends before reaching a definite closure, dictate the termination of the story. He, and the third person narrator that explains everything in the second part of the book, also seems to know that characters outlive their creators and readers. As he describes the dismantlement of the fictional world in the last pages of Part 1, LC tells the reader that he could feel the woman breathing behind the wall: 'the bridge between inspiration and expiration had become wider. The cycle would reinitiate always with the same cadence' (Carmelo 2015: 96). In fact, as soon as readers reach the end of the book, the narrative is ready to begin again without including them in the process. This time, only characters are given access to the world built around LC and the mysterious woman. The paper barrier imposed by the last page of the book prevents them from also 'taking a peek' at the fictional world running endlessly in some other dimension.

*Gnaisse* consciously (even sadistically) undermines readers' expectations, thus equating the process of reading this novel with an attempt to sketch an approximate map of its fictional world. By depicting 'life in progress' (Carmelo 2015a), *Gnaisse* mercilessly challenges the notion of narrative as a coherently organized and self-explanatory chain of events, as well as the notion of a book as a sealed container for a story. Carmelo's novel is a celebratory and complex exploration of the ability of fiction to create alternate worlds. Together with experimental and postmodernist literature, this Hypercontemporary novel exposes the mechanism of fiction and extrapolates its paper sheets by playing metaleptic and intermedial games with the reader. Subliminally, *Gnaisse* also tells readers about the fictional essence of memories, and about the stories we tell ourselves to survive. According to LC, 'the world is a blade that can, from one moment to the next, cause wreckages' (Carmelo 2015: 14).

# References

Arnaut, A. P. (2016), 'A Insólita Construção da Personagem Post-Modernista', *Revista Abusões* 1 (3): 7–34.

Arnaut, A. P. (2018), 'Do Post-Modernismo ao Hipercontemporâneo: Morfologia(s) do Romance e (Re)figurações da Personagem', *Revista de Estudos Literários* 8: 19–44. Available online: https://doi.org/10.14195/2183-847X_8_1.

Bruhn, J. (2016), *The Intermediality of Narrative Literature*, London: Palgrave Macmillan.

Carmelo, L. (2015), *Gnaisse*, Lisboa: Abysmo.

Carmelo, L. (2015a), *Gnaisse* [blurb]. Available online: https://abysmo.pt/produto/gnaisse/ (accessed July 2022).

Iser, W. (1980), *The Act of Reading*, Baltimore: Johns Hopkins University Press.

Jensen, K. B. (2016), 'Intermedia', in K. B. Jensen and R. T. Craig (eds.), *The International Encyclopedia of Communication Theory and Philosophy*, New Jersey: John Wiley & Sons, Inc.

Lévi-Strauss, C. (1987), *Introduction to the Work of Marcel Mauss*, London: Routledge & Kegan Paul.

Manguel, A. (2018), *Packing My Library: An Elegy and Ten Digressions*, New Haven: Yale University Press.

Ryan, M-L. (n.d.), 'Possible Worlds', *The Living Handbook of Narratology*. Available online: https://www-archiv.fdm.uni-hamburg.de/lhn/node/54.html.

Ryan, M. (1991), *Possible Worlds, Artificial Intelligence, and Narrative Theory*, Bloomington: Indiana University Press.

Rudenstine, A. Z. (1976), *The Guggenheim Museum: Paintings 1880–1945*, vol. 1, New York: The Solomon R. Guggenheim Foundation.

Rudenstine, A. Z. (1976), *The Guggenheim Museum: Paintings 1880–1945*, vol. 1, New York: The Solomon R. Guggenheim Foundation.

Stephan, M. (2019), *Defining Literary Postmodernism for the Twenty-First Century*. Cham: Palgrave.

# 4

# Representations of *elsewhere* and New Forms of Dystopia in Hypercontemporary Portuguese Literature

Silvia Amorim

Research in contemporary literature implies a selection of works that are representative of trends in that field, which is far from obvious. Indeed, the main difficulty is to avoid being influenced by passing fads. In academia, this approach is problematic, as suggested, for example, by the publication of *Du "Contemporain" à L'Université* (2015), a work that offers a reflection on how to tackle contemporary literature. As Marie-Odile André, a specialist in French literature, reminds us, choosing from a rich and heterogeneous panorama can lead to 'set literary corpora and critical categories',[1] while establishing a canon determined in part by 'the normative role of Literary Studies' (André 2015: 23). Beyond this process, leading to classicize works, the elaboration of a literary history based on contemporary works is problematic because it risks generating, paradoxically, an 'ageing' of the contemporary. With these preliminary considerations and warnings in mind, we venture to select two contemporary novels that we believe are representative of current trends in Portuguese fiction, which is marked, as literary critic Miguel Real points out, by its cosmopolitanism, and aimed at a 'global reader'.[2] *O Destino Turístico* (The tourist destination) ((2008) 2015), by Rui Zink, and *Depois de Morrer Aconteceram-me Muitas Coisas*, (Lots of things

---

[1] Unless otherwise stated, all quotations originally in French or Portuguese are translated by the author.
[2] In an essay in which he presents a large corpus of contemporary novels published between 1950 and 2010, Miguel Real highlights a trend towards the internationalization of content: 'The Portuguese novel, in the first decade of the twenty-first century, became cosmopolitan, eminently urban, aimed at a global reader, exploring universal themes, focused on geographical spaces outside the national reality' (2012: 22).

happened to me after I died) (2009), by Ricardo Adolfo,[3] both evoke, in the form of dystopias and not without a certain irony, today's globalized world against a background of economic crisis. This context, conducive to travel and intercultural contact, is also marked by new forms of precariousness and incommunicability. In addition, the authors reflect current events, addressing contemporary issues such as the rise of mass tourism, terrorism, and illegal immigration.

Miguel Real highlights the trend towards spatial openness which, in the contemporary novel, translates into 'expansion beyond national borders' or 'minimisation of their importance' (Real 2012: 28). Adolfo and Zink draw attention to issues related to the blurring of borders in a globalized context. The links between *here* and *elsewhere* are regarded in all their ambiguity, and these two categories sometimes cease to be operative, confused in an indeterminate space that does not allow individuals to find their bearings. The impact in terms of identity is notable, as the border between identity and otherness is itself destabilized. But paradoxically, the porosity of borders does not translate into greater openness or tolerance: on the contrary, indeterminacy seems to exacerbate attitudes of rejection or negation, and it does not cancel out certain cleavages such as those opposing centre and periphery. Finally, as we shall see, both novels indirectly reflect an image of present-day Portugal. Thus, by talking about *elsewhere*, they both propose a reflection on contemporary Portuguese society, as if, in order to talk about the local, it is now necessary to look at the global.

## Representations of *Elsewhere*: Stereotypes and Imprecision

The two novels are, at first sight, representations of *elsewhere*. The reader adopts a particular point of view, that of the tourist or illegal immigrant. This perspective, which conveys a sense of strangeness, is a construction that can be approached through *literary imagology*, a method of comparative literature. Jean-Marc Moura defines it as 'the study of representations of elsewhere in literature', and adds that it is particularly interested in 'works of fiction that either directly feature foreigners or refer to a more or less stereotypical overview of a foreign country' (Moura 1998: 35). This approach seems relevant to us because it focuses on the societal images that underlay the recreation of foreigners or

---

[3] The novel has been published in Hungary, Spain, Sweden, Japan, and France.

foreign countries in literary works. It thus brings to light the stereotypes that condition the representations of the other, or on the contrary, the conceptions that, in a critical approach, tend to go beyond the collective representations.

It seems to us that the unveiling of the beliefs, prejudices, and stereotypes that underlie the representations of the foreign country and its inhabitants is an essential issue in both novels. The countries described are not immediately identified, but only perceived as strange, even hostile, by the characters. However, the reader is led to make a critical judgement on the perspective itself: throughout the pages, he understands that he is not observing the country, but the perception of it by the tourist or migrant who thus passes from the status of subject to that of object of representation. In both cases, the name of the country is not specified, as if the location is not important. This vagueness reflects a certain lack of knowledge, an absence of curiosity, or even a form of contempt on the part of the observer, whether a tourist or an immigrant, for the country he is in. This situation is reduced to a simple antinomic reality, and it does not really matter which country it is, since it is above all *elsewhere*.

In *Depois de Morrer Aconteceram-me Muitas Coisas*, this vagueness is particularly visible in the onomastics: the country is called 'the island' and the inhabitants are the 'islanders'. Knowledge of the country is mostly based on stereotypes[4] embedded in the characters, in particular the narrator, Brito – a Portuguese immigrant living on the island with his wife, Carla, and young son. It is through stereotypes (rainy weather, 'pink islanders', etc.) that the reader locates this island which turns out to be Britain.

The character of Brito can be studied as a 'mind picturing the otherness' (Moura 1998: 41) whose perception is conditioned by his own economic and social precariousness. For him, the country is reduced to a land of immigration whose horizon is a rented room without comfort, a supermarket, and a café frequented by other Portuguese immigrants. Apart from that, a few bazaars in the working-class neighbourhoods and, for Carla, the offices she cleans. Any foray outside this perimeter is a perilous journey into *terra incognita*: *Fomos directos para a estação do metro que ficava a três paragens dali. Podíamos ter apanhado outro que nos deixasse na nossa estação, mas era arriscado* (We went

---

[4] We adopt here the definition of the stereotype proposed by the linguist Henri Boyer (2019: 70), who presents it as 'a modality of representation which fame, frequency and simplicity have imposed as self-evident to the whole of a community (or a group within the community). It is therefore a *fixed socio-cognitive structure*, whose practical relevance in discourse depends on its reductive and univocal functioning and on a stability of content that is reassuring for users'.

straight to the underground station three stops away. We could have taken it closer to get off at our station, but it was risky) (Adolfo 2009: 20).

Beyond the known universe, therefore, we find only places that are out of reach (the real *elsewhere*?) in view of the cultural, economic, and social shortcomings of the characters. The places belonging to the perimeter frequented by the couple are populated by other immigrants: many Indians and Chinese, and those whom Brito inappropriately names 'arábios' (Arabs), perceived as violent and dangerous. Even his Portuguese compatriots are colloquially referred to as 'imigras' (immigrants) and reduced to a few stereotypical traits. Ultimately, they are all reduced to their condition of foreigners, of minority, in a country considered as central.

Thus, the country is observed from the inside, but from an eccentric perspective which reveals the character's inability to overcome his marginal condition as an immigrant and suggests the persistence, in the globalized world, of situations of exclusion and strong splits between centre and periphery. The utopia of a welcoming land, providing upward mobility, fulfilment, and prosperity, is transformed into a dystopia for those who, like Brito, do not have the means to integrate into society. Consequently, as it is presented, the country is not the bearer of alternative models or knowledge, of cultural wealth or new horizons, but is perceived as poor and excluding. The characters, far from blossoming, lose themselves in this country which never ceases to highlight their own weaknesses.

The extremely reductive representation of *elsewhere*, to the point of making its location grossly imprecise, also is at work in O Destino Turístico, where Zink uses a series of clichés about war-torn countries. Fighting spreads for no apparent reason as these 'uncivilized' countries are unable to curb endemic violence. Lines of tanks on the roads, burnt-out cars, ruins, and people wandering aimlessly evoke a permanent state of war whose causes are unknown. Of course, these countries are far from the western nations, which the narrator calls 'normal countries', and have obvious characteristics of underdevelopment, such as heavy bureaucracy, corrupt authorities, and summary executions. These distant countries can only be vaguely located: Middle East? Horn of Africa? Central Asia? It does not matter, in the end, because in the eyes of foreigners these places are all the same.

In the novel, the observer is Greg, a man who practises dark tourism or what is also called reality tourism. The character suffers from the *taedium vitae* that affects some people in rich countries: living with an overabundance of goods and an overexposure to screens and images, they end up finding existence insipid, which pushes them towards ever more extreme experiences. By entering what the French essayist Gilles Lipovetsky calls 'the era of hyperconsumption', the individual falls into a spiral of boredom and existential dissatisfaction that leads into a perpetual quest for novelty. With little exposure to frustration, discomfort, and insecurity, people experience a kind of pleasure exhaustion (2009: 175-9). In the novel, war tourism not only allows Greg to relieve his boredom by becoming a kind of onlooker, but it also allows him to satisfy his suicidal impulses, a self-destructive drift that speaks volumes about the loss of meaning in contemporary society.

It is interesting to observe the perception of the other, the inhabitant of the war zone, by the tourist from a so-called 'civilized' country. Although this is a third-person novel, the perspective is that of Greg, for whom the other is embodied in the figure of a native taxi driver, Amadu. The latter is immediately suspected of being an illegal taxi driver, inevitably dishonest, so it is natural to be suspicious of him. From the tourist's point of view, proficiency in English and facility for languages are a given in poor countries, as the narrator ironically reminds us: 'As pessoas pobres, ao que parecia, tinham muito jeito para as línguas' (Poor people, it seemed, were very good at languages) (Zink 2015: 16); which, in passing, underlines the hegemony of the English language. Similarly, the lack of hygiene and care is part of the usual attributes of foreigners: *Amadu riu e o passageiro ficou algo surpreso por reparar que ele ainda tinha a dentição toda* (Amadu laughed, and the passenger was somewhat surprised to see that he still had all his teeth) (Zink 2015: 17). Before meeting the other, before even knowing him, the character already has a ready-made image of him. However, this image is shaped by Greg's imagination and by a context that pushes him to see the other as a subordinate, in a world still very marked by dividing lines such as North/South, colonizer/colonized, civilized/primitive ... The societal images that orient perceptions of the other and *elsewhere* can, according to Jean-Marc Moura, be guided either by utopia or by ideology. Consequently, representations of the other can oscillate between two poles: *alter* (a fellow human being, a utopian representation of the other) or *alius* (a radically different being, an ideologized representation of the other) (Moura 1998: 53-5). It is clear here that the other appears as an *alius* whose image is forged by a particular system of representation (an ideology).[5]

---

[5] Henri Boyer points out that a construction with a dominating aim proposes 'a certain vision of things', it is 'likely to legitimize performative and normative discourses and thus individual practices and collective actions with a view to conquering, exercising, maintaining power (politically, culturally, spiritually, etc.), or at least having a strong (coercive?) impact' (2019: 68-9).

The hierarchies, essentialist perspectives and stereotypes embedded by Greg and Brito do not allow them to perceive the other as a fellow human being, but as an empty shell into which their own fantasies are projected.

In Adolfo's novel, Brito's contradictions and bad faith are revealed through his representations of the other. As an inhabitant of a prosperous and advanced country that welcomes immigrants, the islander should be a role model. Yet, in Brito's eyes, he does not live up to his reputation as a 'civilized' man, despite his apparent good manners. When entering the metro, for example, he is not particularly courteous. Brito does not hesitate to mention the alleged defects of the islanders: *os ilhéus deixavam muito a desejar no que tocava à educação ... Ou então, eram mesmo ligeiramente atrasados. As feições incestuosas ninguém lhas tirava* (the islanders left a lot to be desired in terms of education ... Or maybe they were really a bit retarded. They couldn't deny their incestuous features) (Adolfo 2009: 160).

Brito constructs an image of a rather hostile and closed-minded islander, thus finding a way to justify the rejection he feels. Nevertheless, when Brito tries to convince his wife to stay in the country, he repeats common clichés about opportunities to be seized in rich countries (although he acknowledges he is talking 'bullshit'). So, he mentions *as coisas da cultura que só havia ali, os monumentos, as coisas com história e interesse* (the cultural stuff, monuments, things with history and interest) and adds that *[T]udo era maior, melhor e mais avançado na ilha* ([E]verything was bigger, better, and more advanced on the island) (Adolfo 2009: 110). Although the characters hardly benefit from the resources and opportunities offered by British society, these representations are sufficient to justify the presence of the family on the island, which suddenly becomes a somewhat utopian ideal, far removed from everyday reality. Thus, representations of *elsewhere* are changing, sometimes contradictory, but are always guided by 'collective imaginary patterns' (Moura 1998: 45). Both novels denounce visions conditioned by the divisions of today's world: in *O Destino Turístico*, the oppositions between a barbaric, poor, and subaltern South (in the broadest sense of the term) and a civilized, prosperous, and hegemonic North; in *Depois de Morrer ...*, quite similar oppositions, and equally simplistic, between countries of emigration and host countries, centre/periphery, etc. In both cases, though, we are not faced with 'a writer blinded by the clichés of his own culture' (Moura 1998: 45), but on the contrary, with an author who keeps his distance from his characters and the global representations they convey, subtly criticized.

In both novels, *elsewhere* does not stimulate curiosity and dreams, as if all the islands had already been discovered and explored in a world now devoid of utopian dimensions. Elsewhere is the subject of poor, superficial, and stereotyped representations that the traveller does not question. In the end, while travelling, he finds nothing really new, but observes a reality that is very much in line with his expectations and the structures that he himself conveys. Now, it may be assumed that the location of this *elsewhere* is perhaps itself problematic.

## *Zone* and *Non-place*: Solitude and Spaces of Transience

Both novels draw our attention to the representation of *elsewhere* and the image of the other; and in so doing, they offer a reflection on the notion of space in the contemporary context. Indeed, the places represented are marked by a certain indeterminacy, the reader having difficulty in locating them. In both cases, there is no real mention of a 'country', as if this geographical designation were no longer operative. In *O Destino Turístico*, the narrator notes, about Greg's location: *Era um facto sabido que o país estava um fanico, que já nem um país era mas uma zona, uma zona de morte, um terreno de caça selvagem e brutal* (It was a known fact that the country was just a fragment, that it wasn't even a country, only a zone, a zone of death, a savage, brutal hunting ground) (Zink 2015: 9). The distinction between 'zone' and 'country' is clearly underlined: the 'zone' is not really a place to live, it does not guarantee security.

In an enlightening article, Jeanne Ételain explains the uses of the concept of *zone* since the nineteenth century and emphasizes the uncertain character of this space: 'Outside of time, the zone also seems to escape geography and appears as a non-locatable and unbounded place' (2017: 125). According to the researcher, the *zone* is mobile, dynamic, non-rational, and anarchic. Finally, it is a transition area: 'It is an intermediate space, an in-between, where the act of separation disappears in favour of a space of indeterminacy' (Ételain 2017: 133). This definition confirms the imprecise nature of the *zone*, a space where the characters are out of place, outside the geography, unable to establish links with the territory. In the case of Zink's war zone, the space is defined by its dangerousness as the individual is likely to be attacked, kidnapped, or killed at any time. Zink underlines the multiplication of *zones* in the contemporary world and reminds us that some people have no choice but to live there in a precarious way.

In *O Destino Turístico*, *elsewhere* is presented as elusive, all the more so as new technologies and images interfere between the space and the characters. Smartphones, in particular, uproot individuals from reality by projecting them into a virtual space. Tourists do not look at *elsewhere* directly, but through a filter that prevents them from being anchored in time and space. When they attend a public execution, they do not look at it directly but through their phone screen: *[Greg] fez como os outros — filmou o momento. Telemóvel na mão feito livrinho vermelho do Presidente Mao* ([Greg] did as the others — he filmed the moment. Phone in hand, turned into Chairman Mao's Little Red Book) (Zink 2015: 57–8).

Once back in their vehicles, the tourists who witnessed the scene immediately view and share the footage, as if they had not seen it live. Zink suggests that new technologies and the omnipotence of images are uprooting us from space: we are, most of the time, in the in-between of a semi-virtual space. Moreover, the sham nature of the *zone*, which is in fact a gigantic set, is revealed at the end of the novel. Everything is fictitious: attacks and executions are simulated, explosions are controlled, the inhabitants are extras, etc. Under pressure from Europe and due to strong economic and environmental constraints, Portugal has given up traditional tourism to become a vast theme park for reality tourism. Paradoxically, in order to have realistic experiences, tourists are immersed into a virtual universe.

In Adolfo's novel, the characters frequent a space that does not coincide with the island as a whole: the space of their wanderings, a buffer zone between *here* and *elsewhere*, populated by foreigners, the seat of an asymmetrical relationship between migrants and inhabitants. The notion of *zone* gradually leads us to that of the *non-place*. Although the two are different, they come together to the extent that they are out-of-place. In his famous essay, *Non-Places: Introduction to An Anthropology of Supermodernity*, the anthropologist Marc Augé invites us to relearn how to think about space by distinguishing between places and *non-places* (Augé 1992: 100). The former are socially and culturally marked spaces, anthropological places (places of identity, relationships, and history) that are opposed to *non-places*, which are increasingly numerous in the contemporary era and favour the 'solitude of supermodernity' (Augé 1992: 118). In *Depois de Morrer …*, Brito and his family wander through public space and cross a series of *non-places*: the underground, the street, the bus, the airport, etc. The characters thus evolve in a neutral, anonymous space, where they interact mostly with abstract entities or institutions (road signs, posters, images, etc.).

In short, *elsewhere* is represented as a gigantic *non-place* in which the characters are trapped, condemned to anonymity and solitude.

The two novels implicitly deal with utopia as a genre and as a representation of a place outside geography. In his essay, Marc Augé reminds us that the *non-place*, unlike utopia, does not house any organic society although it is a real space (Augé 1992: 140), thus showing that utopia is the opposite of *non-place*. In Adolfo's novel, this inversion is clear: the reference to the island, an Eldorado for immigrants, immediately puts us on the track of utopia. However, when the characters reside there, they fail to understand the functioning of the island society, let alone integrate into it, relegated to the margins, in places of anonymity and solitude. Thus, for the immigrants, the island turns out to be a *non-place*, not a utopia. The island is a recurring theme in Adolfo's work; for example, in *Tóquio Vive Longe Da Terra* (2015), an autobiographical work in which the author, although well integrated, remains irreducibly an 'alien' in Japan (as he calls himself). The island is not an abstract ideal, but the individual, unable to find his place there, is condemned to marginality. The social dimension of utopia is discarded in favour of representations of isolation and solitude in spaces devoid of human cohesion.

Zink's novel, on the other hand, strongly resembles a dystopia. Nevertheless, what seems to be an abstract space, a *zone*, due to the interference of new technologies and the consumers' taste for virtual reality, is in fact a concrete space: Portugal. But the society that lives in this country turns out to be a gigantic simulacrum.

We no longer dream of models of organized and harmonious societies, located in a distant *elsewhere* that stimulates the imagination. *Elsewhere* is within reach, but it merges with *here*, destabilising identities.

## Otherness and Uncertainty of Identity

Factors such as technological advances, migration, and geopolitical and geoeconomic reconfigurations are changing the very nature of space. Borders are no longer stable lines, in-between situations are frequent, *elsewhere* is here, and *non-places* are multiplying, so much so that one may wonder how the individual can identify with a given territory, especially if he is a migrant. This point is subtly raised in the two novels, which question the process of identification with the territory and, more broadly, identity itself.

The new configurations of the shifting space where we live interact with questions of identity which, according to Zygmunt Bauman, are coming back in force in the unstable era of 'liquid modernity'; that is, at a time when the place of individuals in society is uncertain. The challenge for the individual is no longer to achieve social fulfilment, but to determine what he wants to be (Bauman 2001:15). In both novels we can see how the authors correlate the instability of identity and the instability of the relationship to the territory in the contemporary world.

In *Depois de Morrer ...* the characters roam *non-places* from which they cannot escape, as if they were in a labyrinth, unable to return to a familiar home or to find the slightest identity marker in spaces where individualization is impossible. Their precarious status as illegal immigrants, without the tools that would allow them to integrate (knowledge of the language, professional training, self-confidence, etc.), condemns them to a form of exclusion symbolized by this wandering in *non-places*. In order to determine their identity, they would need to integrate into a *place*; that is, a culturally and historically marked space in which it would be possible to establish links with the other. However, the impersonal space of the *non-place* is hardly conducive to individualization because it constructs the 'average man' (Augé 1992: 126): the information it displays and the norms that govern it are aimed at the greatest number, a public considered as homogeneous. Everyone has to adapt by putting their identity in brackets. Marc Augé speaks of a 'passive joy of disidentification' and, paradoxically, of an 'active pleasure of role playing' (Augé 1992: 129). Yet the role assumed does not consist of becoming someone else, but precisely of being no one in particular. This process of 'disidentification' is constantly recalled by Brito, who experiences it as a death: *Devia ser transparente ... Num dia de desespero, cheguei a pensar que teria morrido* (I must have been transparent ... One day of despair, I even thought I was dead) (Adolfo 2009: 81–2).

Brito feels socially dead and, of course, this situation is accentuated by mutual incomprehension and incommunicability. The character realizes that he is not even an *other*, a stranger, clearly belonging to a different culture, but *nobody*. Furthermore, he is aware that in the public space he and his wife are perceived as 'a young couple of undefined origin' (Adolfo 2009: 153). He even comes to envy immigrants belonging to more visible minorities, such as Indians: *Se fôssemos índios não seria difícil, agora assim, transparentes, era tudo mais complicado* (If we were Indians it wouldn't be difficult, now like this, transparent, everything was more complicated) (Adolfo 2009: 39–40). Communitarianism taken to the extreme is a temptation for Brito who dreams of becoming Chinese (or what he thinks Chinese is): *Eram contra a integração. Sabiam que eram diferentes e orgulhavam-se de ser assim. Não achavam os outros mais* (They were against integration. They knew they were different and proud to be so. They didn't think the others were better than them) (Adolfo 2009: 171). Veiled women are also enviable because, according to Brito, they manage to ignore the island completely, dressing according to the customs of the 'new imaginary village to which they now belonged' (Adolfo 2009: 74). In fact, outsiders develop strategies that allow them to transform *elsewhere* into *here*, which indicates an absence of 'shared spatial awareness'.[6] For Brito, however, this does not work, as he remains in an empty space which is an identity vacuum. His identity is unstable, he is an immigrant, but sometimes he shows prejudice and contempt towards other immigrants (those who settle in Portugal): *Recordei-lhe que a enchente de imigras na terra levara o trabalho e só trouxera problemas para os que lá andavam* (I reminded her that the wave of immigrants back home had stolen our jobs and had only caused problems for those who lived there) (Adolfo 2009: 111). Besides, back in Portugal, Brito ends up feeling like a stranger in his own country, as if he had become an islander: *Achei estranho não me sentir em casa de imediato* (I found it strange not to feel at home right away) (Adolfo 2009: 188). At any moment the roles can be reversed: Brito can be at the same time the immigrant or the native, himself or the other ... and ultimately *nobody*.

The symbol of Brito and his family's identity wandering, as permanent travellers, is the cumbersome suitcase they drag with them, bought not to travel, but simply because it was a good deal. The suitcase only has utilitarian purposes, as a pushchair for the child and as a wardrobe at home. Brito's wandering is reminiscent of the search for identity described by Zygmunt Bauman: 'The purpose is to choose the least risky turn at the nearest crossroads, changing direction before the road ahead becomes impassable, or before the course of that road changes' (Bauman 2001: 19). The family does not know where to go, passing through obstacles and opportunities without a clear idea of their goals.

Not really knowing who he is, Brito does not fit in on the island, constantly subjected to a strong sense of illegitimacy. Instead of making a fresh start, reinventing himself *elsewhere*, he remains in his status as an illegal immigrant

---

[6] We borrow this expression from geographers France Guérin-Pace and Yves Guermond (2006: 289–90), who indicate that one can 'inhabit the same territory without having the same relationship to it in terms of belonging, appropriation or claims'.

and murderer on the run. Moreover, the space accentuates this sense of guilt because in the *non-places* one must constantly 'show one's innocence' (Augé 1992: 133) (one's legitimacy to be there), by striving to 'be like everyone else in order to be oneself' (Augé 1992: 136) and not to behave suspiciously. Brito's uncertainty about his identity then translates into inappropriate attitudes, as the underground scene at the beginning of the novel reveals. When the family is about to return home, the train stops and all the passengers get off. Instead of waiting on the platform like everyone else, Brito decides to get back on the train for fear of losing his seat: *Era uma opção contra a maioria, uma opção visionária* (It was a choice against the majority, a visionary choice) (Adolfo 2009: 23). When the metro starts again, Brito, in a panic, commits an offence by activating the alarm. His choices always turn out to be wrong, inappropriate, and his plans absurd. Finally, in order not to make any more mistakes, Brito decides to do the opposite of what seems logical to him, a new strategy that constitutes a negation of his identity.

Identity is also questioned in *O Destino Turístico*, situations of in-betweenness and identity uncertainty are revealed throughout the novel. Indeed, the figures of the self and the other tend to merge; whereas at first, they seemed to be poles apart. The foreigner we reject, the one we don't want to resemble in any way, is in fact a European, since behind the war zone lies a western country: Portugal. Greg, on the other hand, chooses to experience the violence first-hand, both as a bystander and as a candidate for suicide, becoming the other, the violent barbarian. The Swiss tourist, for his part, is not really who he claims to be, since behind his false identity is Servejit Duvla. This foreign-sounding name does not correspond to a geographically locatable identity, which places him in an uncertain *elsewhere*. On the other hand, Amadu (which sounds 'African') actually corresponds to the Latin name Amado … The reversal of perspective in the novel, where the narrator ends up taking Amado's point of view, suggests this blurring of identities. The author thus highlights the relativity of the boundaries between oneself and the other.

The novel also emphasizes the fictional part of our representations of ourselves and the other. Greg sees the locals as *alius* and simply expects them to fit the stereotypical images he has of them. The democratization of tourism and the ease of travel have made us lose sight, as Franck Michel reminds us in his book *Désirs d'Ailleurs* (2000), of the authentic encounter and the human bond that should constitute any journey. On the contrary, today's travellers tend to depersonalize the other, who becomes a fiction. In the same way, *elsewhere* becomes a setting, reduced to a few coarse features. Amado also highlights the inconsistencies that tourists fail to notice: *esta gente é estúpida. Como podem não se sentir enganados?* (those people are stupid. How can they not feel cheated?) (Zink 2015: 211). Furthermore, as an inhabitant and worker of a country entirely devoted to the tourist industry, he becomes a kind of extra and loses his authenticity in favour of a fake identity in a world of simulation. Torn between global constraints and personal imperatives, the individual must constantly readjust his identity.

Both novels suggest precarious identities, closely related to territories that are themselves unstable. The boundary between *here* and *elsewhere*, identity and otherness, is blurred. The representations of the other and the world are reductive, guided by the characters' own flaws and prejudices.

*Depois de Morrer ...* and *O Destino Turístico* offer a reflection on the contemporary world, and in particular on the new configurations of *elsewhere*. As Paul Virilio had already observed in 1997, under the effect of globalization, multiple displacements, and new technologies, geography tends to be abolished. The essayist notes that under the influence of generalized interactivity, which throws us into a constant 'telepresent', geographical reality is becoming virtual. The consequence is the disintegration of locally situated cultures in favour of a 'virtual hypercentre whose centre is everywhere' (Virilio 1997: 17), like a fruit with the skin on the inside and the pulp on the outside. In both novels, it is clear that understanding contemporary Portugal is not possible without considering foreign countries. This erasure of geography takes place through borders that are no longer defined lines, but rather *zones* or *non-places*, spaces of transition or transit that become more generalized and where identities are blurred.

Ricardo Adolfo and Rui Zink thus propose new dystopias where the fruitful *elsewhere*, provider of dreams and ideals, no longer exists. It is replaced by an omnipresent *here*, where nothing is to be discovered because everything is known, albeit often in a reductive or virtual way. Indeed, this (mis)knowledge is conditioned by ideological frameworks that convey essentialist visions and widespread stereotypes. Devoid of human bonds and social cohesion, this *elsewhere* only reflects one's flaws and limitations. Plunged into loneliness and identity uncertainty, depersonalization threatens the individual. True otherness, which opens up new perspectives, proposes alternative models, stimulates dialogue, and allows self-fulfilment, now seems a distant utopia.

# References

Adolfo, R. (2009), *Depois de Morrer Aconteceram-me Muitas Coisas*, Lisboa: Alfaguara.

André, M.-O. (2015), 'Configuration(s) du "Contemporain"', in M.-O. André and M. Barraband (eds.), *Du "Contemporain" à L'Université. Usages, Configurations, Enjeux*, 17–24, Paris: Presses de la Sorbonne Nouvelle.

Augé, M. (1992), *Non-Lieux. Introduction à une Anthropologie de la Surmodernité*, Paris: Seuil.

Bauman, Z. (2001), 'Identité et Mondialisation', *Lignes* 6 (3): 10–27.

Boyer, H. (2019), 'La Place du Stéréotype dans la Pensée Sociale et les Média', *Hermès* 83: 68–73.

Ételain, J. (2017), 'Qu'Appelle-t-on Zone? À La Recherche d'un Concept Manqué', *Les Temps Modernes* 692: 113–35.

Guérin-Pace, F. and Guermond, Y. (2006), 'Identité et Rapport au Territoire', *L'Espace Géographique* 35: 289–90.

Lipovetsky, G. (2009), *Le Bonheur Paradoxal: Essai sur la Société d'Hyperconsommation*, Paris: Gallimard.

Michel, F. (2000), *Désirs d'Ailleurs. Essai d'Anthropologie des Voyages*, Paris: Armand Colin.

Moura, J.-M. (1998), *L'Europe Littéraire et l'Ailleurs*, Paris: Presses Universitaires de France.

Real, M. (2012), *O Romance Português Contemporâneo 1950–2010*, Lisboa: Caminho.

Virilio, P. (08/1997), 'Un Monde Surexposé', *Le Monde Diplomatique* 521: 17.

Zink, R. (2015), *O Destino Turístico*, Porto: Afrontamento/teodolito.

5

# *Charon Awaits*: Do All Things Come to Those Who Wait?

Ana Isabel Martins

*Neither the sun nor death can be looked at unwaveringly*
—*Sentences et maximes morales* (1664),
François de la Rochefoucault

*First God created travel, then came doubt and longing*
Theodoros Angelopoulos

## Mapping an Itinerary through the Hypercontemporary Novel

Cláudia Andrade, in her first novel, *Charon Awaits*, invites us to travel backwards, in tension, resistance, and friction with the world because, not being an infallible method, at least it consents and *authorizes all hopes* (Andrade 2020a: 51). At the same time, let us *rub salt into the wound we are* (Andrade 2020b), because in getting (re)acquainted with ourselves, we are forced to revisit our failures and fallibilities.

Andrade's prose is intense and exuberant, avoids flabby and superfluous phrasing, and explores a range of tones, from the loftiest forms of erudition down to everyday slang. The sheer richness of her language, its multiple meanings, and her plays on words make offering any sort of interpretation of her work a challenge. Her syntax and style of narration weave together elements of the fable and the parable, dealing with plural meanings. As the author herself has said, 'When I write I want to say something, but I also want to construct something aesthetic, and I find that for me the aesthetic is found in compression and concision. I still think that the short story enables a wonderful density, intensity, and depth' (Andrade 2020b).

In this way, Cláudia Andrade's writing privileges the rhetorical functions of *docere* and *movere* over that of *delectare*; her work confronts the world in a challenging way and charts an almost psychotherapeutic course for her characters – and perhaps for the reader too. In 'A Little Ash and Glory' she does not hold back the imaginative side of her work, she develops multiple narrative possibilities, directing the reader to figure out which are the likely ones. There is no guarantee of peace or reconciliation, no matter the dedication or determination of the reader; the endpoint is not a comfortable place, but is designed to be a difficult one so that the more visceral feelings could be celebrated and driven by the vital instincts.

The recurrence of gerunds exemplifies, at a grammatical level, the formal concision of her writing and suggests the incomplete path, always *in fieri*, that is the hallmark of any rite of passage (Hricsina 2015: 267–84). Her writing seems to be continually negotiating with time, something that we see in the slowness of how narrative events unfold: 'I can't see any reason to narrate life with the same horrible speed with which we are obliged to live it; the god of chance had plenty of time to play dice' (Andrade 2020a: 66). The size of the novel is thus a little bit misleading as it is impossible to consume its 130 pages in a single burst; it requires interludes, pauses, and moments of silence to begin untangling the multiple layers of intrigue and intertextuality that are knotted together therein.

Before even starting to read the book, the choice of colour for the cover of the first edition, published by Elsinore, calls to mind the painting *Charon crossing the Styx* (1520–1524) by the Flemish artist, Joachim Patinir, who was himself a link between the Gothic and the Renaissance, the past and the future, with Dürer as one of his influences. The outline of the mythic, deathly boatman, Charon, also signals to us that Artur, the protagonist, is going to prepare for a crossing, a transformative journey, a rite of passage, although it might end up being a Quixotic quest where the final destination will be laughing at and seeing the irony of that very journey. Etymologically, Charon (Χάρων) comes from the word for light and shining because the final moments of our lives are (or ought to be) a kind of epiphany when we make sense of our existence (Bailly 1935: 2126). The boat trip brings on an awareness of our errors, in the same way that shipwreck is often tied to the idea of punishment: Charon does not take us on a pleasure cruise, he always takes us to the underworld. There is no heavenly boatman.

The focus of the narrative is seemingly straightforward: Artur, a retired man fed up with life, wants to kill himself. Suicide is a recurring theme in Cláudia Andrade's work; she is an author who likes to call into question life's purpose and to examine death and the ideas associated with it: the fragility of the body, the precarity of the human condition, old age, solitude, the monotony of relationships, libido, and the weight of the past.¹ Put simply, suicide is a refusal to buy into the game of devising and resignification of the meanings for life (a game that we all inevitably play).² It is a way of quitting existence. If humans face so many insoluble, perplexing contradictions when it comes to death and the finitude of life – both fascination and terror, and curiosity and repulsion – it is exactly those contradictions that we have to examine.³

Artur's doubts and worries make him into a kind of anti-hero, a little bit like Virgil's protagonist, a vexed and unwilling Aeneas.⁴ Artur represents the tedium of domestic life and especially the dullness of the interior, emotional life associated with it, the apathetic thoughts of a Sisyphean drudgery. Beatriz, his wife, is the watchkeeper who personifies the repetitive, monotonous day-to-day life, the guarantor and the embodiment of the emptiness of life and everything that has been lost over the years. 'As on many other occasions, Beatriz, in response to some minor thing from the past that she herself had brought up … went to fetch their wedding album. Artur didn't have the strength either to go along with or to reject the endlessly repeated performance of this ritual … Beatriz told the story for the umpteenth time and Artur, lost in thought, paid no attention' (Andrade 2020a: 7).

Artur's *abulia* hovers between the desire to put an end to his life and his weakness in actually doing so. At the core of this concept in Greek is the idea of the cutting off of the ability to act: 'It is above all the meaning of irresolution, the weakening of the will, the decrease or inhibition of the ability to move from reflection to action' (Kapsambelis 2016a: 15–19). In the same lexical field as *abulia*, we also have the idea of apathy: 'the word apathy appears during the fourteenth century, borrowed from the Latin apatheia, and will initially be associated with philosophical vocabulary. From the eighteenth century, it most often takes on a pejorative connotation, meaning rather softness, indolence, indifference, insensitivity, absence of activity, lack of initiative' (Kapsambelis

---

[1] 'Then it was the man's turn to introduce himself and say hello. Artur was sincere in the astonishment that he showed in the face of the ever-surprising transformations that ageing brought in others (especially in those who used to be young) and that has the tendency to take such sudden, giant strides forward' (Andrade 2020a: 32).
[2] See the author's début, the book of short stories *Quartos de final e outras histórias*. At present, Cláudia Andrade says that she is writing a new novel that focuses on a nomadic and somewhat mad character.
[3] 'Had Christ put down the cross and run away, would his father have helped him? Suddenly cowards, they suspect death has some hidden agenda other than the clear intention to give them back their freedom, that they had lost the moment they arrived in this world screaming and with reason' (Andrade 2020a: 57).
[4] In Book II of the Aeneid, the hero is taken by force of destiny into exile against his wishes. See: André 2020.

2016b: 59). Artur's state of mind produces a kind of passive disenchantment, he becomes alienated from the world and from himself (Barrento 1995: 163; Soares: 39–40).

In terms of the narrative's *res*, all of its themes, explored in the morbid delirium of the characters, are characteristic of Hypercontemporary fiction. At the level of *verba*, the dense, fragmentary narrative, broken up by ambiguities or omissions, is also symptomatic of Hypercontemporary fiction. This idea of hypercontemporaneity has emerged out of a need for new terminology to understand recent changes in society and the way in which texts have explored new ideas and situations in response to things that are changing or intensifying in our world. These Hypercontemporary narratives privilege the multiple, plural, heterogeneous, and ambiguous, disrupting anything that is unified and whole, and favouring juxtaposition and disjunction.[5] And yet, while there are certainly new styles and literary movements that respond to the contemporary world, we cannot ignore the fact that the legacy of Classical Antiquity still persists and finds new ways of being relevant. It still lies ingrained in the cultural identity of the West. It is this symbiosis of the old and the new that I will explore in what follows.

## Metamorphosis of Charon: An Intertextual Process of Reading, Reception, and Transmission

Intertextuality has been approached in many ways. There is no space to go into the various approaches to how ideas are conveyed and reworked in literature here. My approach to Cláudia Andrade's work follows Michel Riffaterre and acknowledges that the act of weaving together ideas makes a text a rich tapestry of potential meanings that dialogues with various influences and has a host of resonances.[6] Philippe Sollers (1971: 51) argues that 'the text is situated

---

[5] For a discussion of the idea of 'hypercontemporaneity', see Arnaut and Binet 2018 (orgs); Martins 2022: 80–101; Martins 2020: 167–90.
[6] Riffaterre argues that the connections that a work makes with others, through its intertextualities, are rooted in parallels between semiotic structures, without necessarily conforming to a strict chronological sequence between text and intertext, which allows for the idea that later intertexts can also shift our understanding of the original text. This gives a certain freedom to the reader to bring their own experiences to bear. Subtexts are texts within a text that are not necessarily subplots or themes but narrative structures that activate forms of symbolism and enable re-readings of the main plot. On this matter, Riffaterre departs from Kristeva and Baktin when they define an intertext as a direct reference to another text through citation, allusion, or wordplay (Riffaterre 1990: xvii; Riffaterre 1981: 4–7).

at the juncture between various other texts which it re-reads, condenses, displaces, deepens, gives emphasis to'. Indeed, *Charon Awaits* not only alludes to the original myth, but also adds to it a range of new meanings and layers that are themselves entangled with each other: Dante (*The Divine Comedy*), Guimarães Rosa (*The Third Bank of the River*), Fernando Savater (*Charon Is Waiting*)[7], Tolstoy (*The Death of Ivan Ilyich*), Victor Hugo (*The Last Day of a Condemned Man*), Mikhail Bulgakov (*The Master and Margarita*), Thomas Mann (*Death in Venice*), Virginia Woolf, and the stream of consciousness of *The Voyage Out*.[8]

In Greek mythology, Charon is the boatman who ensures a person's crossing over the river of suffering to their final resting place, Hades, as long as a few conditions are met. His duties were restricted to greeting the dead person, however, as it was the souls themselves who would row themselves across the river, in a similar way to how suffering in Purgatory in the Judaeo-Christian tradition is also individual and untransferable.[9] This figure of the *portitor*, intimately associated with the idea of the final voyage and the finitude of the human condition, has had a long tradition since Plato (*The Republic*, 621a), Pindar 44, Aristophanes (*The Frogs*), Virgil (*Aeneid*, Book VI), Homer (*The Odyssey*), Luciano de Samosata, as well as during the Renaissance and the centuries afterwards. Over the course of history the myth has gained new layers and been through many incarnations; sometimes parodic or comic, sometimes epic or tragic. Consider, for instance, the Athenian philosopher, author of the *Dialogues with the Dead*, when he depicts a Charon who plans to leave his watch post to ascend to the land of the living to see what its advantages might

---

[7] The quest of a man on an interminable journey as part of a revenge narrative about the forms and transformations of evil in the contemporary world.

[8] 'Ivan blocked out the sun with his copy of *The Master and Margarita*, and Artur, lying on his stomach and smiling at the blond children who were collecting little shells, flicked through *Death in Venice*, something that they had dug out of the small and disorganized local library' (Andrade 2020a: 80); 'Acquiescing, he offered examples like that of the woman, who, like Artur, suffered from an unhealthy lack of practicality and who, faced with the traditional and erroneously romantic conception of death and enjoying the rocking of Virginia W's waves, would opt in a split second for the common option of putting their feet together and jumping into a nearby river' (Andrade 2020a: 77).

[9] 'Charon is therefore specialized in the "passage of the river". The image is well attested in mythology, but it is often associated with life and initiatory transformation. This relative passivity of Charon makes him as much, and even more a guardian of the threshold than a ferryman, because he does not intervene in the post-mortem evolution of souls. Its role, negative, is above all filtering (no one can pass who does not have the obole, and the burial). This is probably why, in some stories involving him (but not in Virgil), he steers the boat, but it is the souls of the dead who row' (Thomas 2002: 200).

be. He presents himself as *xenos* (a foreigner) and asks Hermes to guide him in his explorations. This version of the myth, where the boatman becomes a traveller in a strange land, is a model that Cláudia Andrade works with. Artur stops wanting to direct his own life and embarks instead on a journey under the tutelage of the demonic figure of Ivan (thereby perhaps recalling Hermes and Charon) (Samósata 2012). This kind of mentor, in the guise of a tour guide, will take him through a number of misadventures and hardships. The reader is never quite sure of the reality of the character of Ivan. He could be a product of Artur's hyperawareness or a hallucination, the fruit of his imagination. The protagonist realizes that the most difficult thing is not letting go of the pains in his body or the big annoyances in life, but rather to escape the shadows and minor troubles of the soul so that he can reckon with the past: 'when the accounts are settled, perhaps the only things that are truly ours are our sorrows' (Andade 2020a: 55). Our only destiny is to walk down the gravel path, through that maze we call memory, which is so unclear, perishable, laughable, fragile, and fallible. This kind of self-absorption is always the most painful and solitary of encounters: memory is a crossroad where the riddles of the oracle at Delphi are unravelled only to reveal not what truly happened, but what could have been. These cracks and scars in the human condition make the *Hypercontemporary* individual an atom in the universe, a descendant of Sisyphus throughout his sacrificial labours, and also a descendant of Tantalus throughout his endless torments.

Artur pauses his thoughts about putting an end to his life when his wife, Beatriz (an allusion to Dante's *Divine Comedy*?), goes to fetch their wedding album and makes him engage in an act of reminiscence and reconstruction of the past. It is then that his journey begins:

> 'Who's this?', he asked, pointing to the unknown person with two little taps of his index finger. He saw his wife slowly come to the boil and become suddenly younger ... he was astonished. It seemed to him an unnecessary jibe of destiny's that a man, in the week when he decides that he is going to die, notices that his wife is still able to blush at the grainy image of a lover from the past ... It was an agonizing addition to his imagination and it ended his calm.
>
> (Andrade 2020a: 7)

Troubled by this unidentified thing that ravaged his mind, this retired man decides to set off alone on a journey – all real journeys are taken alone. He begins the inescapable cathartic descent (Darmon 2011): 'he slipped easily down the inevitable tunnel ... until he came out into the light, a neon light remorselessly illuminated his confusion at seeing himself minuscule' (Andrade 2020a: 21). The cathartic process – separating the good from the bad – involves melancholy, but we should not reduce this concept to a saturnine or depressive malaise as how it manifests itself is wrought with ambiguous contradictions. On the one hand, it involves a series of black thoughts, an obsession with death and with the dark side of life and being, but on the other it also brings on a frenzied passion, wild, intoxicated thoughts and creative euphoria.[10] It is in the mixed feelings of these moments that the protagonist finds himself again and on his way he meets Ivan: they help each other out[11], coming to know one another's vulnerabilities, their most cavernous silences, and their most intimate desires.[12] One day, Ivan gives him a letter that is as perplexing as it is revelatory, leading to the following moment of anagnorisis:

> You won't believe it: I have already been here. Not always upright, though. Sometimes, fed up with walking or flipping my fins, or tired of moving my wings and of all these ontological regurgitations, I pick a damp and quiet spot and let myself be, arms wide, in a slow, vegetal state. But it's really in this bipedal vertebrate situation that I have the most fun. Sometimes I missed articulated thoughts, the delights of irony, the secret pleasure of hatred. And laughter, above all, laughter. Now I'm not quite sure whether I've been an executioner, or if I dreamt that in this life ... What I do recall, though, and an old sorrow that comes with the memory lets me know it's legitimate, is the shameful part of my incompetence. I don't have nor have I ever had the right constitution to be an executioner. I don't have the required simplicity, I end up imagining things that don't matter, estimating distances, forces, speeds ... On the road a bunch of youths appeared in party clothes. Three girls came in front of me, laughing under their breath and looking at me sideways, and I stumbled because they got in my way ... I think it was those girls who put me on edge and dealt me that vague blow.
>
> (Andrade 2020a: 58–91)

---

[10] Yves Bonnefoy, in his preface to an exhibition about melancholy at the Grand Palais (Paris, 2005/2006), once wrote: 'Melancholy, genius, madness, yes, we are used in our Western countries to associate these three notions'. Aristotle also considered melancholics to be exceptional individuals.

[11] 'Artur smeared cream on all the parts of his body exposed to the sun. Ivan was adept at partial protection, his nose, shoulders, and the sensitive part behind his knees. They helped each other out with the bits that were hard to reach, they strolled along where the waves break and stretched out on the sand', 'Ivan helped Artur to compose himself and escorted him to the door, tucking a small manuscript under his arm' (Andrade 2020a: 58).

[12] '[H]e slipped easily down the inevitable tunnel ... until he came out into the light, a neon light remorselessly illuminated his confusion at seeing himself minuscule' (Andrade 2020a: 21).

Ivan's letter raises another possibility about his role in the novel: what if those three girls were the *parcae* and he was the incarnation of death, *Thanatos*?[13] In this family portrait we should not forget Hypnos (god of sleep), who lived in the underworld, and Morpheus (god of dreams), his son.[14] The Greeks associated sleep with death, either through Hypnos, the god of peaceful slumber, or through Thanatos, the god of a peaceful death.[15] In *Charon Awaits*, references to sleep and dreams proliferate at various moments:

> After dinner, Artur wakes suddenly with a sense of weightlessness in his knees, in the throes of a vague, physical pain. He had dreamt that a little boy pedalling on a bike and with a pair of angel wings sewn onto his shirt was running him over multiple times inside a small, perfect circle surrounded by the flames of a hundred torches; 'A parade of equally sluggish ghosts, which emerged from the shadows, stumbled over Beatriz and the inexplicable mystery of her peaceful slumber to reach Artur and to remind him of old forgotten anxieties'. During this night of strange dreams and premonitions he had to get up several times to go and eat some crackers and other sedatives. Haunted, he went into the living room, where he suddenly recalled another old dream, a daydream that he might never have remembered if it hadn't had as its backdrop that same partition and the sofa on which Arthur was now hesitating to sit; while he was sleeping, the landscape had been bucolic and was lit up by a springtime glow overcast with

---

[13] 'Long before the living confided themselves to the waves, was not the coffin put into the sea, the coffin to the torrent? The coffin in this mythological hypothesis, would not be the last boat. It would be the first boat. Death would not be the last journey. It would be the first trip. It will be for some deep dreamers the first real journey' (Bachelard 1974: 100).

[14] 'As a proper name, Hypnos is in Greek mythology the god of sleep (Somnus in Roman mythology). Hypnos is the son of Nyx (the Night), twin brother of Thanatos (dead), father of Morpheus' (Kapsambelis 2016c: 441); 'As a proper name, Morpheus designates in Greek mythology the um of the thousand sons of Hypnos (Sleep), especially the one who is responsible for embodying this or that person in dreams' (Kapsambelis 2016d: 571).

[15] 'The new moon would hide us and offer its full support for our necessary secrecy, but unfortunately it falls on a night that is poor for sailing, according to the almanac. We will be noticeably beyond, can you see in the water the reflection that looks like Icarus still on fire? It's true, did I forget to ask him if he prefers Pinot Noir or Chardonnay? When we fall into a pleasant drowsiness, I invite him to sit with me at the stern. We continued our conversation and laughed, we abandoned a thought halfway through, without being bothered by this and without returning to that thankless toil of spouting ruminations ... Even still I can't stop myself from chatting away, I'm excited for your next rite of passage' (Andrade 2020a: 98); 'in the morning, thrown out from dreamless sleep with a noisy slap' (Andrade 2020a: 93). 'Μορφεύς' – One of the many sons of Hypnus (of 'Sleep', Latin Somnus) who personify the dream life of people. With his brothers Icelus and Phantasus, M. is responsible for the realistic form of dream images. M., who appears to Alcyone in the form of her dead husband Ceyx, in particular, became proverbial in the tradition of Ovid ('lie in M.'s arms'). The 'dream artists', mentioned only by Ovid (Met. 11, 633-76) in his description of the caves of sleep localized in Cimmeria, are among the *poetological* figures in the 'Metamorphose' (Walde 2016). On Hypnos, see Renberg 2017: 677–88.

watercolour clouds … a rare, specific fragment of an urban childhood devoid of adventures.

(Andrade 2020: 16–17)

If we decide, then, that Ivan, this shadowy and obscure figure, represents *Thanatos*, who is Charon in the story?[16]

It is then that at the end of the novel, a new character, Victor, arrives, to shed light on some of our questions:

> Wishing to end a journey full of difficulties and suffering and without any compass points, I help you get from the other side to the place from where you set off and to lightly touch down at the place where you started. And so the intended circle gets drawn with ridiculous simplicity, and there is redemption … To free them from the snares of wanton desires, dark thoughts, ill-considered decisions, to teach them simplicity and then lead them with an infinite kindness toward their triumphal return to happiness and life.[17]

Victor might just be an inverse Charon, someone who makes the crossing in the opposite direction and instead of taking one to the underworld, takes one back to the surface. Indeed, as we have seen already, the very etymology of his name suggests this redemptive possibility.

In Classical Antiquity, one of the requirements for Charon to undertake his journey was the payment of an obol, the fee for the journey. Cláudia Andrade did not neglect this detail. Consequently, she had a beggar approach Artur: 'A beggar came up to him to ask for some money. Artur shooks his beach bag to show that there was no jingle from any coins inside, and the other man followed him. That came to him as a revelation.' According to the Stoic thinking of Seneca, it is not the final drop that makes the water clock overflow, but all the others that came before imperceptibly filling it up. In Artur's mind this was the last drop,

---

[16] 'Ivan was irritable. The month by the sea that we had planned to spend together dragged on and his protégé didn't properly prepare. He scribbled in the margin: highlight the North Star and other maritime reference points relevant for the ornamental arrangement of future pelagic gentians. The image of a water nymph, lying dead in floral repose … He had already checked out the quay. No one rented boats for the night, so they would have to unmoor whatever was closest to hand. It would be best to have a small elegant yacht, with its own bar and with a sailor who'd be able to take them to the point where the blue becomes deep by day and immeasurably black by night, an abyss in whose depths blind creatures grope about' (Andrade 2020a: 83).

[17] 'Victor spoke with a soft, soothing voice. He made a confession. He revealed that he had, in his words, a special talent that Ivan would probably have some difficulty in understanding. It consisted of being able to detect, with mathematical precision, the cracks in the foundations of individuals who looked sturdy to the untrained eye, but that he knew were about to collapse under the weight of unhappiness, corroded from within by the untrammeled proliferation of groping anxieties with voracious mouths born of a ravenous imagination' (Andrade 2020a: 26).

he had the realization just there when he had to give a coin to the beggar, but found he did not have one. But perhaps he was already not quite so determined to end his life, perhaps some kind of feeling of resistance had begun to take shape inside him, a kind of momentum that comes from stopping, the sudden urge to dawdle on his path. This perception begins to deepen and changes the way that he considers the world around him. Suddenly, for no clear reason, he starts to experience everything as though he were savouring it for the first time, as though the numbness in his body were beginning to lose its effect. A strange feeling of calmness comes over him 'beneath the bright and lonely dawn' (an echo of the dawn and the first bright and whole day of Sophia de Mello Breyner) initiating a new beginning, breaking out of the silence 'to inhabit the essence of time'.[18]

It was time to salvage what was lost along the way; he needed to follow Ariadne's thread out of these labyrinthine spaces in which he had been immersed. Artur desperately tries to speak with his wife, Beatriz, from a public telephone. Deep down he needed to tell her that evening, a Thursday, a day of the week that was so symbolic for the both of them, that he had reconnected with her and that he was coming home: 'Don't hang up, my love, I'm on my way, I'm on my way; she felt the growing surprise in his voice, the incredulity, the joy, promising her that he would never leave her again. It was their cleaner on the end of the line but she revealed herself to be so delighted to hear him, and so comforting in her rebukes, that Beatriz, if he had been at home, could not have done any better' (Andrade 2020a: 74).

He tries again, with the same intensity and outpouring of emotions, with the same desire to listen, but, unfortunately, fails once more: 'He couldn't contain his tears. He spoke of regret, of the joy that was to be found, ought to be found – I'll find it, I promise you – in all the little aspects of their life together. He spoke of their love on Wednesday, of the plans he had to make it better, sweeter, to make it last longer, to expand it into an addition to the symmetry of the week. Living,

---

[18] 'Artur began to make the dawn unfold with the power of his awakening. The first time this happened to him … he realized that it was the first time he had witnessed this phenomenon, even though the dawn had probably come in secret on many other mornings during his lifetime. The desire to wander returned … He abandoned the slow drumming of the breakwater and the village alleys he was well-acquainted with and started to imagine straight paths marked out in dotted lines … Artur performed his ablutions in a completely placid sea … it floated a little further ahead of him, which made him take three steps forward and submerge most of his chilly thighs to grab hold of it. The thing he captured and dragged from the water was a disappointment, just a lifeless jumble of things … He noticed that it was the third time in a few days that he had experienced something entirely new … That recently discovered sea where he had played a few minutes ago was destined to become his grave' (Andrade 2020a: 95, 96, 97).

Beatriz, you can't imagine how much I want to live. She tried to interrupt him, but he wouldn't let her, until she eventually did and told him that he had got the wrong number' (Andrade 2020a: 105). Artur had hoped that Beatriz had turned into a sort of Penelope and that she had waited all this time for him or perhaps, like Eurydice, would be able to rescue him from the shadows with the simple incantatory power of her words.

## Cause of Death: Dying from Death

'What comes out of me is Thanatos masquerading as Eros' (Andrade 2020a).

Some final questions: Who is Charon in Cláudia Andrade's book? Who is the 'condemned' in this crossing? What is the rite of passage and how is it described? And, finally, who was the man in the photograph? This is perhaps the most important question, or, maybe, it is the only one that does not need an answer because it is only by not answering it that Artur's journey can continue.[19] Coming up with complete answers to all these questions is impossible, given the depth, allegorical richness, and multiple possibilities of the narrative.

Ivan is that shadowy, hesitant, diffuse character who leads Artur to a secret opening into the past and detonates an explosion that will push him towards emptiness, diverting him from the insoluble ending that was announced at the beginning of the novel. The rite of passage through the twists and turns of memory, self-knowledge, self-soothing, and self-fulfilment is successfully completed. The attempt to negotiate with time is always illusory and fruitless. We deceive ourselves in this treacherous exercise from which we always emerge betrayed:

> [E]ven after it has been uncovered and reconnoitered, it remains a labyrinth, it seems to transform itself like a sentient serpentine being, remaking itself, turning the corners inside out. This tubular creature, just as the traveller is about to find the depths he has been seeking, regurgitates itself and puts him with childish merriment right back at the place he set off from.
>
> (Andrade 2020a:41)

---

[19] "The thought of one of those seaside resorts where Artur was supposed to find the main in the photograph was simply fabulous, but Artur could not neglect the other trip, the great journey for which he hadn't yet found a concrete itinerary. He didn't forget that he didn't yet have – and he rebuked himself for this – the most rudimentary practical idea of how he could get in the way of his heart's habit of beating' (Andrade 2020a: 77).

A sense of humour and irony runs throughout the work as a tragicomic foil to the misfortunes that are inherent to our calamitous condition and that can only be sublimated by being put into perspective. Horace said *ridentem dicere verum*, and Voltaire suggested *ridendo castigat mores*. Terry Gilliam says that serious thinking makes the world seem more real than we do ourselves and it is only our playful imaginations that can do the opposite and make us larger and more powerful when faced with the world. Perhaps that is why this book is so elusive; just as we think we are beginning to reach some sort of clarity in our understanding of the novel, the pages that follow quickly pull the rug from under us.

Charon undeniably awaits us all, but he also hides from us every time we try to grab hold of him, has many different forms, and, like Janus, is found at the juncture between the past and the future. The catalyst for the imagination is our childish side – that search for mythical beasts – that desire to keep going, which Artur gradually rediscovered. In the end 'what he needed was just to have fun, to pretend to be a child playing the gods in control of the storms' noisy insurrections'. And yet this levity is only achieved through a raw confrontation with reality, after catharsis, and with the return of an immovable semblance of the truth. This was the role of the therapist, to bring on a collision with the world, a sense of vertigo so that the protagonist could find his feet again: 'Artur was frightened. He felt the need to go back on himself a little, saying that it was sometimes, only sometimes, that life became truly unbearable'.

What is the opposite of nostalgia? This is a question that reverberates throughout the novel and not innocently when one of the protagonists walks through a room between two lines of bookshelves. There is also another related quandary: 'what is the word for that comforting idea of having arrived, miraculously and safely, at another distant moment in irreversible time?' Speaking of going back in time, we still have the problem of identifying the man in the photo album to deal with, given he is a leitmotif in the narrative and the impetus for Artur's actions. Since Artur would be in the role of the groom at the wedding, the man cannot be him, so this man might be a kind of spectral presence, a consciousness that is always with us, in the moments we take decisions, that relative who is both present and yet unplaceable in our lives and in our family history. There will always be a face in a photo album that makes us feel distant from ourselves; there will always be a face that changes and becomes unrecognizable and that thus leads us in pursuit of unknown places.

*Charon Awaits* offers us a moral: just as easily as disaster, good fortune can appear and rushing, pressing on, setbacks, and interruptions are all ultimately immaterial. Our will cannot force a particular end as it is not what determines our arrival at a safe haven or at least not at the moment when we make our plans. Along the way there will always be storms and unexpected events and the only thing that really matters is the strength that we still have after we have been shipwrecked, the energy we still have after we have been crushed. All that is expected is that we seize this remaining energy and figure out what to do with it on this journey which defies any Herculean or foolish ambitions. You have to put down your weapons, with good humour, so that in the end you can die of death and 'without Artur realizing how, this became his newest, most secret, and most ambitious project'.

# References

Andrade, Cláudia (2020a), *Caronte à espera*, Amadora: Elsinore.
Andrade, Cláudia (2020b). 'Esfregar Sal na Ferida que Somos', [Interview by Teresa Carvalho], *Jornal i*, February. Available online: https://ionline.sapo.pt/artigo/686648/claudia-andrade-esfregar-sal-na-ferida-que-somos?seccao=Mais_i.
André, C. (2020), 'Eneias, Herói a Contragosto de uma Estranha Epopeia'. Available online: https://www.uc.pt/en/cech/training/seminars/2020/eneias-heroi-a-contragosto-de-uma-estranha-epopeia/.
Angenot, Marc (1984), *Intertextualité, Interdiscusivité, Discours Social*, Paris: Les Editions Trintexte.
Aristote (2013), *Problèmes XXX*, Trans. J. Pigeaud, Paris: Gallimard, Folio classique.
Arnaut, A. P. and Binet, A. M. (orgs) (2018), *Revista de Estudos Literários 8*, Coimbra: Imprensa da Universidade de Coimbra.
Bailly, A. (1935), *Le Grande Bailly: Dictionnaire Grec-Français*, Paris: Hachette.
Bachelard, G. (1974), *L'Eau et les Rêves*, Paris: Librairie José Corti.
Barrento, J. (1995), 'O Astro Baço: a Poesia Portuguesa sob o Signo de Saturno', *Colóquio Letras* 135 (136): 163.
Crépon, Marc (2008), 'L'Imaginaire de la Mort: une Responsabilité Éthique et Politique', *Cairn* 33: 53–61.
Darmon, J.-C. (2011), *Littérature et Thérapeutique des Passions: la Catharsis en Question*, Paris: Hermann.
Hricsina, J. (2015), 'Análise Corporal do Gerúndio em Português', *Études Romanes de BRNO* 36: 267–84.

Kapsambelis, Vassilis (2016a), 'Aboulie', *Dictionnaire de la Fatigue*, directed by Philippe Zawieja: 16–19.
Kapsambelis, Vassilis (2016b), 'Apathie', *Dictionnaire de la Fatigue*, directed by Philippe Zawieja: 58–62.
Kapsambelis, Vassilis (2016c), 'Hypnos', *Dictionnaire de la Fatigue*, directed by Philippe Zawieja: 441.
Kapsambelis, Vassilis (2016d), 'Morphée', *Dictionnaire de la Fatigue*, directed by Philippe Zawieja: 571.
Martins, M. (2020), 'Gonçalo M. Tavares' Histórias Falsas (False Stories: Encountering Tradition and Confronting Fragments of Truth)', in M. F. Silva, D. Bouvier, and M. G. Augusto (eds.), *A Special Model of Classical Reception: Summaries and Short Narratives*, 167–90, Cambridge: Cambridge Publishing Press.
Martins, M. (2022), 'Misadventures and Detours of a Contemporary Ulysses in José Miguel Silva', in M. F. Silva and L. Hardwick (eds.), *The Classical Tradition in Portuguese and Brazilian Poetry*, 80–101, Newcastle-upon-Tyne: Cambridge Scholars Publishing.
Ovid (2015), *Metamorphoses*, Ed. A. D. Melville and Edward J. Kennwy, Oxford: University Press.
Piégay-Gros, N. (1996), *Introduction à l'Intertextualité*, Paris: Dunod.
Renberg, G. (2017), 'Hypnos/Somnus and Oneiros as Evidence for Incubation at Asklepieia: a Reassessment', in *Where Dreams May Come*, vol. 2, 677–88, Leiden: Brill.
Riffaterre, M. (1990), *On Narrative Subtexts*, New York: Peter Lang.
Riffaterre, M. (1981), 'L'Intertexte Inconnu', *Littérature n° 41: Intertextualité et Roman en France au Moyen Âge*, vol. 41, 4–7.
Ruprecht, H-G. (1984), *Intertextualité*, Paris: Les editions trintexte.
Samósata, L. (2012), *Diálogo com os Mortos*, Trans. Int. and Notes by Custódio Magueijo, Coimbra: Imprensa da Universidade de Coimbra.
Soares, R. (2005), 'Novo Humanismo', in Carlos Reis (dir.), *História Crítica da Literatura Portuguesa. Do Neo-Realismo ao Post-Modernismo*, vol. IX, 39–40, Lisboa: Verbo.
Sollers, P. (1971), *Théorie d'Ensemble*, Paris: Seuil.
Thomas, J. (2002), 'Les passeurs dans l'Énéide, in P. Carmigrani (dir.), *Figures du passeur*, 199–216, Perpignan: Presses Universitaires.
Walde, C. (2016), 'Morpheus', in Brill's New Pauly, Antiquity volumes edited by Hubert Cancik and Helmuth Schneider. Available online: https://referenceworks.brillonline.com/entries/brill-s-new-pauly/morpheus-e810010.
Zawieja, Philippe (2016), *Dictionnaire de la Fatigue*, Genève: Droz.

Part Two

# Memory and Post-Memory in the Hypercontemporary Novel

# 6

# 'What's in a Name?' Reading the Hypercontemporary

Isabel Cristina Rodrigues

*What's in a name? That which we call a rose*
*By any other name would smell as sweet*
W. Shakespeare, Romeo and Juliet

(act 2, scene 2)

If we read the text of the inaugural lecture which Giorgio Agamben presented in the theoretical philosophy course at the Faculty of Art and Design in Venice in 2009, we find the author questioning what is by no means an infrequently considered concept:

> 'Of whom and of what are we contemporaries'? And, first and foremost, 'What does it mean to be contemporary?'. In the course of this seminar, we shall have occasion to read texts whose authors are many centuries removed from us, as well as others that are more recent, or even very recent. At all events, it is essential that we manage to be in some way contemporaries of these texts.
>
> (Agamben 2009: 39)

In fact, merely by way of example, Agamben's thinking appears to follow Pessoa's notion, under the problematizing legacy of which the writer Mário de Carvalho also seems to seek shelter, recalling that our contemporaries are, after all, those 'giants that carry time on their backs' (Carvalho 2014: 24). Pessoa's words are these: 'Who are my contemporaries? Only the future can tell. Many people who live with me coexist with me just because they last with me. These are just my fellows in time; I don't want to be parochial in matters of immortality' (Pessoa 1980: 3).

Pessoa posited that our contemporaries are not necessarily only those authors who endure with us (in a parallel that would, in each one's life, be instituted on the sidelines of the intersubjective transit that provides the meaning of being human). If this is the case, in the meaning of contemporaneity which I intend to touch on here, the temporal dimension cannot be discarded, since it underlies the purpose of considering a literary era that coincides with that of my own existence. And if immortality is indeed averse to parochialisms of dubious critical relevance, the coincidence between time and literary writing, and between literary writing and critical reading, does not exempt us from questioning or systematizing our own time.

It also so happens that Agamben, who declared himself a contemporary of Nietzsche's thinking and specifically of his *Untimely Meditations* (published in 1874, in which the German philosopher formulates a kind of ontology of the *contemporary* based on the principle of inconsistency, apparently more consistent with the conceptual reason for the extemporaneous), has no hesitation in attributing the practical or methodological reason for this dyssynchrony to the sense of contemporary itself:

> Nietzsche situates his own claim for relevance [*attualità*], his 'contemporariness' with respect to the present, in a disconnection and out-of-jointness. Those who are truly contemporary, who truly belong to their time are those who neither perfectly coincide with it nor adjust themselves to its demands. They are thus in this sense irrelevant [*inattuale*]. But precisely because of this condition, precisely through this disconnection and this anachronism, they are more capable than others of perceiving and grasping their own time ... Contemporariness is, then, a singular relationship with one's own time, which adheres to it and, at the same time, keeps a distance from it ... Those who coincide too well with the epoch, those who are perfectly tied to it in any respect, are not contemporaries, precisely because they do not manage to see it; they are not able to firmly hold their gaze on it.
>
> (Agamben 2009: 40–1)

Thus, a critical reading of the contemporary (of which we may or may not later discover ourselves to be contemporaries in the sense attributed to it by Agamben and Pessoa) seems to stem as much from inevitability – that of knowing the other side of time that belongs to us – as from choice: we subject our perceptive outlook to a distance that does not coincide with the object of our perception, or to a kind of interval that is also a voluntary hesitation or withdrawal. Agamben marks this with the use of the metaphor of darkness, a darkness whose meaning fatally escapes us yet never ceases to enlighten us:

> In an expanding universe, the most remote galaxies move away from us at a speed so great that their light is never able to reach us. What we perceive as the darkness of the heavens is this light that, though travelling toward us, cannot reach us, since the galaxies from which the light originates move away from us at a velocity greater than the speed of light.
>
> To perceive, in the darkness of the present, this light that strives to reach us but cannot – this is what means to be contemporary ... And for this reason, to be contemporary is, first and foremost, a question of courage, because it means being able not only to firmly fix your gaze on the darkness of the epoch, but also to perceive in this darkness a light that, while directed toward us, infinitely distances itself from us.
>
> (Agamben 2009: 46)

The Italian philosopher imports this concept of darkness from the epistemological field of astrophysics and extends it into the domain of contemporaneity. He seems, thus, to establish a studied step of discontinuity between individuals and the time that belongs to them; it allows us to look at a time which we can only approach in the exact measure by which we are distanced from it: an analytical distance and a critical distance. Fate or method, the rhetoric of discontinuity that the perception of the contemporary demands from us is fundamental if we are to undertake a critical reading of the literary texts of our time. It has come to be commonly referred to as Hypercontemporary literature, a term that requires reflection. In the mid-1980s, the time of the joyously turbulent waters of Portuguese postmodernism, Jorge de Sena called his fellow critics' attention to what he called 'the plight of taxonomy' (Sena 1986: 22). With one nuance or another, this can be seen as mildly applicable to the circumstances that have shaped the epistemological domain of so-called Hypercontemporary literature in the last twenty years.

Adapting Sena's notion to today, the troubles we confront when faced with more recent literature do not necessarily coincide with the taxonomic wrangles that, at the height of the postmodernist wave, (de)marked the strategy of setting literary genres. After the *plight of taxonomy*, we are now, in the middle of the twenty-first century, also confronted with what could be termed the plight of prefixes. Being assigned to the name under which they are grouped leaves the epistemological core untouched, which that prefixation should, after all, evidence – from a categorical point of view, a prefix is a critical non-place.

I therefore turn to Shakespeare as much as to Ana Luísa Amaral:[1] What's in a name? Or, to paraphrase, what's in a prefix? They say what they say, merely indicating a position, and therefore the paucity of their message has no distance; they are opaque signs in relation to what they intend to designate.

The opacity of prefixes clearly does not only affect designations such as Hypercontemporary literature. This kind of mute label, which has been given to literary texts published in the first decades of the twenty-first century, seems intended to re-edit, for example, the identical sense of indetermination that has touched so-called hypermodern times, the functional dilution of which Lipovetsky has striven to undertake over several decades. In fact, more than a clarification, Lipovetsky's thinking has always seemed like an instigating gesture of non-elucidation: a critical-analytical stalemate that makes the potential orientation assumed by hypermodernity more or less undecidable; a break from modernity (and also post-modernity) or an expression of its epistemological radicalization. It may not be possible (or even desirable) to conclusively answer this question, not least because, as Saramago reminds us with the character Lídia in *The Year of the Death of Ricardo Reis*, 'there are many truths and they are all opposed to one another' (Saramago 1998 (1984): 380).

In truth, this type of cataloguing, in relation to the texts that it is supposed to regulate, constitutes a kind of added value, yet does not engender an explicit critical balance; it therefore constitutes a kind of 'diversion[s] of abstract thought' (Baudelaire 1995 (1863): 4), in the sense Baudelaire attributed to this expression, which shows how the greater or lesser artificial convenience of labels tends to leave the objects that they are supposed to classify inviolate.

In his essay *The Painter of Modern Life*, Baudelaire refers to his contemporary experience (in the second half of the nineteenth century – the essay was published in 1863) as a time marked by a sense of ephemerality or acceleration, not because this was a quality particularly evidenced by the time in question, but because this is always the view imposed by the contemporary world on those who ponder it:

> Modernity is the transient, the fleeting, the contingent; it is one half of art, the other being the – eternal and the immovable. There was a form of modernity

---

[1] I refer here, in the case of Ana Luísa Amaral, to her book of poems *What's in a Name*, published in 2017, which re-evaluates not only the Shakespearean formula, but also the poet's belief in the irrelevance of a name to fix the identity of an object.

for every painter of the past; the majority of the fine portraits that remain to us from former times are clothed in the dress of their own day. They are perfectly harmonious works because the dress, the hairstyle, and even the gesture, the expression and the smile (each age has its carriage, its expression and its smile) form a whole, full of vitality. You have no right to despise this transitory fleeting element, the metamorphoses of which are so frequent, nor to dispense with it. If you do, you inevitably fall into the emptiness of an abstract and indefinable beauty, like that of the One and only woman of the time before the Fall.

(Baudelaire 1995 (1863): 7)

So, if modernity (and, in this sense, contemporaneity) places us against the transitory and the fugitive (a matter of contingency, therefore), it is certain, as Agamben argues, that the light we hope to gather from it will never reach us. We are left with the experience of the darkness that trails behind it, which (as also typical of the physiology of vision) will always be a product of our retina.[2]

And so the words hypercontemporaneity or Hypercontemporary (which have been used in various languages as a provisional label to refer to the literature – and especially the novel – of the first decades of the twenty-first century) induce a chronological circumscription of the concreteness of literary texts. Yet they seem to lack a broader critical-analytical property which could convert those terms into concepts and provide them with an informative nucleus to aid contemporary readers in making a reading of their time and the literary texts that their own contemporaneity imparts.

Ana Paula Arnaut, who has devoted careful critical attention both to the compositional ethos of postmodern narrative and to the more recent Hypercontemporary drift of the novel as a literary form, has sought to defend the correlation between the concept of Hypercontemporary and the postmodern orientation that she designates as celebratory (cf. 2018: 21). This, in turn, would

---

[2] Cf. Agamben (2009: 44): 'What happens when we find ourselves in a place deprived of light, or when we close our eyes? What is the darkness that we see then? Neurophysiologists tell us that the absence of light activates a series of peripheral cells in the retina called "off-cells". When activated, these cells produce the particular kind of vision that we call darkness. Darkness is not, therefore, a privative notion (the simple absence of light, or something like nonvision) but rather the result of the activity of the "off-cells", a product of our retina. This means, if we return to our thesis on the darkness of contemporariness, that to perceive this darkness is not a form of inertia or of passivity, but rather implies an activity and a singular ability. In our case, this ability amounts to a neutralization of the lights that come from the epoch in order to discover its obscurity, its special darkness, which is not, however, separable from those lights'.

represent a kind of entropic overstepping of the former, of an avowedly more moderate nature:[3]

> This proposed concept of the hypercontemporary therefore seems to result both from the more systematic cult of this variant and from a need for a change in terminology. This corresponds to the very evolution of the socio-historical dynamic and consequently to the imperative for laying down new themes and new scenarios that mirror behavioural, (inter)individual and (inter)social inflections, arising from a new, globalized world in constant transformation, and also in a progressive escalation of violence.
>
> (cf. 2018: 22)

Undertaking a genealogy of the concept of Hypercontemporary, or of the term that will have to be converted into a concept (as with the designations of Romanticism or Neorealism), is obviously important. However, this is only the case to the extent that, with the darkness that belongs to it, its trajectory may prove capable of illuminating the present literary era.

In the introductory text of his recent *Judge for Yourself. Reading Hyper-Contemporary Literature and Book Prize Shortlists* (2020), Nicholas Taylor-Collins makes a point of referring to what he considers the most relevant merit of Hypercontemporary literature – its poignant novelty. This makes it naturally apt to engage in a type of healthy inaugural reading (assisted by a useful analytical innocence) – a merit that, on the other hand, may well become its own means of resistance:

> '[H]yper-contemporary literature' characterizes texts that have just been published, that have just reached bookshelves, and just been devoured by a brand-new readership. Hyper-contemporary literature is exciting, brand-new writing whose merits also lead to problems for the critic – regardless of whether that critic is an academic in a university, a student in the seminar room, or a book-club member who reads the latest bestseller. The merits of hyper-contemporary literature are clear. These texts have not yet been read, pored over, or digested. They are fresh and their stories are new. The ways those stories are told are as yet

---

[3] 'The first [type of postmodernism] is moderate, in which a certain connection to reality is maintained, despite evident subversions (parodic or not), related for example to (non)compliance with genological standards or (dis)obedience to narrative categories; the second is celebratory, more creative and effusive, if not delirious, and in some cases therefore it intensifies the entropic dimensions of this art of writing in number and variety, although it must be emphasized, without losing the ties to a certain reality which the intends to reproduced. Yet this is less fixed, because it is given in a decreasingly linear way and often has to be guessed at or investigated by the reader. The game then becomes even more of a game, and the stakes are forced to rise: for the author and for those who read it.'

unknown. The characters are either formed out of an imaginative nothingness or develop previous characters in ways that are unforeseen or long-awaited. Hyper-contemporary literature is unread, untouched, and exciting … But hyper-contemporary literature also comes with its problems. The frameworks for analysing and examining the texts are either non-existent or insufficiently developed. The subjects are unknown in their specifics and they may offend or (worse yet) bore the reader. The unseen nature of hyper-contemporary literature also means that few people have had eyes on the text and had – let alone taken – the opportunity to amend or improve the writing, either in its subject, characters, style, or form … Hyper-contemporary literature is not the same as 'twenty – first-century literature', such as that expertly surveyed in books like Daniel O'Gorman and Robert Eaglestone's The Routledge Companion to Twenty-First-Century Literary Fiction (2019). For one, that text is concerned with a particular type of literature called 'literary fiction' that, as I detailed above, entails thinking about critically as a type of writing that has been co-opted by.
(Taylor-Collins 2020: 8)

Taylor-Collins employs an argument to distinguish Hypercontemporary literature from twenty-first-century literature. But it is as instigating as it is liable to be contradictory, due to what is profoundly incoherent about it. In Taylor-Collins's understanding, Hypercontemporary literature concerns a type of textuality that opens up to the reader without the mediating intervention of critical discourse and, he also argues that 'hyper-contemporary literature is therefore literature that has … to gather a critical consensus' (Taylor-Collins 2020: 9). The implication is thus that Hypercontemporary texts would always be subject to an irrevocably provisional status, prior to being inevitably placed onto the critical-symbolic shelf of *twenty-first-century literature*. One way or another, the truth is that, in terms of the perceptive body that they designate, neither the label *Hypercontemporary* nor *twenty-first-century literature* can institute the mode of distance that Agamben considers fundamental to induce a human cognitive experience of the contemporary, that dark that illuminates us without us receiving the sense of light itself. So the (self-)imposition of a certain caution or reluctance in the act of categorizing what is still in the process of becoming may be a side effect which the darkness in which we walk imposes on the dim light of our cognitive ability. In the introduction that Daniel O'Gorman and Robert Eaglestone wrote for the volume of which they were also editors (*The Routledge Companion to Twenty-First Century Literary Fiction*), they set out this necessary warning:

This field begs questions. For example, when, after all, does the contemporary begin? Often in academic texts and university modules, and in our case here, the year 2000, the 'Common Era' millennium, is chosen, but this is an open issue. Should 'mere chronology' define a period? Or do significant political events (an election, a war) inaugurate it? Or, perhaps more appropriately in this context, should a major literary event begin a literary period? And, perhaps more saliently for this volume, when do contemporary texts stop being contemporary? Or, most of all: can the contemporary even be characterized?

(O'Gorman & Eaglestone 2019: 1)

In trying to respond to the questions put forward by Eaglestone and O'Gorman, I have very few reservations in my belief that a literary period is in fact indefinable exclusively by its chronology. That is why I defend the legitimacy of answering the two authors' latter question in the affirmative: yes, the (Hyper-)contemporary can and should be characterized, beyond the inevitable transience of the critical judgement to which it is exposed. One should therefore seek to endow the perception of literary hypercontemporaneity with more substantial critical force. The hinges of a prefix which is becoming detached from its own meaning should be broken and the critical cartography of a time that, from my point of view, seems to call for more specialized attention within the epistemological spectrum that it itself provides, should be expanded (beyond the studies on multimodal orientation that the novel has come to assume).

In recent decades, the relevance of the material dimension of the text in literary semiosis has taken on a hitherto somewhat unprecedented critical-analytical prominence (note, for example, the exercise of critical consideration that has been developed within the scope of the multimodal narrative). Yet the same has not happened in relation to another dimension of the Hypercontemporary that is of particular interest to me and that has garnered merely passing critical attention until now: the rhetoric of violence in the domain of the novel, which has become particularly evident in texts published in the first decades of this century.

In 2014, Helder Gomes Cancela, in whose work the issue in question carries perhaps more importance than any other work of current literature, published a small book of essays entitled, very significantly, *O exercício da violência* (The Exercise of Violence). In this book, the author goes into some detail on what we might designate as the ground zero of violence – the understanding of culture as a form of violence:

> Of all forms of violence, the most fundamental to the idea of culture is that produced in the name of a representation of the world. No representation is neutral. Whether religious, political, ideological or otherwise ... Conflicts between representations are those that most profoundly have shaped civilizations. There are as many names for violence as there are ways to justify it: god, education, state, order, truth. In any of these cases, the paradox is that the alternative to the violence of representations is often another, even more aggressive form of violence: the chaos that emerges from the crumbling of representations.
>
> (Cancela 2014b: 16–17)

This notion effectively ends up subscribing to the exercise of violence as a grammar of a domesticated world via the more or less provisional authority of the various paradigms by which its cognitive or representative grasp is legitimized: 'perhaps what we call civilization is nothing but the confrontation between different models of organization of violence' (Cancela 2014b: 17). Science and art, therefore, are modes of violence that endorse the sense of their own threat by means of the cognitive and epistemological balance that both impart to human possibilities, that is, through the utility of a force which can be called either truth or beauty:

> [T]rying to hide the blood behind art or science is no more than a way of justifying it, making violence something useful ... It is a heavy toll, but one that, from a distance, runs the risk of appearing all the fairer as from it rise the peaks of a heritage of knowledge or art on which we base our identity.
>
> (Cancela 2014b: 16–17)

It may then prove possible to assess the legitimacy or illegitimacy of the violence that underlies every representative exercise through the operational practice of concepts such as truth or beauty. Indeed, this aspect would, ipso facto, justify the opportunity for a fictional recomposition of the violence evidenced by the Hypercontemporary novel as a condition of our own imaginative rationality. Up to the present day, the thinking of the scientific community on this question has constituted little more than descriptive signalling of the problem; that is, the more or less declarative grasp of certain thematic and compositional evidence, the critical-analytical reach of which is still to be revealed. A more systematic approach to literary texts is called for, where the problem is represented as a function of a narrative process of ambiguous neonaturalist literary affiliation.

One of the first critical comments in Portugal that aimed to highlight the epistemological urgency of this issue dates from 2006, authored by Miguel Real. At the time (with regard to the work of Valter Hugo Mãe) he had no hesitation in attributing the resolute label of neonaturalist to this 'literary perspective' (Real 2006: 22). This classification merits some reservation for some recent novels, such as those by H. G. Cancela or Ana Margarida de Carvalho, for example, but also those of Gonçalo M. Tavares, including the author's first books, published in the early years of the twenty-first century. This categorization indication was also echoed by Ana Paula Arnaut (Cf. Arnaut 2018: 23–4), who deemed it fit to associate the neonaturalist vision of Valter Hugo Mãe with the memory of a type of character recorded in the prologue to the second edition of *O Barão de Lavos*, by Abel Botelho (1898): 'a type in which 'imbalances, [the] aberrations and [the] pathological abnormalities' are found' (1898: 24).

In fact, in the work of these three authors (but especially in H. G. Cancela and Gonçalo M. Tavares), the rhetoric of violence goes hand in hand with a powerful sense of notable restraint, like a tempered blade that wounds the reader's thinking soul with the action of a constantly fierce verbal gesture, albeit with the precision of a clock or a dagger. It is a form of writing that both saves and at the same time makes bearable the compositional structure of violence that novels like *O escuro que te ilumina* (2018) by José Riço Direitinho, or like *Impunidade* (2014a) and *As Pessoas do Drama* (2017), both by Cancela, lay down as foundations. Indeed, this floor is not made for bare feet, but imposes on the walker the need to learn to move over the inalienable hardness of the ground. In these novels (as in many others; for example, in the astonishing *Torto Arado* (Crooked Plough) (2019) by the Brazilian writer Itamar Vieira Júnior) no redemption is possible nor is there even a glimpse of it, because the *pathological abnormalities* on display are not a feature of any pedagogy of reading.

The novelist Ana Margarida de Carvalho, who burst onto the Portuguese literary scene as if she were not a new arrival (I refer here to the publication of her first book in 2013, *Que importa a fúria do mar*), published the novel *Não se pode morar nos olhos de um gato*, the core of whose world impressively echoes Saramago's *Ensaio sobre a Cegueira* (Blindness) (1995). Saramago's novel was written under the categorical baton of postmodernism, yet it already foreshadowed the entropic drift that the novel of the first decades of the twenty-first century would undergo and which finds one of its uncomfortable touchstones in the fictionalization of violence. Ana Margarida de Carvalho's second novel has the simultaneously acute and impassive starkness of an auto-da-fé, exposing the journey of the characters to acts of 'baseless cruelty' (Carvalho 2016: 205) consented to by an 'evil God' (Carvalho 2016: 93). It accepts the legitimacy of human bestialization in the context of confinement that is not only spatial, but also moral, similar to the one imposed by the walls of the asylum in *Blindness*, which confines the blind to a siege of their own violence: in this novel, it first concerns a slave ship (a Guineaman) and then, after the shipwreck, the small strip of sand between the rocks and the daily threat of the tide:

> The bosun had examined the cliffs. He was interested in a recess in the rock and was trying to climb up there; in fact, he was the first to realize that the tide was rising, and that only a thin layer of sand was left, burnt dry by the sun … Soon, that strip would be submerged and they would be under siege, between the waves and the hard place.
>
> (Carvalho 2016: 87)

However, the castaways in *Não se pode morar nos olhos de um gato* are primarily castaways of their own making, dragging within their tight geographic boundaries the violence of a past with no possibility of remission: Teresa, Father Marcolino, but above all the slave Julien, who, on the verge of being rescued, deals a mortal blow to Nunzio, and thus to any belief in human potential:

> Nunzio begged for help. There were still a few kilometres of sand to cross before reaching the end of the cliff, Nunzio was getting farther and farther away, and Emina realized that the boy was not among them in that unbridled race. Their throats dry with air and salt, she asked Julien to stop; they had to help him … Nunzio broke into a smile of relief when he saw someone coming towards him … Julien, however, did not smile. There was an urgency in his eyes, the kind that can sometimes be confused with indifference … Julien stopped suddenly and headed to the shoreline. He picked up a rock and when he turned around there was an urgency in his eyes, the kind that can sometimes confused with mercilessness. He caved in Nunzio's head with three blows of the rock and Nunzio slumped to the floor, blood pooling around him, dyeing his hair the colour of molasses, like a dead beetle turned on its back.
>
> (Carvalho 2016: 342–3)

In Cancela's words, hiding blood behind art is merely an artifice for legitimizing it. Perhaps then this ambiguous purpose of legitimation will take the form of the cognitive balance that necessarily supersedes it: that of knowledge itself as a way of inhabiting the Earth.

# References

Agamben, G. (2009), 'What Is the Contemporary?', in *What Is an Apparatus and Other Essays*, 39–54, Stanford: Stanford University Press.

Amaral, A. L. (2017), *What's in a Name*, Porto: Assírio & Alvim.

Amaral, A. L. (2014), 'Carta', in *Escuro*, 52–4, Porto: Assírio & Alvim.

Arnaut, A. P. (2018), 'Do Post-Modernismo ao Hipercontemporâneo: Morfologias do Romance e (Re)figurações da personagem', *Revista de Estudos Literários* 8: 19–44. Available online: http://impactum-journals.uc.pt/rel/article/view/6168/5052.

Baudelaire, C. (1995 (1863)), 'The Painter of Modern Life', in *The Painter of Modern Life and Other Essays*, 1–34, New York: Phaidon Press.

Binet, A. M. and Angelini, P. K. (2016), 'Literatura Hipercontemporânea', *Letras de Hoje* 51 (4): 447–9.

Botelho, A. (1898), *O Barão de Lavos*, Porto: Livraria Chardron. Available online: http://purl.pt/232. (accessed 03 October 2022).

Bruss, R. (2019), *The Time Is Now: Embodiments of the Hyper-Present in Contemporary American Literature*. Theses and Dissertations. Available online: https://dc.uwm.edu/etd/2291?utm_source=dc.uwm.edu%2Fetd%2F2291&utm_medium=PDF&utm_campaign=PDFCoverPages.

Caires, C. (2011), 'O Hiper no Modernismo e na Ficção', in Sabarís, X. N. (coord.), *Diálogos ibéricos sobre a modernidade*, 25–40, Ed. Húmus: V. N. de Famalicão.

Cancela, H. G. (2014a), *Impunidade*, Lisboa: Relógio d'Água.

Cancela, H. G. (2014b), *O Exercício da Violência*, Lajes do Pico: Companhia das Ilhas.

Cancela, H. G. (2017), *As Pessoas do Drama*, Lisboa: Relógio d'Água.

Carvalho, A. M. de (2013), *Que Importa a Fúria do Mar*, Lisboa: Teorema.

Carvalho, A. M. de (2016), *Não se Pode Morar nos Olhos de um Gato*, Lisboa: Teorema.

Carvalho, M. de (2014), *Quem Disser o Contrário é Porque tem Razão*, Porto: Porto Editora.

Cruz, D. N. da (2018), 'Pós-modernidade ou Hipermodernidade? Pensando o sujeito contemporâneo sob as óticas de Lipovetsky e Bauman', *Sapere Aude* 9 (18): 351–71.

Direitinho, J. R. (2018), *O Escuro que te Ilumina*, Lisboa: Quetzal.

Júnior, I. V. (2019), *Torto Arado*, Lisboa: Leya.

Lipovetsky, G. (2004), 'Tempo Contra Tempo ou a Sociedade Hipermoderna', in *Os Tempos Hipermodernos*, 50–101, São Paulo: Barcarolla.

Magalhães, C. A. (2018), 'Desigualdade, Exclusão e Violência Urbana em Narrativas Hipercontemporâneas', *Revista de Estudos Literários*, 8: 75–100.

O'Gorman, D. and Eaglestone, R. (2019), *The Routledge Companion to Twenty-First Century Literary Fiction*, London: Routledge.

Pessoa, F. (1980 (1923)), *Ultimatum e Páginas de Sociologia Política*. (Recolha de textos de Maria Isabel Rocheta e Maria Paula Morão. Introdução e organização de Joel Serrão), Lisboa: Ática.
Real, M. (2006), 'O Neo-Naturalismo', *Jornal de Letras, Artes e Ideias*, July 19: 22.
Sena, J. de (1986), *Sobre o Romance*, Lisboa: Edições 70.
Saramago, J. (1998 (1984)), *O Ano da Morte de Ricardo Reis*, Lisboa: Caminho.
Taylor-Collins, N. (2020), *Judge for Yourself. Reading Hyper-Contemporary Literature and Book Prize Shortlists*, London and New York: Routledge.

# 7

# Paulo Faria's Wars: Owning Experience, Violence, and Postmemory

Felipe Cammaert

Chronicling the sites of memory of the Great War in France, Paulo Faria wonders about the transmission of traumatic experiences associated with violence perpetuated in armed conflict from the perspective of artistic representation:

> How is it that the experience of war is conveyed? The horror of war, the emotions of war? Through words? Through images? And what does it serve to describe them, represent them, show them? Is it so that they are not repeated? But has passing on the knowledge of war to those who have not lived it ever averted new wars? Has anyone ever become a pacifist, having read the *Iliad*, or having watched *Apocalypse Now*?
>
> (Faria 2019a)

The apparent scepticism of this excerpt contrasts with the aims set elsewhere by the Portuguese writer and translator, born in Lisbon, in 1967. Paulo Faria is the son of a doctor who fought in the colonial war as an ensign of the Portuguese Armed Forces in Mozambique. His works are grounded in the reconstitution of a familial past amidst the colonial war, as well as in the possible consequences it might pose for contemporary Portuguese society. In his novels and short personal essays published to date on this topic, two main, interconnected, concerns stand out: on one hand, the artistic representation (with a special emphasis on literary representation) of violence resulting from armed conflicts, in particular in contexts related to the wars of decolonization in Africa and in the two world wars of the twentieth century; on the other hand, the intergenerational transfer of memories related to these topics, and their subsequent appropriation in written form by those who did not live through these violent events.

In *Estranha Guerra de Uso Comum* (2016) and *Gente Acenando para Alguém que Foge* (2020a), Faria approaches Portuguese colonial memory through Carlos Silveira, an autobiographical character who, from the point of view of a descendant, narrates the experience of a father living in Africa, in an introspective journey that aims to unveil the silence that looms over those traumatic events. The first novel alternates between letters that Silveira writes to his deceased father, and interviews with combatants who fought alongside his father in the colonial war. The second book focuses on an account of his journey to Mozambique in search of his father, and particularly on a quest to find a Mozambican man whom his father supposedly adopted during his term in the military, when he was just a child. As for the short essays Faria regularly publishes, they likewise serve to reflect on the immanency of war in the public and private memories of European societies, particularly the generational trauma associated with it.

Paulo Faria is one of the loudest voices in postmemory literature in post-colonial Europe and is one of the writers who has reflected most on the legacy of Portuguese colonialism in the twenty-first century. Alongside other authors such as Dulce Maria Cardoso, Djaimilia Pereira de Almeida, Joaquim Arena, Isabela Figueiredo, or Bruno Vieira Amaral, Faria brings the topic of the Portuguese colonial past to the forefront. In fact, this generation of 'artists under the condition of postmemory' (Ribeiro 2021: 8) has been able to breathe new life into the contemporary Portuguese novel by dramatizing through literature a traumatic heritage that still looms large over Portuguese society. In his approach to post-colonial memory, Faria comes across his own status as a descendant who did not experience first-hand the events that his works enact. Contrary to what happens with direct testimonial works from that period, in which writing assumes a cathartic function, the setting-off point of these descendants is marred by the absence of a biographical experience. As an adoptive witness of that troubled past, Paulo Faria must reach the 'ownership of experience' through writing, in order to appropriate his father's past in the colonial war. As such, the appropriation of borrowed memories causes representations of war in writing to undergo a fictionalization process that places the writer of postmemory in an interstitial space.

## Representations of the Ownership of Experience: 'My African War'

The so-called 'literature of the colonial war' has occupied a dominant position in the recent history of Portuguese literature. Following the end of the *Estado*

*Novo* dictatorship and the consequent fall of its empire overseas, many were the literary voices of the participants in the wars that Portugal fought with its colonies in Africa (Ribeiro 2004). The works of António Lobo Antunes are, perhaps, the most important example of this attempt to approach, from a literary standpoint, the Portuguese colonial debacle in the African continent. The brief reflections that follow, concerning the relationship between the experience of war and writing in the works of Lobo Antunes, will contextualize not only Faria's own relationship to the colonial war, but will also be useful to demonstrate that the updating of these memories at the hands of descendants marks both a continuity and a breaking away from previous representations of colonial memory.

*Os Cus de Judas* places the war at the forefront of the narration, with the intention of describing the traumatic experience of 'learning the agony' (Antunes 2004: 39) that the narrator went through during his term in Angola. This early novel admirably presents the relationship between the experience of armed conflict and the fictionalization of the biographical event. Aside from its testimonial function, *Os Cus de Judas* reflects on the power of literature to translate into words the moral collapse of the individual, as a consequence of armed conflict. In this book, the war is described as a disease that, aside from reaching Lisbon 'aboard the military vessels that returned, dizzy and bewildered, from a gunpowder inferno' (Antunes 2004: 174), triggers a physical and moral metamorphosis of both the narrator and his comrades, transfigured into 'dumb fishes inside aquariums of metal and fabric, simultaneously feral and tame, trained to die with no contest' (Antunes 2004: 103). Conversely, the act of transposing this experience into fiction is seen as 'a painful relearning of life' (Antunes 2004: 54). Both diegetically and in a broader dimension, Lobo Antunes's first books (understood to be acts of resilience) fulfil a cathartic function, capable of rescuing the autobiographical narrator of *Os Cus de Judas* from the hell of the Angolan battlefront. Moreover, in this paradigmatic text about Portuguese colonial violence, healing through writing is associated with the memory of the African homeland, namely the figure of the Black woman who incarnates the character of Tia Teresa in the novel (Cammaert 2019: 28).

In a post-colonial context, the writings of Paulo Faria constitute a paradigmatic example of what is known as a 'postmemory' approach to literature, according to Marianne Hirsch. In summary, the concept of postmemory speaks about how subsequent generations turn to artistic representation to appropriate their families' traumatic pasts, to the point that those memories present themselves to these descendants as if they were their own.¹ According to Hirsch, postmemory works reappropriate past traumatic cultural experiences, to reactivate and re-embody them through familiar and individual affective mediation devices (Hirsch 2012: 33). Initially coined in a post-Holocaust context, the concept of postmemory has recently been applied to other historical and cultural purviews, such as the postcolonial European context.

Postmemory literature such as Paulo Faria's exist in the wake of these earlier works (such as Lobo Antunes's), which openly criticize the phenomenon of colonialism. However, the spatial and chronological distance that separates them from the testimonies of those who took part in the colonial war means that these two literary manifestations differ substantially from one another. In his writing, Faria must approximate the reality of Africa through mediated testimonials, archives, and objects of memory, with the goal of (re)living his father's war. Thus, it is through writing that the heir will then recreate *ex post facto* the memory of an alien memory. In fact, in his journey to Mozambique in search of the theatres of war his father experienced – which makes up the plot of *Gente Acenando para Alguém que Foge* – the African space unveils a novel reality for the heir. When Carlos sees himself as the 'son of an executioner-victim' (Faria 2020a: 35) of the war, his presence in Africa reveals a completely different meaning for one who looks to recreate his father's memory *in situ*: 'I thought I came to Mozambique in search of the time when my father, executioner-victim, could still openly say that he was only a victim. Maybe I came to heal my urge to compartmentalize. And to leave my dead here if I can' (Faria 2020a: 35).

As with Lobo Antunes's work, there is hope in recovering and finding redemption through writing by invoking the African land. However, it is clear from the beginning of the book that, for Faria, re-enacting his father's war will ultimately lead to an intimate process, the effects of which will be particularly tangible for the person who inherits the colonial memory.

One of the main concepts connected to the notion of postmemory is that of 'ownership of experience' (Ribeiro and Ribeiro 2013: 25–36), which aims to signal the epistemological void characterizing the generations that did not live through the Portuguese colonial war, but that have somehow inherited that

---

¹ Here is Hirsch's definition (2012: 5): '"Postmemory" describes the relationship that the "generation after" bears to the personal, collective, and cultural trauma of those who came before, experiences they "remember" only by means of the stories, images, and behaviours with which they grew up. But these experiences were transmitted to them so deeply and affectively as to *seem* to constitute memories in their own right. Postmemory's connection to the past is thus not actually mediated by recall but by imaginative investment, projection, and creation'.

historical trauma. This kind of individual is presented as 'the symbolic heir of an open wound' (Ribeiro and Ribeiro 2013: 30), about which he elaborates a testimony created both from public and private narratives. The ownership of experience can be understood as the operation through which the generations who did not experience the colonial trauma directly can appropriate alien memories by resorting to conscious mediation mechanisms such as those that Hirsch mentions for the post-Holocaust context, although, according to Ribeiro and Ribeiro, the so-called 'sons of the war' do not objectively possess the ownership of experience, since they were neither actors nor immediate victims of the colonial system. Yet, the fact that they inscribe these foreign testimonials into their own identities means that, at least symbolically, the transmission of the colonial memory takes place in the heirs themselves.

In Paulo Faria's work, the ownership of experience of the Portuguese colonial memory is materialized via two concurrent narrative techniques. On the one hand, through the introspection of familiar memory, for example, through accounts and private archives (writings, photographs) belonging to the military father, which the writer will appropriate in his writing, and on the other hand, through recreating a composite discourse whose original holders are other African ex-combatants, and with whom the writer dialogues by way of interviews, looking to achieve what, in a recent essay, Faria calls 'the choral symphony of our African war' (Faria 2020b: 2).

The first of these devices is described in detail in *Estranha Guerra de Uso Comum*, thanks to a scientific metaphor, according to which the memories reincarnated in the descendant are the result of a physical process of crystallization.[2] The emergence of a postmemory is thus grounded in a process of purification according to which the substance it aims to achieve (i.e., the memories of the colonial war engrained in the narrator) will be free from any residue, following a process of depuration: 'Without my noticing it, the first crystals had already started to gather around the little wire. That wire was your photos of Africa, laid out on top of my bed, as I'd never seen them before. That wire was your African war, which I felt I could make somehow my own' (Faria 2016: 33).

In this letter, the narrator of *Estranha Guerra de Uso Comum* turns his father's photographic archives from Africa into the main element through which the past materializes itself in the consciousness of the heir of the colonial war.

---

[2] I have already had the chance to comment on this topic. See Cammaert 2021: 79–94.

In fact, the appropriation of the father's memory brings with it the illusion of additional knowledge on the son's consciousness, triggered by his imagination from looking at the photos: 'I felt I could see in those images things that you yourself had never seen, that I was tearing through veils that shrouded your eyes. I felt I was beginning to know more than you' (Faria 2016: 34), as Carlos tells his absent father. Achieving the ownership of experience is then described as such: 'Without being able to emigrate to escape conscription, since I have a wife and daughters and my life in Portugal is a complete mess, I then left to fight my war Overseas, looking for you' (Faria 2016: 39).

As for the second narrative device – the statements of his father's brothers in arms that the writer-narrator is collecting in order to construct his own narrative – there is a fundamental element that opens the way for noticing the presence of a mediated testimony, an inherent trait of postmemory narration. On multiple occasions, when confronted with the accounts of direct witnesses of the colonial war, Faria admits to being satisfied in accessing the intimate universe of those who do not belong to that specific group. However, the fact that these witnesses share their stories with the writer does not mean that they are fully assimilated. The final letter reads as follows:

> When I'm sitting there, listening to them, I know that before me no one listened to them like this, someone who was not Overseas, who does not have his own war histories to exchange, who only has a set of ears and a piece of paper, a pen, and time, all the time in the world, and this is my African war, I owe no allegiance to any narrative, only to the impressions I've harvested.
>
> (Faria 2016: 292)

Faria's narrator is aware that, in his role as a recipient, he will not be able to achieve knowledge like that direct witnesses hold. However, by considering the act of writing as the ground on which to fight a new war (his own Overseas war), Faria is also reclaiming the autonomy of his own narrative concerning the various stories he has heard.

In his most recent texts, Faria explores this idea even more explicitly, in a concept that, in a way, could be seen as his own definition of postmemory. In a short narrative essay titled *This is not your war III*, Faria refuses to be fully identified alongside the victims of the Portuguese past in Africa, without denying the gripes that, at present, his own generation still displays towards the victims and the executioners of colonial violence: 'Saying goodbye, they all ask me to send them the texts that I may write. I will do that. I will disillusion them again, perhaps lay them low. I do not write their memories; **I write my memories of their memories**' (Faria 2021: 4) (my bold).

With this formulation, Faria insists on the vicarious nature of his artistic representations as a consequence of intergenerational transmission. Analogously to the matter of justifying writing as a vital need that emerges from the earlier works of Lobo Antunes, the works of colonial postmemory such as Paulo Faria's also suggest a process of unlearning on the writer's part, who is not exempt from violence. Accessing the ownership of experience that allows the heir to convert his father's past into his own African war presupposes a unique epistemological construct, in which the intergeneration reupdating of memory occupies the forefront of this new narrative.

## Representations of Colonial Violence in Paulo Faria: 'The Struggle Goes On'

When, in a postmemory approach, the writer symbolically reaches the ownership of experience in the realm of writing, there occurs what Catherine Coquio calls 'the passing of testimony' in the act of transmission, which corresponds to the moment when the memory becomes testimony. Coquio adds that the incarnation of a descendant into a 'witness of a witness' simultaneously implies a 'moral mutation' (Coquio 2015: 149) in the addressee of the discourse. This transformation is especially visible in the representations of colonial violence within the Portuguese context. In the works of Paulo Faria, the re-enactment of colonial violence through writing has radical repercussions for the heir. Although the writer is not remembering situations that he actually experienced, the way in which the fiction universe depicts the episodes of colonial violence means that the literary representations of postmemory actually succeed in reappropriating, in their own way, the experience of violence.

*O rosto que falta*, a short narrative essay by Paulo Faria, is a paradigmatic example elaborating a narrative from the reconstitution of an encounter with an ex-combatant. The central element of the text is a photograph from the colonial war, captured by Portuguese soldiers, which depicts two Portuguese soldiers in Guinea-Bissau holding the body of a dead African combatant, which occupies the foreground of the image. In its opening lines, the text unveils the tension between the significance that this image holds for the witnesses of this scenario and the meaning that the postmemory writer can attribute it:

'This is war', he said when he showed it to me. As if this photo summed up everything, as if it was enough in itself, without needing to add anything to it. As if this image expelled words, made them superfluous. Or, worse still, noxious. But I, who was never in the war, have only words to counter this image.

(Faria 2019b: 22)

As an heir to a reality that he did not live through, Faria tries to understand the inherent violence of this photo that, even for its protagonists, represents the 'edge of inhumanity' (Faria 2019b: 22). However, the writer is immediately faced with a difficulty in overcoming the obstacle of (non) ownership:

I cannot speak of 'us' … 'What if, before pressing the shutter, we asked someone to hold the body up, so that we could get a better photo?' Makes no difference. There remains between me and the ensign the moat that the photograph digs out. I seek a common ground between me and the grammar of this photograph.

(Faria 2019b: 23)

Here, the distance that separates him from the ownership of experience is formulated by the warlike metaphor of the moat and is made clear through a linguistic marking: between the 'us' of those who witness a situation that belongs to themselves (a collective 'us', brought together by the war) and the 'I' of the writer who can only refer to these facts at a distance, there stands a gap so wide that to question it would seem to be doomed to fail.[3]

However, Faria intends to overcome the obstacle of non-ownership by resorting to the potential that literature has to reincarnate alien memories. The passing of testimony takes place when Faria appropriates the inherent violence of the war image, transposing into writing the historical significance that the situation conveys. Through an overtly fictional process, Faria centres his observer's gaze by focusing on the details of the photograph that escape the violence of the event depicted:

My gaze turns to what is missing in the photo, to what is absent from the image. The soldier's left eye with the mosquito netting around his neck, to Caselas, which the snapshot's edge cuts off … And, of course, Penedo's face is missing, he is holding the dead man, and who was, I'm afraid, tempted to smile … Could the expression on Penedo's face, which the photo denies me, be the key to evaluating the inhumanity of that gesture?

(Faria 2019b: 23)

---

[3] For a more detailed analysis of this matter, see Cammaert 2022: 57.

If this second-hand witness cannot truly grasp the 'why' of the situation, if the desire to relive this violence in its original state is rendered moot, then all the writer has left is to go looking for the elements that make up the background of the composition:

> I leave soldier Casela's gaze to its own fate, which I imagine simply tired and relieved, I remove myself from the closed eyelids of the nameless dead man, avoid his atrocious agony. I outline the face that is missing from the image, the face of soldier Penedo, cautiously avoiding his potential smile.
>
> (Faria 2019b: 23)

Here, the narration moves through the various levels of the image until it symbolically surpasses the spatial borders of graphical representation. The reader witnesses the transmutation of the writer's eye into the *hors-champ* of the photographic image, which is to say, into the absent face of the soldier which, when all is said and done, could hold in itself the ultimate meaning of not only the photo, but most of all the violence it implies.

In Faria's novels, the violence inherent to colonial memory also brings with it the heir's need to find a discourse that is able to re-enact past situations. In *Gente Acenando para Alguém que Foge*, the relationship between his writing and the reappropriation of his father's memory is explicitly described:

> I wrote my novel on the war to rob my father of the exclusive of the warlike narrative, to dethrone him, to write the book he was not able to write himself. To rewrite his war stories, to extirpate them from the ulterior lie. To ennoble him. I did it at the cost of the other veterans, who have seen their narratives reformulated, subordinated to the unhappiness of my father, usurped by me. I wrote my novel in order to, using the colonial war as a bait, tell the veterans of another war, my war. The one who goes out to search for war already has a war within himself.
>
> (Faria 2020a: 156)

Here, the descendant's narrative achieves, in a way, relative autonomy in relation to the subject matter from which it draws. The writing would, at the same time, be both a way to get closer to his combatant father's memory and the scenario of the descendant's moral mutation as a consequence of reappropriating violence through fiction. The transmission of memory is somehow effective when the descendant shares with his father the capacity to narrate his own war.

Now, note that the register of fiction is itself the element that seems to differentiate between the two positions, when direct and indirect witnesses meet on the same plane, regarding the ability to narrate the traumatic past. In the same novel, the author mentions a conversation with one of the ex-combatants, in which the interviewee expresses his doubts about the truthfulness of the heir's narrative as it appears in his first book. Despite Carlos's insistence on the conformity of his initiative, the conclusion is clear:

> I do not repent anything I wrote. I am only sorry that the book did not fulfil its function. I thought it would give me peace, but the war does not stop, does not slow down, gives no truce. The only thing that remains is for me to go on telling the story, to cause new victims, to reopen old wounds, to prevent cicatrisation. It was not me who spilled blood in the first place, but now I am not capable of stopping. It was not me who started the fire, I have my back against the wall. I start a counterfire, I sit down and suffocate. The struggle goes on.
>
> (Faria 2020a: 167)

At this stage, the warlike register used to describe the act of writing reaches its full potency. For Paulo Faria, literature presupposes a confrontation both *with* the memory and *for* the memory of the Portuguese colonial war. If, in the case of Lobo Antunes, writing appears as an antidote with which to fight off a past that weighs an individual down with traumatic memories, in the words of the descendants who reincarnate the colonial past writing is a space for re-enacting alien suffering. After all, this is an example of a cathartic situation in which the ownership of experience produced by the fictional enactment of postmemory allows the adoptive witness to experience colonial violence through writing, like that of the direct witness. In other words, in postmemory the transmission of the traumatic past necessarily requires a re-embodiment (to recall Hirsch's terminology) of the traumatic experience within writing, in a double motion of continuity and rupture compared to war literature.

Finally, it is necessary to point out that this identification between the writer-witness (who, like Lobo Antunes, writes through his own biographical memory) and the adoptive witness (who, like Faria, writes after other people's memories) does not imply a complete melding of the two witnessing entities. Commenting on the memorialization of the colonial war in Portugal, Ribeiro and Ribeiro state that, more than simply pointing out a continuity, the prefix 'post' in the term 'postmemory' symbolizes 'a gap, a reflexive moment … a mark of distance', which is the result of 'a particular kind of labour through which the contemporary relevance of the past can be enacted' (Ribeiro and Ribeiro 2018: 3). This conscious act from the writer, which the same authors call, in a previous text, an 'authorial gesture' (Ribeiro and Ribeiro 2013: 33), is unequivocally present in the works of Paulo Faria. In *Gente Acenando para Alguém que Foge*, the condition of the creator of a post-memorial narrative is referred to in terms of an interstitial space in which the heir moves, thanks to his double condition of non-protagonist and 'witness in spirit'; to use Catherine Coquio's expression (2015: 149):

> The war overseas functioned as an ideal matrix for this attachment of mine for second hand things: … An apocalypse in slow fire of whose chronicle I became an heir, in summary, a place where I can be inside and outside at the same time, be a protagonist and an observer, leave the frontstage to others while not leaving the scene. A place where the first word is always the prerogative of others. A place where, after all, I savoured to the end the pleasure of being and not being at the same time. And being war as it was, a fascinating and mysterious place, repelling and comfortable, a place of tyranny and sickly candour, of love, of unbridled madness, of brutality. Like my childhood, after all.
>
> (Faria 2020a: 88–9)

In this excerpt, the writer of postmemory places himself at the threshold from which he can look both to the past and to the future, thanks to his double condition as the receptor of alien memories and the narrator of a novel, mediated by his own experience as an heir to violence. Moreover, if we take a closer look at the significance that this novel gives to the memory of the Portuguese colonial war, or rather, to the elaboration of a narrative on this sensitive topic, we can conclude that, for Paulo Faria, the purpose of the writer of postmemory largely resembles the activity of literary translation. As with a translator, the writer of postmemory is somehow an intermediary between two realities, that, due to an act of linguistic mediation, transposes foreign words to allow for the cohabitation of consciousness in which their presence is necessarily subordinate to the initial discourse.

## Postmemory, Translation, and Intertextual Relations

In the text quoted above, António Sousa Ribeiro and Margarida Calafate Ribeiro point out that postmemory is not merely a situation in which the heir receptor acts passively, by simply replicating an alien past. On the contrary, this kind of writing necessarily relies on the creative and transformative role of the author in order to be able to articulate the inherited memories with reality and with the current discourses that are its own. Therefore, Ribeiro and Ribeiro consider postmemory as an act of translation:

> Thus, postmemory literally represents an act of translation, if one understands translation as being an epistemological model for strategies of relating to and incorporating discourses and experiences that belong to a framework of reference that is by definition strange and inassimilable.
>
> (Ribeiro and Ribeiro 2018: 3)

Thanks to a conscientious epistemological construction by the writer, postmemory emerges with the intention of combining two realities: the inherited past and the descendant's present.

When Paulo Faria appropriates the traumatic past of his father, in the realm of the text there is a translation of the cultural codes of the direct witness according to the epistemological horizon of the inheriting writer (see Cammaert 2022: 93). Furthermore, as an act of translating a series of common (and yet sometimes conflicting) epistemological codes, postmemory can also be understood as an act of 'decided correction' (Sarlo 2005: 104) of a previous memory, to recall Beatriz Sarlo's formulation for the post-dictatorial context of Latin America. This is to say, the decided correction of a previous public memory that has silenced many aspects of the traumatic European past. In this sense, the 'post' in postmemory would be equivalent to the moment in which the heir achieves critical awareness by elaborating a literary narrative of his country's colonial past. When compared with the literature produced by direct witnesses of the colonial war, postmemory writing somehow adds another element to the equation of the traumatic memory of Portuguese colonialism, while updating the cultural codes for new generations of readers.

In Portuguese literature of the twenty-first century, the formal and thematic innovations that postmemory colonial literatures bring to the literature of the colonial war mean that approaches such as Paulo Faria's claim a certain form of intertextuality. And they do so by suggesting the transmission of the memories of the colonial war as a form of translation. This means that, by appropriating the alien memory of a violent situation, the writer of postmemory is also unveiling a system of textual references that precedes him, while also broadening the relations of co-presence between works of colonial literature and those that depict a second-hand memory. Going back to Paulo Faria's questioning (with which we began this text) about the meaning of representing the experience of the war in artistic representations, we could conclude that 'passing on the knowledge of war to those who have not lived it' (to resume Faria's expression quoted above) is a way of translating for future generations the horror of an inherited memory that is still alive in Portuguese society.

# References

Antunes, A. L. (2004), *Os Cus de Judas*, Lisboa: Dom Quixote.
Cammaert, F. (2019), 'A Visita da Tia Teresa: Experiência da Guerra Colonial e Resiliência pela Escrita em Os Cus de Judas', *Colóquio/Letras* 201: 20–31.
Cammaert, F. (2021), 'Cristalizações de Memórias Alheias: A Guerra Colonial na Escrita da Pós-Memória de Paulo Faria', *Revista Abril. Descolonizações: Memórias Residuais* 13 (27): 79–94. Available online: https://periodicos.uff.br/revistaabril/article/view/50684.
Cammaert, F. (2022), *Passados Reapropriados. Pós-memória e Literatura*, Porto: Afrontamento.
Coquio, C. (2015), *Le Mal de Vérité ou l'Utopie de la Mémoire*, Paris: Armand Colin.
Faria, P. (2016), *Estranha Guerra de Uso Comum*, Lisboa: Ítaca.
Faria, P. (2019a), 'A Guerra Foi o que Tivemos em Vez de uma Infância Feliz (parte II)', *Público*, April 14. Available online: https://www.publico.pt/2019/04/14/mundo/noticia/guerra-infancia-feliz-parte-ii-1868593.
Faria, P. (2019b), 'O Rosto que Falta', *Público*, October 6: 22–4.
Faria, P. (2020a), *Gente Acenando para Alguém que Foge*, Lisboa: Minotauro.
Faria, P. (2020b), 'This Is Not Your War (I)', *Memoirs* Newsletter 120, December 12: 1–4. Available online: https://memoirs.ces.uc.pt/ficheiros/4_RESULTS_AND_IMPACT/4.3_NEWSLETTER/IMAGENS_NEWSLETTER_SEM_LEGENDA/MEMOIRS_newsletter_120_PF_pt.pdf.
Faria, P. (2021), 'This Is Not Your War (III)', *Memoirs* Newsletter 126, March 13. Available online: https://memoirs.ces.uc.pt/ficheiros/4_RESULTS_AND_IMPACT/4.3_NEWSLETTER/MAPS_MEMOIRS_newsletter_126_PF_en.pdf.
Hirsch, M. (2012), *The Generation of Postmemory: Writing and Visual Culture after the Holocaust*, New York: Columbia University Press.
Ribeiro, A. P. (2021), *Novo Mundo. Arte Contemporânea no Tempo da Pós-Memória*, Porto: Afrontamento.
Ribeiro, M. C. (2004), *Uma História de Regressos: Império, Guerra Colonial e Pós-Colonialismo*, Porto: Afrontamento.
Ribeiro, A. S. and Ribeiro, M. C. (2013), 'Os Netos que Salazar Não Teve: Guerra Colonial e Memória de Segunda Geração', *Revista Abril* 5 (11): 25–36.
Ribeiro, A. S. and Ribeiro, M. C. (org.) (2016), *Geometrias da Memória: Configurações Pós-Coloniais*, Porto: Afrontamento.
Ribeiro, A. S. and Ribeiro, M. C. (2018), '"A Past That Will Not Go Away. The Colonial War in Portuguese Postmemory"', *Lusotopie* [Online]17 (2). Available online: http://journals.openedition.org/lusotopie/3249
Sarlo, B. (2005), *Tiempo Pasado. Cultura de la Memoria y Giro Subjetivo*, Buenos Aires: Siglo XXI.

# 8

# The Attraction of Autofiction in *Contra mim*: Paths and Chasms of Memory

José Vieira

*Who cannot remember everything that wants to forget runs the risk to forget about forgetting certain things.*
*Ilja Leonard Pfeijffer,* Grand Hotel Europa.
*There will never be a truth that can be fully shared. It is personal, even private.*
*Valter Hugo Mãe,* Contra mim.

With the world under the shadow of a virus, 2020 was an unusual year for human history. We are still feeling the impact from COVID-19, not really knowing how, where, and when we will have overcome this pandemic. In moments of crisis, the human being looks for answers to questions about the purpose of life. Our identity and the meaning of things become a means to fight oblivion and the annulment of the past, in a time that sees speed as the essence of creation and performance.

Therefore, memories, and childhood memories in particular, are the place, space, and time where the artist, in this case the writer, has to not only find answers, but also to come up with solutions or purposes, real or fictional.

This is where autofiction, and its faint and diaphanous edges, meets autobiography, the autobiographical novel and fiction. More than just an autonomous genre, autofiction is a product of the twentieth century and various revisitations of big institutionalized narratives. It is both a reaction and a response to the autobiographical pact and to the attempt to inhabit the truth through words.

It was in 2020 that Valter Hugo Mãe released the book *Contra mim,* a book of an autofictional and autobiographical nature. Before moving into the text analysis and matters regarding the factual truth and the literary or fictional truth, it is safe to say that in any part of the text we find a description of the literary genre of the book. We don't know, in fact, if it is a novel, which raises, from the start, a few questions, in concurrence with the fact that the title of the book fills a small part of the cover, the bottom-right corner, while the name of the author occupies the central space, followed by a drawing that might be the author himself, siting under a tree – the tree of knowledge, the tree of life, the tree of memory? – naked and holding a crow in his left hand.

The cover invites you to think about and deconstruct the paratextual elements in a literary work. First of all, it is not the title of the book that is singled out, but the name of the author is, as if the name of the writer was in fact the title of the book. Second, the title appears to be an appendix, a subtitle, relegated to a suggestion plan, once self-reflective. *Contra mim* (*Against me*) implies a personal and interior confrontation with what will be written and told, being, then, against the author and narrator, since this is a book of autofictional, autobiographical, and homodiegetic nature. Last, besides the title there's also an image that appears to be the author himself, sitting and completely naked, as if he is telling us that we're about to look at a private and personal disclosure of his own life.

However, it is important that we do not forget that this is a structure. The literary word articulates and creates worlds and realities. If the literary word is indeed a structure, it will raise many questions about what it could be, in fact, the historical truth and the personal truth, built from our own memory and the memory from those around us.

Therefore, the journey of a person's life, in this case the writers' journey, it is built on memories and memory occupies a primordial space in the creation of our own identity. It is through memory that we (re)build our past. The way that we remember places, ambiences and people is, in itself, a narrative, because memory works like a Damocles sword. The memory that we have, for instance, of our childhood is completed with what others say about us. The memories that we create and continue to create are, in part, the responsibility of other people. It is not totally unreasonable to say that what we recount and remember comes from beyond our memory, other people's memories or the combination of both with a little creative imagination.

In this *game* that is memory, a *game* of existence, as in the *game* of the narrative, we are part of what we tell, whether by approximation or separation, and that is why the other person is such a crucial part in creating our identity. Identity, memory, reality, truth, and fiction seem to come together in this book that the author divided into three parts, being the trilogy of his personal life or the invention of 'I'. In the author's 'Note' we find this division that justifies, or pretends to justify, writing. According to Carlos Nogueira (2021), *Contra mim* deals with 'the meanings and the working of memory', with 'childhood and his issue with the adulthood'; ... with 'the concepts of truth and lie in the autobiographical context of the book' and with 'the greatness (in the numerous meanings of the word: extension and elevation, vastness and spirituality) of literature (say, metonymically, "beauty and poems") and art in general'. According to the author, the reader may also read this 'Note' as an explanation both for life and for the poetics of literary autobiography.

Trying to understand and think about the concepts and autobiographical and autofictional genres necessarily requires one to go back in time and examine the texts of Philippe Lejeune and Serge Doubrovsky e Georges Gusdorf among other critics and theorists, who are still searching for consensus on the subject.

The foundational text that opens the way to the study of fictionalization in the biographical narrative is, without a doubt, *Le Pacte Autobiographique* from Lejeune. For the French critic, autobiography is a genre that has been merely used to tell the lives of great individuals with the purpose of 'emphasizing the genesis of their personality' (Lejeune 1975: 323).

The autobiographical pact consists in the protocol of certification led by the author, that undertakes to tell the truth in a sequential and chronological way, at the same time that the reader suspends his disbelief, accepting that what is being written corresponds to the truth and is real.

Autobiography is based on a real person telling his/her own name, and this fact will make the text real, since, according to Lejeune (1984: 37), one does not read a narrative where the main character's name is different from the author's the same way one reads a narrative where both have the same name.

The empire of light and image came to destroy the world of the written word. As a result of television, for example, and more recently smartphones and other digital and electronical paraphernalia, creative imagination connected to the word has lost its place and importance, because now we don't need to read a book or imagine the author and its characters. In this digital world of clicking on images, fiction has reinvented itself. The fictional autobiography metamorphosed not only because of this context, but also as consequence of its own fragmentation of the subject's identity and unity, a long phenomenon that had its awakening in Romanticism, suffered changes and new additions during the nineteenth century, and reached its peak with the arrival of Modernism and the World Wars.

According to Bauman, saying that modern times has led to the breakdown of identity is superfluous, since 'there's never been a time when identity 'would become' a problem, it could only exist as a *problem,* it has been a 'problem' since the beginning' (2007: 88).

According to Lejeune, and we can all agree, autobiography reveals one of the biggest and fascinating 'myths of Western civilization, the myth of MOI' (1971: 105). It is the I, the subjectivity inherent in it that leads, in a paradox, to autofiction and to the empire of the image that is nonetheless a world excluding the other. To fight these paradigms or realities is why there are books like that by Valter Hugo Mãe, but also the most recent novel from Mário Cláudio, *Embora Eu Seja um Velho Errante* (2021), or even *Astronomia* (2015) e *Tiago Veiga. Uma Biografia* (2011) and the saga from Norwegian writer Karl Ove Knausgård, *My Struggle* (2009-11).

In the book *Contra mim* we find the author's drawing on the cover as well as his name almost serving as a title; in the books of Mário Cláudio there are repeated photographs of the author himself throughout the chapters, as well as secrets and stories of personal experiences and a stylized image of the author on the cover of *Astronomia*. In Knausgård, on the other hand, the six volumes of the autofictional saga have a real photograph of the author appearing to stare at the reader, like a painting in a museum that follows its visitors with its mysterious look.

It is against those times that deny the Other that these authors write, along the lines of the autofictional theme. The writer, by deconstructing his reality and daily life, reinvents reality from facts, such as events, dates, and names of people or places, creating in turn, uncertainty, thus not allowing the reader to fully understand if such events actually happened to those people on those dates, turning the fiction of the 'I' to a level that does not refute the other, but makes it think about him/herself, like a mirror in search of a reflection and an image.

According to Knausgård, 'writing is bringing out of the dark what we know. Writing is about that. Not what happens here or there, not what happened here or there, but the *actual here and there*' (2012: 168). Trying to establish the nature of reality through fiction seems to be one of the purposes of autofiction, complimenting fiction rather than historical or scientific truth. Autofiction follows the path of literary truth, the truth of the word.

The term autofiction came about in 1977, on the cover of the novel *Fils,* from Serge Doubrovsky, as an immediate response to *Le Pacte Autobiographique* (1975) from Lejeune. Doubrovsky ironically responds to Lejeune, stating that his book cannot be an autobiography since this is a genre destined 'to the important of this world, in the evening of their lives, and in a beautiful style'. His book, on the other hand, is 'Fiction, report of events and strictly real facts; If you will, *autofiction*' (Doubrovsky 1977: 63).

In 1989, in his doctoral thesis called *L'autofiction (essai sur la fictionalisation de soi en Littérature)* (1989: 9), Vincent Colonna begins by affirming that '"The fictionalization of oneself" is an approach that consists in making oneself an imaginary subject, of telling a story by putting oneself directly to contribution, by collaborating in the fable, by becoming an element of one's invention'.

This way, the author uses his autobiography as raw material for his novel, converting his life's episodes, the various moments, dates, and characters into literary-fictional text, so that it becomes difficult to understand where fiction and the truth begin.

In two articles following *Fils*, Doubrovsky again discussed the term autofiction. In 1980, he comes back to the notion that the autobiographical genre was intended for great individuals, in a way that 'The humble who do not have the right to history, have the right to the novel' (Doubrovski 1980: 90), bringing to mind the words that Saramago would come to use years later, when raising the question: 'In another words: why can't literature have its own version of History?' (Reis 2015: 90). What is important to keep in mind about the reflection of Doubrovsky is that he classifies the term autofiction as being part of the novel genre.

However, he and Vincent Colonna proceeded with their reflections on autofiction, eventually overcoming, on the one hand, the literary genre barrier of the novel, whilst opening doors to the multiple definitions of the term.

For Vincent Colonna, it is possible to classify autofiction in four different categories: fantastical autofiction, biographical autofiction, specular autofiction, and intrusive autofiction (authorial).

When addressing the biographical autofiction, one needs to emphasize the intrusive autofiction that seems to cut across other forms, as illustrated by Valter Hugo Mãe's book.

In biographical autofiction, the author continues to be the hero of the story, the main character, 'the centre of the narrative but fables about his existence from true facts, remaining closer to the verisimilitude and gives to his text a truth at least subjective or even more than that' (Colonna 2014: 44). This type of autofiction marks an evolution from and insight into the 'I', since truth and precision are not more than 'theological virtues' (Colonna 2014: 46). One of the big innovations of autofiction seems to be the assumption and revelation of the first name and the overvaluation that our era gives to this fact and to the total uncovering of intimacy that, at the same time, is present and reflected on television, in the political world, as well as the habits and private and professional lives of everyone.

In a sense, the effect of biographical autofiction does not fully diverge from that of the *roman à clef*, since the people involved recognize each other, but for readers they are nothing more than characters. Speaking about other people might not be a great distinctness, but concerning the author, who is also the narrator and main character, this is where the big transformation takes place, because from that moment on we have access to all of his world, his secrets and intimacies, real or fictitious.

Autofiction is nonetheless a manifestation of the singularity of the writer in a world that seems more and more to exclude the other from a supposed democratization of society, in which we wear the same clothes, listen to the same songs, eat the same food, and have the same thoughts.

For the reader of *Contra mim*, Valter's mother, as well as his family members and childhood and youth friends continue to be, paradoxically, strangers, because we don't know in fact who they are. What we do know is from the narrator's perspective, which transfigures reality into literary fiction. Therefore, for the common reader, those people acquire the *homo fictus* status, while the author seems to follow a diametrically opposite course, heading towards humanization. This so-called humanization is also a means of the figuration and fictionalization of the author's (and narrators') own life, when in fact there is no difference between these categories in the biographical autofictional universe.

In *Contra mim*, there are many episodes in which family members and friends are axial to the growing and development of the child that was Valter Hugo Mãe. We notice, right away, the aesthetic portrayals and descriptions that are consistent with the narrative structure that leads the little boy from Paços de Ferreira to the writer he will become. What happens in this book is the construction of the childhood image that, paradoxically, works against the writer who is writing about his own past, a past that is as much imaginative as it is real, always filled with personal notes and commentaries that appear as footnotes:

> I wrote somewhere that exercising memory is an effort of companionship … my relationship with the craft of remembering is mostly emotional … I've spent

about fifteen years writing down these texts without a purpose, approaching each one slowly like if I was coming back home … To write about me, after clearly stating that my life is not worthy of a book, was in fact as irresistible as necessary to fulfill the task of reviewing and adjusting myself. I'm not anymore the boy with beautiful intentions that I was, this child so pure that inspires me, but I really want to be, at least, his memory.

(Mãe 2020: 276)

This excerpt enables us to discuss the nature of intrusive autofiction, which consists of the introduction of long commentary and reflections from the author on what he has written. If it is certain that this mechanism is not necessarily innovative or recent – remember the commentary that the narrator of *Viagens na Minha Terra* gives in the novel about characters and intrigue – it is important to emphasize that in the case of intrusive autofiction, the author interferes with what he has written about himself or about something that is closely and directly related to himself and not the others. When writing this commentary about others, it comes from reflecting about himself and the point of view that he has or had.

The narrative of the special, different, and sensitive boy starts with the memory of his grandfather: 'My grandfather asked my mother: take care of this boy. He thought I was important. My childhood would be marked by that worthy impression of someone who listened to me for so long and wanted to instigate my curiosity, rejoicing with my imagination' (Mãe 2020: 32).

The memory of grandfather Alves is part of his imaginary and identity. In both life and death, memory transforms into a revealing episode, of the heightened sensitivity of the boy-writer:

When my grandfather died, people came yelling for my mother on the street. It was early in the morning. And I remember sensing that she was getting up and, well before hearing but her name, she said: my father died. My grandfather would die for years and a thousand times. It was so normal that that could happen that it seemed his way of living forever. When that finally happened, heartbroken, I imagined how the bed and entire bedroom would have to fit in the hole of dirt that would be dug up for him.

(Mãe 2020: 33)

When confronted by the memory of his grandfather, the author starts by stating that the image of him is foggy and uncertain. It is important to mention that, almost at the end of the book, this uncertainty is the result of an undiagnosed eyesight condition. His eyesight managed to conceal or even blur the narrator's memory, when he realizes, at that moment, the damage that has been done to his life in that childhood period:

> I thought it was unbelievable that everybody saw how somebody could walk so far ahead. My childhood was blind to so many things. I knew now, after all, that maybe my own eyes had stolen from me the memory of my grandfather Alves at the big Christmas dinners … I didn't even recognize the exact traits of peoples' faces. … With glasses on, all of the things in the world presented themselves to me as if it was the first time … How solemn to be able to see that way.
>
> (Mãe 2020: 272)

The creation of memories and our own history and identity is made with others and by others. The others are part of our memory. The others are also our memory and history is built from numerous narrations, ours and others'.

The relationship between the writer and the Carnation Revolution is also a memory in itself, but is also, no doubt, a structure that will serve as an identity anchor for an author born during the rise of Portuguese democracy:

> I remember momentary images from that day, and it is with great pride that I keep my oldest memory of him. I know where I was on the moment that the Portugal of the future was created … In a sense, my head was born on April 25th of 1974. What happens before that day acts like an intuitive abstraction.
>
> (Mãe 2020: 25, 28)

Whilst we have the family history and the growth of Valter, with his own incidents, adventures, and memorable moments, the history of Portugal emerges also as a historical reference to which we can pin the narrative, one of, along with a few dates, the only certainties that the reader has in his book. Without more temporal references, the reader is conscious of this being a work of creative imagination, even though the author says that he took notes about various occurrences.

The terror of school, violence, and the teacher's aggression when she hit the students left a mark in the narrator; however, what stands out is a conversation with his mother and the value given to the words, helping, once more, the structure of the author's ongoing narrative:

> So, my mother asked me if I would like to learn how to keep things inside my head. … Soon after, she said: the things you think about. You must learn how to store the things you think about. If you know how to write, the paper sheets will become little boxes where you can storage with words everything you don't want

to forget. And the paper sheets, so plain and apparently empty, gained depth, an unexpected immensity, because, if I knew how to write firefly, forever a firefly would be there, even with its tail light on, waiting for me. Mine. Without ever leaving ... I agreed to go to school because I accepted being tortured in exchange for the stunning science of learning how to keep the fortune of words.

(Mãe 2020: 51)

In the text we find various episodes and moments that express a child's sensitive and attentive singularity. This way of describing the personality of a boy who would become a writer is biographical autofiction in the making.

The choice of episodes, contexts, and characters interfering with the author's commentaries, making use of the intrusive autofiction, transforms this book into one of the most interesting autofictions of Hypercontemporary Portuguese literature.

Byung Chul-Han writes in *The Expulsion of the Other* that 'we travel everywhere without having an *experience*. We keep up to date about everything without acquiring knowledge. We anxiously search for experiences and incentives in which, however, everyone stays always identical to *their self*' (2018: 11). In a tone as intimate as autobiographical, but sometimes fictional, Valter Hugo Mãe justifies a kind of literature that fights a narrow minded society.

*Contra mim* presents itself as a narrative that is also a journey through the author's experience as a child; it portrays the experience of an adult writer who bends over himself in search of much deeper roots, capable of identifying the man, the writer and the artist, he who questions himself and plays with the truth and memory, amniotic fluid of our identity: 'when I get stuck in my memory, by all means, I don't do it without surprise. Great wonder that was once. If we do not remember it, then we're wasting it, frivolous and reckless like the boys in those noisy motorcycles and girls with nothing to lose' (Mãe 2020: 64).

The passing of time is the great engine on *Contra mim*, the same time that gives consciousness, experience, and perspective, perspective of a world that, as Knausgård writes:

[I]t increases not only ... the pain it inflicts on you less but also its meaning. Understanding the world requires you to take a certain distance from it. Things that are too small to see with the naked eye, such as molecules and atoms, we magnify. Things that are too large, such as cloud formations, river deltas, constellations, we reduce. At length we bring it within the scope of our senses and we stabilize it with fixer. When it has been fixed, we call it knowledge. Throughout our childhood and teenage years, we strive to attain the correct distance to objects and phenomena. We read, we learn, we experience, we make adjustments. Then one day we reach the point where all the necessary distances have been set, all the necessary systems have been put in place. That is when time begins to pick up speed.

(2012: 14–15)

The consciousness of the memory's purpose and the way the writer not only gains perspective with the passing of time, but also knowledge from experience, are key factors that contribute to the writing of biographical autofiction from Valter Hugo Mãe. It does not matter anymore if he cannot justify, whether from dates or historical events, the gestures and attitudes that the writer had or the action of a character. Contrary to what happened in the nineteenth century, for instance, under the mantle of Realistic aesthetics and historiography, in which was necessary to resort to official and credible sources, able to certify what was being written, contemporaneity overlooks the truth.

In a letter to Oliveira Martins in April 26, 1894, regarding the book *A Vida de Nun'Álvares*, Eça de Queirós writes the following about an excerpt in which a historian describes Nun'Álvares's attitudes:

> I also don't like certain aspects of the moulded detail, such as the description of gestures, etc. How do you know them? What document do you have to say that the Queen, at a certain point, covered with kisses Andeiro, or that Master thoughtfully put his hand across this face? Where you there? Did you see?

(1983: 314)

Eça de Queirós intends to draw his friend's attention to the lack of data and factual information that might confirm the gestures and attitudes of the characters, with a logic that does not want to misinterpret the realistic code of historiography and biography through the idea of rudimental scientists and positivists. Although the book by Oliveira Martins is a biography and has a strong historiographical trend, Eça de Queirós establishes a clear distinction between what belongs to the universe of fiction and what should be that of history and biography.

These borders have now faded, whether concerning genres, or the search for the truth and the effect of the real. It interests the Hypercontemporary writer, in general, and the autofiction writer, in particular, not the historical truth, but the personal truth, the one that makes sense in a senseless world and without anchors or narratives that confirm our identity and a possible unity of subject.

The roads and chasms of memory are constructed from the writing, the past and the evidence, but above all else, it empowers the imagination, the power of fiction and the search for a purpose or a narrative justifying the actions and the journey of one who writes. Progress and setbacks, just like editing and commentary are part of the world of autofiction, as Valter Hugo Mãe demonstrates:

> All lives are, after all, the imitation of a novel. They imitate a book. My life's journey until the end of my adolescence is, in part, this truth with strangeness and effort. Once I've chosen what attracts me now, what deserves my attention, either disturbs me or leaves me inescapable. I found out once before that I got wrong so many details. I rectified what I could and what I knew. But I also enjoy the misunderstanding and that splendour of imagining more than we know, and that in itself, is real enough to lead guide our way and define it. It is worth it. The way we are real authors is also worth it.
>
> (2020: 279)

The attraction of autofiction is connected with a moulding opportunity that writing and literature allow, in an open, free, and always available manner, different (re)interpretations. The selection of episodes, commentary, and the characters that fill the autofictional narrative are part of a much bigger plan of the writer's goal to (re)design and (re)invent his own fiction. In the confrontation with the past and the places that have marked his identity and trajectory, Valter Hugo Mãe creates a mythology elevated to character, raising the question whether it is the characters and places that shape the writer's creative imagination or, if, in turn, it is the novelist the prestidigitator of the many figures that populate the narrative universe.

The fiction of the 'I' is, indeed, the biggest temptation of Hypercontemporary literature.

# References

Bauman, Z. (2007), *Life in Fragments: Essays in Postmodern Morality*, Lisbon: Relógio D' Água.

Colonna, V. (2014), 'Tipologia da Autoficção', in Noronha, J. (org.), *Ensaios sobre Autoficção*, 39–66, Belo Horizonte: Editora UFMG.

Doubrovsky, S. (1977), *Fils*, Paris: Éditions Galilée.

Doubrovsky, S. (1980), 'Autobiographie/Vérité/Psychanalyse', *L'Esprit créateur* XX (3).

Han, B.-C. (2018), *The Expulsion of the Other*, Trans. Miguel Serras Pereira, Lisboa: Relógio D'Água.
Lejeune, P. (1971), *L'autobiographie en France*, Paris: Éditions A. Collin.
Lejeune, P. (1975), *Le Pacte Autobiographique*, Paris: Seuil.
Lejeune, P. (1984), *Moi Aussi*, Paris: Seuil.
Knausgård, K. O. (2012), *My Struggle*, Book One, New York: Archipelago Books.
Mãe, V. H. (2020), *Contra mim*, Porto: Porto Editora.
Nogueira, C. (2021), 'Valter Hugo Mãe, Contra Mim', *Colóquio/Letras*, 207: 256–9.
Queirós, E. de (1983), *Correspondência*, coordination, preface and notes by Guilherme de Castilho, vol. 2, Lisboa: Imprensa Nacional-Casa da Moeda.
Reis, C. (2015), *Diálogos com José Saramago*, Porto: Porto Editora.

# The Shattered Narrative of Mafalda Ivo Cruz

Paulo Ricardo Kralik Angelini and Samla Borges Canilha

Tracing a narrative typology has never been an easy task. That is because there is a necessity for organization and classification inherent to the studies, the research, and even to the subjectivity of the investigation. To rationalize a certain concept, to think about literary examples and to convey that thought in a didactic manner promotes categorizations, and every system of classification implies a process of inclusion and exclusion.

The theory of literature obviously has literature itself as the object of analysis and is a diverse and everchanging field of study. That is why new writers and new works end up demanding new perspectives and new research, new classifications. That is also why one can say that tracing typologies has never been and will never be an easy task, considering that one of the core materials of that construction of concepts is contestation itself.

One of the examples of classification and contestation may be illustrated by the discussion that began in the nineteenth century and extended to the first half of the twentieth century around the concepts of *to show* and *to tell*. On one side, some theorists defend a supposed objectivity in the construction of narrative, with the participation of a neutral narrator. On the other side are those who perceive in the doings of a demiurge narrator – including comments even if spurious to the plot – a better communication with the reader. Whoever has read *The Rhetoric of Fiction* by Wayne Booth can see a theorist rescuing different names who defend one or the other side, and pointing the normative exaggerations of both sides which lead them to, accidentally or not, fall in the same trap of standardization – because categorizing necessarily implies taking sides and sometimes when we state that an element does not fit into one category, we create another one to place those elements which were removed from it. Booth complains, for example, about the classification which came before him about the point of view, calling it *embarrassingly inadequate*.

It is not our intention to dwell long on this still controversial dispute about point of view, the focalization, but Pierce Lubbock, Norman Friedman, Gérard Genette, Mieke Bal, Booth himself, and more recently Seymor Chatman, Gerald Prince, and James Phelan, among others, have questioned each other's concepts to debate, for instance, why the narrator may or may not be a focalizer.[1]

In the preface to *The Rhetoric of Fiction*, Booth admits the arbitrariness of the process. He admits the subjectivity in the choice of the theoretical corpus to be researched and exemplified, calling attention to what attempts to be 'illustrative' and not 'definitive', thus demonstrating a more open attitude.

In order to illustrate what was said, it is relevant to observe how, for example, Wayne Booth sees his own work two decades later, when in 1983 he launches a second updated edition – an idea which he had refused so far. He highlights in 'Foreword to the second edition' what made him change his mind: 'the rapidly aging bibliography' (Booth 1983: xi). Because of that, a great number of his students and researchers of literature followed a work which was outdated,[2] facing a 'silence about those two decades' (Booth 1983: xi), reminding us of the constant renewal of the object of analysis about which we spoke: the literary work.

Despite being one of the most referenced books, there is a great deal of dispute about Booth's concepts. Perhaps one of the best known is that of Paul Ricoeur, who notices a certain harshness in the gaze of the American theorist regarding the 'unreliable narrator' whose role 'here may perhaps be less perverse than Wayne Booth depicts it' (Ricoeur 1985: 163). Ricoeur comments in the volume 3 of *Temps et récit*: 'There is no denying that modern literature is dangerous. The sole response worthy of the criticism it provokes, of which Wayne Booth is one of the most highly esteemed representatives, is that this poisonous literature requires a new type of reader: a reader who responds' (Ricoeur 1985: 163). Ricoeur's perspective is directed to a more *dangerous*, more *poisonous*, and more *disruptive* object.

When, for instance, decades later an important author of post-classical narratology, Brian Richardson, states, 'It should be readily apparent that a model centered on storytelling situations in real life cannot begin to do justice to these narrators who become ever more extravagantly anti-realistic every decade' (Richardson 2006: 3), he is actually reinforcing the necessity of widening the narrative categorizations, once there is a whole new manner of writing, and

---

[1] For an interesting theoretical discussion about it, see Prince 2001 and Phelan 2001.
[2] The first issue of *The Rhetoric of Fiction* is from 1961, and the second from 1983.

here we think about the literature of the twenty-first century, unconcerned by questions which in the past were considered fundamental to the labour of writing, like dealing with verisimilitude in composing of characters and narrators who obey the basic rules of *real life*. Richardson is one of the pillars of a theorization which researches non-mimetic (or *unnatural*) works and elements in those narratives. In his pages there is the recovery of names like Wayne Booth and Gérard Genette, many times as a way of contestation like, for instance, about the point of view:

> Summing up nearly all of the theorizing on 'point of view' since the time of Henry James and Victor Shklovsky, Gérard Genette writes that the novelist must choose between two narrative postures, either 'to have the story told by one of its 'characters', or to have it told by a narrator outside the story'. It is, however, precisely this choice that is rejected by so many contemporary authors.
> (Richardson 2006: 5–6)

Genette's classifications would then be for Richardson limited for all the narrative stratagems explored by inventive writers like António Lobo Antunes or Mafalda Ivo Cruz. As Brian Richardson points out, there is a whole new lineage of fictional texts which overflow from the buckets methodically created by the theorists of the twentieth century. Narratives neither mimetic nor anti-mimetic, therefore, challenge not only readers but also critics of literary theory.

However, let us be fair. Just as Wayne Booth sees the limitations of his writings due to the diversity and novelty of the objects of analysis, so does Genette, who offers some 'words of self-criticism', emphasizing that his categories are not 'without defects', but obey a choice *between two inconveniences*, alerting in the postface of *Figures III*: 'This arsenal, like any other, will inevitably be obsolete before a few years, and all the faster as it will be taken more seriously, that is to say, discussed, tested, and revised in use' (Genette 1972: 325). Genette did predict strange artifices which break a natural pact like, for example, the concept of metalepsis he developed or how animals and objects in an *unnatural* attitude can narrate. About that, there is an interesting footnote in *Figures III*, when Genette problematizes the term character exactly in this passage quoted by Brian Richardson. He says:

> This term is used here for lack of another more neutral, or more extensive, which would not unduly connote like this one the quality of 'human being' of the narrative agent, while nothing prevents in fiction to entrust this role to an animal (Memoirs of a donkey), or even to an 'inanimate' object (I do not know if

we should classify in this category the successive narrators of the Indiscreet Jewels).

(Genette 1972: 322)

To finalize this topic on what the construction of narrative typologies takes into consideration, one needs to pay attention to another last debate which shows that the contestation does not cover only the attention of the twenty-first century on the narrative theories of the twentieth century. Brian Richardson himself has theorizations discussed by names like Gerald Prince, who at the start questions, for instance, the terms 'unnatural narrative theory' and its cousin 'natural narrative theory', stating that both 'may be unfortunate (I prefer 'narrative theory' *tout court*)' (Prince 2016: 475–7). He states that many of the 'assertions made by Richardson likewise invite examination and lead to a number of questions' (Prince 2016: 477), besides finding many of his examples problematic.

Finally, this is a debate which is always renewed, and some theorists seem to express some resentment for having been disputed, like Booth in 'Afterword to the second edition: twenty-one years later' (Booth 1983: 402)[3] of *The Rhetoric of Fiction*.

There are many examples of contestations to show a matter which needs to be opened up, its borders broken, to get some fresh air onto objects which no longer obey pre-established standards. The Hypercontemporary narrative,[4] works released in the last few years, the first ones in the twenty-first century, bears different marks which demand new critical and theoretical approaches. As Ana Paula Arnaut suggests, the term

> hypercontemporary which is proposed seems to result therefore from the most systematic cult of that variant as well as from a necessity of terminological change corresponding to the very evolution of the historic-social dynamics, and consequently the imperative of including new themes and new scenarios which mirror behavioral, (inter)individual and (inter)social inflections resulting from a new world.

(Arnaut 2018: 19)

---

[3] 'Why should I remain silent when a famous reader-critic implies that my book deals wrongly with the relevance of belief?', he questions, to state later: 'Biting my lip, then, I have chosen instead to extend and clarify the book'.

[4] About that, see the debate promoted in the magazine *Letras de Hoje*, by the Catholic Pontifical University of Rio Grande do Sul, from 2016, volume 51, number 4, organized by Ana Maria Binet and Paulo Ricardo Kralik Angelini, and in *Revista dos Estudos Literários*, by the University of Coimbra, number 8, from 2018, organised by Ana Paula Arnaut and Ana Maria Binet. Both issues present special dossiers about Hypercontemporary literature.

Hypercontemporary works are produced in times of vertiginous changes, of a globalization that no longer brings surprises in its complexity of connectedness, but reinforces the perception of fractures caused by different inequalities – social, economic, and cultural – which that globalization feeds. These are works which make an allegory of economic and environmental crises, which carry dystopic messages that debate the depletion of our planet or which problematize migratory movement, voluntary or not, the refugee crisis, the processes of deterritorialization, and identity erasing: works which have as their theme the transformations and the deterioration of labour and the workers in 24/7 (Crary 2014) journeys in informal jobs, and which discuss the mechanization of the individual, their dehumanization; works produced in times in which science is questioned, culture and the arts are attacked, and journalism is relativized in favour of narratives fabricated on social networks, *fake news*; works which bring subjects, therefore, that are broken, more and more individualized and isolated in a world more and more connected[5] by virtual contacts amid diverse technologies, social networks, artificial intelligence, amid growing social inequality and urban violence, amid significant political changes in many nations, which again turn to regimes with autocratic leaderships that question democracy and some basic issues of human rights; works which carry this turmoil, which give voice to minorities, fighting against silencing and censorial ideas; works which deepen autobiographical or autofictional issues, mix public and private, include the author's biographical data and shuffle the reader's perception; works which create tension with the historical past – and, in the specific case of literature in Portuguese, the identification of a barely – buried colonial legacy – and with the personal, in the perception of memory as a complex and at the same time always blanked system; works which revisit with more or less verisimilitude a lived or invented childhood in the creation of voices of children (Angelini, Silva and Canilha 2021); and works whose formal deconstruction reflects, then, this world, external or internal.

More than the thematic, what interests here is the narrative archaeology that those works present. In that sense, there is the rapid development of conceits which break with fixed criteria of narrative categories like character, narrator, and author in the construction of strange and disruptive narrative voices.

---

[5] Impossible not to refer to the horror that the year 2020 brought, along with a pandemic with devastating effects, never seen before, evidencing even more the fragility facing the supposed omnipotence of the human being, defeated for endless months by a minuscule virus with a gigantic and deadly effect. Certainly, in the future many narratives will resignify the year 2020, whose protagonists were COVID-19, fear, and death.

It is in this context that the work of Mafalda Ivo Cruz is included. She began to publish her novels near the twenty-first century and continues today. The plots of her books may not take place in technological contexts – actually they seem suspended in a diffuse moment, even when it is marked, in an almost analogical reality which intensifies the loneliness that involves the characters – but they have many of the characteristics of Hypercontemporary literature. We can highlight among them a tension with the past: with Portuguese history, especially in the first novels (which will be replaced by an increasingly interest in global subjects, in the sense of no longer having a specific spatial reference), and with the subjective, when her novels are seen from the standpoint of memory, the recovery of one's own past by the main characters. A brief introduction to them allows us to glimpse those issues: in *A Portuguese Requiem* (1995), the main action of the narrative is the escape from prison and hiding of a group of revolutionaries in Salazar's Portugal; in *The House of the Devil* (2000), the story of Nancy is told from the perspective of a detective narrator who investigates her and to whom she is connected through the ex-husband. The investigation ends up causing in the narrator the recovery of his own past; *The Boy of Botticelli* (2002), based on the work of a journalist, is centred on the ballet dancer Efron Cage, famous in 1970's Portugal, whose decadence leads him to work as a gravedigger in a cemetery; *Red* (2003), to which we will give special attention, is about the reconstitution of the family's history by the protagonist-narrator – a search, also, for autoidentification; in *Oz* (2006), the rape of a woman, supposedly committed by the titular character, initiates a narrative around the uncertainty about the character's guilt or innocence; *The German Cook* (2008) is a novel about the ambiguous relationship between a rural woman and the characters around her – among them the war refugee Kopf, the German cook from the title; and finally *Little Europe* (2016) is a novel with an essayistic tone which discusses art in Europe and its connections with politics from the context of an asylum directed by a priest, of which the protagonist is a patient.[6]

Additionally, the theme of violence, pointed out by various critics as a staple of the most recent literary production, is present in all Cruz's stories at some level. It appears interwoven in the aforementioned remembrance of subjects with complex psychologies, who are traumatized and who, for guiding the narrative as a narrator as well as characters, function as a way to make a very

---

[6] It is worth mentioning that Cruz's whole work deals with the arts (besides literature, visual arts, and music especially).

specific aesthetic: extremely fragmented, non-linear narratives, with time and space overlapped, with narrative voices and points of view which get mixed – in some cases, voices and perspectives of narrators which would be impossible – and several interruptions, repetitions, and a graphic organization that breaks with tradition at various points. The chaos of the characters reflects itself in an apparently chaotic text, but whose complexity can be unravelled with a careful reading, revealing itself as extremely rich in possibilities. They are texts which demand a reader like the one proposed by Ricoeur regarding the poisonous readings, that is, an active reader, to whom a challenging path is proposed:

> Yet it may be the function of the most corrosive literature to contribute to making a new kind of reader appear, a reader who is himself suspicious, because reading ceases to be a trusting voyage made in the company of a reliable narrator, becoming instead a struggle with the implied author, a struggle leading the reader back to himself.
>
> (Ricoeur 1985: 164)

Mafalda Ivo Cruz is a perfect example in the discussion presented at the beginning of this work: the categories, especially the more traditional ones, are not enough to evaluate her work. What can be done is indeed a discussion on the aesthetic innovations which she adopts from those categories and the relationships with realistic mimetic representation. *Red* serves this purpose well because the narration developed by Tito, the protagonist-narrator, is full of apparently disconnected sentences, constant commentary, strange unleashing of memories, temporal overlapping, and sudden changes of time and space – resources which together make Cruz's writing stand out even in such a diverse context as the contemporary literary scene.

In *Red*, what we have is the narration by Tito of his family's history, from his great-grandfather Afonso de Amadeus, a Portuguese settler in Africa who has a slave, Isaura Maria de Jesus, as a lover, passing through his grandmother, and his mother before arriving at himself in a genealogical recovery which serves a purpose: to prove that his wife, Nina, intends to poison and kill him – the same way it is said that his father was killed. That supposition, however, is based on uncertain stories, especially the ones told by his step-father, Mário (Cruz 2003: 17).[7]

---

[7] Since this novel has not been translated and published in English yet, the quoted excerpts have been translated by us.

It is precisely in relation to one of those, perhaps the most important to the narrative, that we can point out a phenomenon described by Brian Richardson as *denarration*, that is, 'a kind of narrative negation in which a narrator denies significant aspects of his or her narrative that had earlier been presented as given' (Richardson 2006: 87). In that sense, it is pertinent to notice how Tito takes as truth through the narrative a memory he has from his childhood which is not very clear, from the women of the family talking, presented in the first pages of the book – and which he deems confirmed in the stories that Mário tells, even if he is an extremely questionable source: the cause of his father's death, poison.

Approaching the end of the novel, though, we find out that the memory had been distorted. Tito remembers what he really – or what he supposes he really – saw, and any pact of reliability we might have made with him may be questioned: 'Dária was the poison that I gave because later I knew how to remove it. Those had been the words. The precise words' (Cruz 2003: 33).

That attempt at correction and control of the narrative takes place even before, with the recall of the arrival of Lena, a woman who knocks on his door asking for shelter – and who for him is the personification of death coming to fetch him. It is important to notice how the insistent recovery of the scene does not mean conclusion or exactitude, since the narrator never gives us a definite version. Actually, every time this scene is recovered, it is different; the only information that is obtained from one version to another is that she comes from Vilna.

The repetition of a scene or element does not always work though as a correction or supplement. On the contrary: many are the elements constantly arranged in a loose, disconnected way. Their comprehension originates from the reading of the whole. For example, the sound of the bell that 'rings' several times through the narrative reminds us of the father figure, and consequently of death. It is a constant reminder of the end that Tito believes is in store for him. Besides that, we can mention the image of the passing horses, animals associated with the figure of Isaura, who used them to run away from the farm.[8] If we think of them in association – something only possible when reading the entire book – those elements reinforce the fear and the eagerness to escape the supposed destiny by the narrator-protagonist.

That technique of repetition, recurrent in Mafalda Ivo Cruz, along with the commentary made by the narrator about the narrative process, can be associated

---

[8] Those repetitions also work as a form of echo of the memory: the stories mark the narrator so much that different triggers in his experience bring them back. The result is that he incorporates some memories which are not his to his own memory discourse.

to *pentirsi* (pentimento), strokes remaining from an artist's previous painting that slowly start to be visible again. Cruz in a way scrapes the writing and shows those alterations in the process in which it is elaborated. They are not erased, not deleted, but overlayed: echoes. We believe that the metaphor of *pentirsi* serves the writer well, as there are many references she makes to works of art. In *Red*, for example, *Winter*, by Pieter Bruegel, and *La Mort de Marat* or *Marat Assassiné*, by Jacques-Louis David, are explicit references.[9]

Both repetition and intertextuality lead us to the discussions of Tiphaine Samoyault because Cruz works with a wide range of artistical references which become an important characteristic of her work. Samoyault notices that the 'perpetual reiteration of identical thoughts' (Samoyault 2001: 51) (those sometimes dissonant echoes in *Red*), but also the recovery of other texts, brings 'a definition of literature as necessary repetition as well as appropriation' (Samoyault 2001: 51). In Mafalda Ivo Cruz, those associations of ideas converge to a kind of *mémoire de l'écriture*, a term discussed by Samoyault when recovering the concept of 'la mémoire des œuvres' by Judith Schlanger as 'un espace instable, où l'oubli, le souvenir fugace, la récupération soudaine, l'effacement temporaire jouent à plein' (Samoyault 2001: 50).

The corrections mentioned before enable the perception of Tito as a self-conscious narrator: 'a narrator who is aware of the distance between his current and former self is also likely to be aware of himself constructing the story of how he moved from one place to the other' (Phelan 2001: 61). Evidence of that are the various comments made by Tito throughout the text about the development of the narrative, showing full awareness of an ongoing construction as in 'Ready. Change register now' (Cruz 2003: 98) or in 'I think I've already said it' (Cruz 2003: 16).

It is also worth highlighting how those commentaries are bound together and how they reinforce the tone of uncertainty which characterizes the protagonist's narrative voice. There are several passages in which he admits that uncertainty and therefore his unreliability, as in 'I think I will never know how to distinguish true from false. Or to distinguish one dream from another dream' (Cruz 2003: 22) – which is reinforced by admitting that he bases himself on his *feelings* about what he hears and decides to tell: 'I didn't know. I will never know. I will never know anything, anything and in spite of that – I feel, sometimes I feel' (Cruz

---

[9] In other novels, other artistic references can be identified. For example: in *The Boy of Botticelli*, the indication is obvious in the title; and in *The House of the Devil*, we can notice the references to the paintings of French impressionist Pierre-Auguste Renoir.

2003: 18–19). Finally, he admits his confusion: 'Yes, I can confuse it all. Places as well as time' (Cruz 2003: 66).

The narrator of *Red* serves the categories proposed by Booth, in the sense of his self-consciousness – very similar to Phelan's narrator self-consciousness, he conceptualizes self-conscious narrators – as well as (and mainly) his unreliability. He agrees with what Booth calls 'unreliable narrator', one who does not act according to the norms of the work – and who is not necessarily a liar narrator, a concept as we have seen expanded by Paul Ricoeur. In the case of Tito, by recovering a genealogy and placing himself as responsible for transmitting the family history, we expect that he will present us with a well-structured, cohesive story, with proofing, but what we have is an extremely fragmented, confused narrative, based on stories, often contradictory told, without registers that may attest for them. Also, the fact that he consumes liquor and drugs reinforces that characteristic: he is chemically altered, besides being obviously delirious, for Nina at no moment seems to be a real threat.

That unreliability is a rhetorical, aesthetic resource which contributes to the reader's confusion. Once again, we maintain that literature becomes a challenge, demanding more from the reader. Tito (and Cruz, in the whole of her work) does not simply want to present us with a story: he wants to involve us in his madness; he wants us accompanying the elaboration of an idea, remembering it with him; and he wants to drown us in confusion, and the impact of that experience is inevitably destabilizing.

An important observation is that Tito's narrative is all elaborated from an interlocutor's projection: the mother, already dead. That (impossible) attempt at dialogue is marked by several commentaries and expressions, but mainly by the repetition of the question 'Can you hear it?'. The narrator tries insistently to get some attention which, by natural logic, he will not have, and by doing it he adds an interesting tone to the narrative. The act of speaking to someone else, of elaborating what happens in our minds so that we can communicate it, involves an attempt to organize which does not succeed – or, it succeeds only in the *attempt*, not as an actual organization. Besides, if we think about the conceptualization proposed by Brian Richardson that the interlocutor 'is a disembodied voice that poses questions which the narrative goes on to answer' (Richardson 2006: 79), we should wonder: what are the questions Tito is trying to answer? Are not those questions much more his than his interlocutor's? That technique somehow speaks directly with the reader, makes them also interlocutors, especially if one considers that at some point he no longer addresses his mother, but a plural which can be thought of as the readers of and listeners to the story he narrates.

Another relevant aspect, pointed out before, is that Tito admits he confuses time and space. That confusion can be invoked as the reason for the constant overlap of those categories throughout the narrative. In a general way, we always have a tension between the diegetic present and the recovered familiar past, with changes happening suddenly but marked by narrative breathing. Many are the cases in which that change happens after a simple comma or with a simple change of line.

Another element which reinforces the confusion is the very narrative voice of the novel. Despite involving many characters, and even though it carries the perspective of other characters (like Mário's, for instance, when he tells Tito the stories of the family's past), it is always through the mind of the narrator-protagonist, and there are no moments in which we can think of a heterodiegetic narrator: he controls the whole discourse. Complicating is when the voices of other characters appear and interfere. It is also worth wondering to what extent they might be Tito's projections, in that they also convey his perspective, and also have his focalization – even though they are supposedly different voices. In that case, one could think about the situation proposed by Phelan, when we have 'narrator's focalization and character's voice, as when a naive narrator unwittingly takes on the voice of another character' (Phelan 2001: 59), but that would only happen if we considered that those voices are autonomous. Besides, Tito does not seem to be such a naïve narrator, despite his altered state of mind.

A point of interference of another voice, exemplifying this, is Chapter XII, when Dária, Tito's mother, remembers her own childhood. In it, the content of the memories and the extension of the narrative make one think that it is not a mere projection of Tito attempting to give space to his mother and her story, but another narrative – even if impossible, because it is a dead person. In that moment, close to the end of the book, the origin of a sentence repeated frequently in many contexts and almost randomly, is clarified – '*Dormi ancora, Dormi à quest'ora*', one of the sentences Dária's father said to his daughter that Tito ends up incorporating in his discourse and that ends up intensifying the confusion about who the narrator of the chapter is. After all, if the sentence is permeating all the narrative, he knows its origin and, by knowing its origin, he may try to recreate the context, pretending to give space to his mother, but in reality giving her only, once again, the opportunity to appear under a specific gaze – her son's.

In this case, such a voice and perspective can fit the conception of 'impossible narration', 'metaleptic texts that contain discourse that cannot possibly be spoken or written by their purported narrators and may involve the kind of ontological framebreaking typical of postmodern works' (Richardson 2006: 76). That intrusion of voices also allows Tito to be characterized as a 'permeable narrator', a phenomenon described by Richardson as 'the uncanny and inexplicable intrusion of the voice of another within the narrator's consciousness' (Richardson 2006: 95).

More than nomenclature, more than attempts to fit parts of Mafalda Ivo Cruz's work into comfortable categorizations, it matters to think that all those strategies lead to an experience of defamiliarization and discomfort. The experience of reading *Red*, of which we have briefly tried to pinpoint some of the many narrative techniques, dives in aesthetic vertigo, demanding from the reader undivided attention, requesting another type of reader, as Ricoeur wants, one who *responds*.[10]

Cruz's text – and we believe it is in that sense an exemplar when we think about Hypercontemporary literature – constructs and deconstructs itself among echoes, strange images, sensations, and contradictions, in such a way that when we get lost in her books, in the chaotic mentality of her characters, we also face our own chaos, and with the chaos inherent to the world around us, which we insist on trying to organize.

# References

Angelini, P. R. K., Silva, R. B. da, and Canilha, S. B. (2021), *Inventário da Infância: o Universo não Adulto na Narrativa*, Porto Alegre: EdiPUCRS.

Arnaut, A. P. (2018), 'Do Post-Modernismo ao Hipercontemporâneo: Morfologia(s) do Romance e (Re)figurações da Personagem', *Revista de Estudos Literários* 8: 19–44.

Arnaut, A. P. and Binet, A. M. (eds.) (2018), *Revista de Estudos Literários*, 8.

Binet, A. M. and Angelini, P. R. K. (eds.) (2016), *Revista Letras de Hoje* 51 (4).

Booth, W. (1983), *The Rhetoric of Fiction*, 2nd ed., Chicago: Chicago Press.

Crary, J. (2014), *24/7: Late Capitalism and the Ends of Sleep*, New York: Verso Books.

Cruz, M. I. (2003), *Vermelho*, Lisboa: Dom Quixote.

Genette, G. (1972), *Figures III*, Paris: Seuil.

Peer, W. van and Chatman, S. (eds.) (2001), *New Perspectives on Narrative Perspective*, Albany: State University of New York Press.

---

[10] Reading becomes a game, a challenge. Ricoeur says (1985: 168): 'This strategy consists in frustrating the expectation of an immediately intelligible configuration and in placing on the reader's shoulders the burden of configuring the work'.

Phelan, J. (2001), 'Why Narrators Can Be Focalizers – and Why It Matters', in W. Peer van and S. Chatman (eds.), *New Perspectives on Narrative Perspective*, Albany: State University of New York Press.
Prince, G. (2001), 'A Point of View on Point of View or Refocusing Focalization', in Willie Van Peer and Seymour Chatman (eds.), *New Perspectives on Narrative Perspective*, Albany: State University of New York Press.
Prince, G. (2016), 'Response to Brian Richardson', *Style* 50 (4): 475–7.
Richardson, B. (2006), *Unnatural Voices: Extreme Narration in Modern and Contemporary Fiction*, Columbus: The Ohio University Press.
Ricoeur, P. (1985), *Time and Narrative*, vol. 3, Trans. Kathleen Blarney and David Pellauer, Chicago: The University of Chicago Press.
Samoyault, T. (2001), *L'Intertextualité: Mémoire de la Littérature*, Paris: Éditions Nathan/HER.

# 10

# Of Technology and Lost Connections: A Decolonial Approach to *As Telefones* by Djaimilia Pereira de Almeida as a Hypercontemporary Novel

Emanuelle Santos

The work of Djaimilia Pereira de Almeida has been critically acclaimed since her debut novel *Esse Cabelo* (2015). To date, the author has published eleven books, her work has been translated into nine languages, and she has been awarded several literary prizes. Her narrative range extends beyond the novel, embracing shorter forms such as the novella, short story, chronicle, and essay as well as a transmedia approach indebted to her dialogue with other art forms such as photography. Her fiction, especially the 2018 novel *Luanda, Lisboa, Paraíso* awarded the prestigious Oceanos Prize in 2019, has been praised by critics for the ways in which it decentres the memory of the Portuguese empire (Medeiros 2020; Ribeiro 2019), for its registration of subjective experiences of migration (Franco 2021) and the way it, as such, destabilises – and even decolonizes – the Portuguese literary canon (Rendeiro 2022). In this chapter, I propose to look closely at *As Telefones* (2020), her sixth work, as a narrative that extrapolates the confines of representation in the realm of colonialism and its aftermath – be it Portuguese or in Portuguese – and I maintain that, this work's strongest decolonial potential is of world-systemic proportions. Reading the book against the wider backdrop of the relationship between technology and modernity that marks the Hypercontemporary novel, I argue for a view of the book that situates it in a tradition of the European semi-peripheral novel that sheds light on technology's entanglement with capitalism and international division of labour expressed in economic migration. This approach aims at supplementing the critical discourse about Pereira de Almeida's work, and at opening it up to wider comparative scopes that illuminate the connection between aesthetic choices voicing experiences of groups in minoritized positions and broader transnational historical phenomena.

*As Telefones* is a ninety-page narrative in which the protagonist, Solange, speaks of the constitution of her self at the physical and psychological levels in relation to the relationship with her mother, Filomena, maintained mainly through the medium of telephone conversation, from Solange's childhood to the present. As the reader learns, mother and daughter get separated during Solange's infancy, in what the loose chronology of the narrative suggests to be sometime in the mid-1980s during a phase of particular hardship in Angolan economy fuelled by the civil war (1975–2002). Filomena's lack of employment and means forces her to send her infant daughter to live with her sister, who was established in Lisbon. Told through a number of fragments that can be seen as short chapters, the story also brings a multiplicity of voices including chapters narrated in the first-person, chapters in which we have Filomena's voice – often reproducing what she would have said to her daughter through the telephone – and chapters in the voice of an omniscient narrator. Whilst the relatively recent date of publication of the novel and the disruption in all manners of intellectual activities and publications caused by the COVID-19 pandemic have certainly slowed the pace of critical reaction to this narrative, work published to date attests to its literary quality, mainly in the ways in which it supplements a critical discourse about the work of Pereira de Almeida as a representation of the Afro-Portuguese condition.

Ana Gabriela Macedo's 2022 essay 'Djaimilia Pereira de Almeida, *As Telefones*. Homenagem ao 'género literário da diáspora' e a reinvenção da narrativa poética' (Djaimilia Pereira de Almeida, *As Telefones*. Homage to the 'literary genre of the diaspora' and the reinvention of the poetic narrative) sensitively approaches the tragic disruption in the bond between mother and daughter imposed by the separation. Understood as a poetic narrative that speaks of the theme of *chegar atrasado à própria pele* (belatedly arriving into one's own skin) (Macedo 2022: 22) that undercuts the work of the writer and works as an index of the Afro-diasporic condition of Black Portuguese in contemporary society, Macedo understands the telephone as an intermediator between the two women, who find themselves in a situation of *suprema escassez de materialidade corpórea* (overwhelming lack of physical proximity) where the *protagonistas são, assumem-se, metonimicamente, como o próprio telefone* (protagonists are, and present themselves, metonymically, as the telephone itself) (Macedo 2022: 21).

Margarida Rendeiro's article titled 'On how post-colonial fiction can contribute to a discussion of historical reparation: an interpretation of *As Telefones* (2020) by Djaimilia Pereira de Almeida', in its turn, provides an in-depth reading of the novel that takes the telephone as a generator of two 'metaphorical possibilities' (Rendeiro 2022: 46). The first is that the narrative 'decolonises the experience of loss and interior emptiness that literature published after 1974 has tended to associate with the memory and corporeal experience of Colonial War veterans and returned colonisers, and ... with the feeling of nostalgia or longing (saudade) that is so emblematic within Portuguese culture'; the second is that the focus on the telephone conversation is 'a break with western and Portuguese literary conventions, which tend to take writing as a privileged form of bearing witness' (*ibidem*, 46–7). Both hypotheses by Rendeiro highlight important ways in which the narrative, seen in the context of Pereira de Almeida's oeuvre to date, has the potential to destabilize the very narrative of a literary Portuguese identity in the aftermath of the Portuguese Colonial Empire. Offering effective critical approaches to the work in itself and as part as the work of the author as a whole, the evaluations of both Macedo and Rendeiro are essential for an assessment of the Portuguese literary canon in light of contributions to the Portuguese African diaspora.

Yet, the emergence of a canonical reading of the work of Pereira de Almeida as solely centred around the Portuguese cultural memory that it disrupts establishes a degree of contradiction with a view of her work as a decolonizing force. In what they confine the critical reach of Pereira de Almeida's work to the counter-hegemonic approach to Portuguese colonialism, this critical canon fails to notice her work's potential of putting forward new ways from which to understand the world *despite* its connection with Portuguese colonialism. As she puts it rather openly in the essay *O que é ser uma escritora negra hoje, de acordo comigo* (What does it mean to be a Black writer, according to me), *[s]er uma escritora negra hoje ... é escrever contra esse facto, carregando-o às costas sem deixar que ele me tolha* (to be a Black writer today is to write against this fact, carrying it with me without letting it stop me) (Almeida 2022: 7). While the author refuses to be a Black writer if it means *um género de subgrupo exótico dentro dos escritores do mundo* (an exotic subgroup amongst the writers of the world), she declares: *visto com orgulho a noção que sou uma mulher negra que escreve* (I proudly present myself as a Black woman who writes) (*ibidem*, 12). Between the agency of self-expression and the prison of reification, Pereira de Almeida's work constitutes an essayistic writing of autobiographic projection

(Mata 2018) that not only expresses a double consciousness at work but also deals with the complex awareness of the weight of one's own personal experience in its intrinsic relation to a collective history in the making.

That said, to highlight the tension between subjective and collective, memory and history, or fragment and system underlying the work of Djaimilia Pereira de Almeida is not, in itself, novel. Nonetheless, while critics have often noted how her work transcends national borders, the borders it is seen to transcend are often described as those between Portugal and Angola or, more broadly, between Africa and Europe. The decolonial potential of her work is frequently cited in relation to the Portuguese literary canon, of the Portuguese imperial legacy, or a very specific type of peripheral experience – that exclusive to Black people whose heritage is in former Portuguese African colonies – hence recentring the very coloniality such interpretations of her work intend to dislodge. This not only reduces the reading of Pereira de Almeida's work as that of a 'Black woman in the world who writes' to that of a 'Black writer', to use the author's own terms, it also perpetuates one of the main pitfalls in the study of literatures in Portuguese, which is a tendency for inward-looking analysis often disguised as transnationalism due to the pluricontinental proportions of the Portuguese-speaking world. In an attempt to release Pereira de Almeida's work from the confines of the subsystem of Portuguese colonial economic and social history, this essay proposes to understand how her work registers features of contemporary life of world-systemic proportions in literary form.

In the essay titled 'Do Pós-modernismo ao Hipercontemporâneo: Morfologia(s) do romance e (Re)figurações da Personagem', Ana Paula Arnaut focuses on the concept of hypercontemporaneity as a way to recognize the irreversible impact of late capitalism's technology and globalization in the structures of feeling of the contemporary subject whose literary expression gives way to narrative forms open to intermediality, where character subjectivity lacks clarity and definition (Arnaut 2018: 22–3, 39, 41–2). Drawing from the analysis of important Portuguese contemporary writers such as António Lobo Antunes, valter hugo mãe, and Luís Carmelo, Arnaut's approach is relevant for the understanding of what she calls *uma ficção portuguesa escrita e publicada depois do ano 2000* (a Portuguese fiction written and published from year 2000) (*ibidem*, 22) marked by the *esfacelemento* (crumbling) of the form (*ibidem*, 28), subversion of narrative linearity (*ibidem*, 32), dissolution of classic narrative categories (*ibidem*, 33), metafiction (*ibidem*, 35), and dissolution of the contours of the character (*ibidem*, 38). These categories can all be found in Djaimilia

Pereira de Almeida's *As Telefones*, despite the apparent critical abyss separating the interpretative possibilities of the form in the Hypercontemporary novels analysed by Arnaut and Pereira de Almeida, notwithstanding the author's depiction of subjective experiences in the same society.

Marking the difference between these interpretative horizons is a tradition in literary studies in which art largely identified with the hegemonic ethnocentric values of Western Europe is allowed a weightlessness in regard to socio-historic materiality that is often denied to art perceived as defying these values. In contrast to the lightness that liberates form and aesthetics of art aligned with mainstream definitions of the western (white, cis, male, cosmopolitan, or even hipster as the current discourse would have it), we have the almost determinant excess of material weight given to art produced from counter-hegemonic positionalities. So, while the unbound – or 'universal' as it used to be called before critics knew better – nature of the first kind of literary work enables its travel beyond its place in time and space, open to comparison and saying something about wider phenomena such as a whole transnational aesthetic movement, age, or even humanity itself; the nearly determinant excess of materiality of the latter pins it down so heavily to its time and place of production that it is hardly seen as having anything to say about anything beyond the hegemonic notions it is seen to dislodge. Yet, contrary to a view that would prefer to focus on the separation between these two ways of conceiving literary works, highlighting their opposition from each other in what can, at times, be described as an unsurmountable distance, I propose to study them in their inherently uneven inseparability as they are both part of the same capitalist world-system 'simultaneously *one*, and *unequal*' (Moretti 2000: 56, emphasis in the original). In this sense, neither the aesthetic freedom ascribed to the cosmopolitan, cis, white, male, middle-class writer, nor the grounded sociological framing of the work by the Black woman who writes, happens in isolation. A systemic view of the domestic and international forces maintaining these, or in fact any, categories must focus on their constitutive interdependence to understand both aesthetic form and context together. This has the potential to liberate both approaches from the sterile paradigm of eternally separate, parallel interpretative lines that is easily identifiable by set keywords and concepts, to open them up to the complexities of the world and its global history, hence enabling them to help us understand, through the study of aesthetics and material contexts, the many complexities of the reality they share on so many levels. As such, my approach to *As Telefones* as a literary registration of the Hypercontemporary condition focuses on the role of the telephone itself in the narrative. Seen as an index of the inescapable impact of technology on the intersubjective relations of those partaking in the technological revolution of the end of the twentieth century in subaltern positions, this reading proposes that the narrative's most powerful decolonial critique of systemic proportions lies in its portrayal of technology's betrayal in fulfilling its utopian promise to mitigate the alienating effects of uneven globalization.

The embodiment of historical contradictions (Mata 2018) found in Pereira de Almeida's work is seen here as a literary index of peripheral experiences common not only to people like the protagonist, Solange, who see themselves in minoritized social positions due to the meaning of their skin colour or heritage connected to the historic horror of slavery, but also in the most recent experience of the international division of labour in the form of migration and diaspora caused by late global capitalism. This experience marks contemporary Portugal in its double position as both core, in the post-imperial relationship it maintains with the African countries that were once its colonies, and peripheral to the core economies of Western Europe. From this angle, the telephone acquires a meaning that goes beyond established readings limiting its interpretative possibilities to the nuanced realm of the colonial binaries. Referred to as a 'homenagem ao género literário da diáspora, o telefonema' (Almeida 2020, back cover) the telephone's metonymic relationship with Solange and her mother speaks of the Faustian bargain of the reliance on technology to mitigate the distance between mother and daughter in the contexts of migration driven by capitalist unevenness.

More than a simple figure of speech, the reference to Faust's deal with the devil in the eponymous landmark European epic poem by Goethe sheds light on technology's relevance to transitional moments in the longue durée of the capitalist world-system visible in Djaimilia Pereira de Alemeida *As Telefones*. Many critical works highlight the tragedy of Faust's (1808 and 1832) inherent relationship with the time of change in the semi-peripheral space that would become Germany as we know it. Marshall Berman, for one, dedicates the first chapter of his seminal book *All That Is Solid Melts Into Air* (1982) to an analysis of *Faust* as a *'tragedy of development'* (1988: 40, emphasis in the original) of an 'epoch whose thought and sensibility are modern in a way that twentieth-century readers can recognize at once' thus 'express[ing] and dramatiz[ing] the process by which, at the end of the eighteenth century and the start of the nineteenth, a distinctively modern world-system comes into being' (*ibidem*, 39). This recognition feels yet more concrete in the context of *As Telefones* if we consider that Berman's own intervention is published at around the time in which the novel's protagonist is a child about to have her own relationship with her mother mediated by technology. The backdrop of combined and uneven development where the eighteenth-century Faust can be seen between pre-modern working tools and large-scale sophisticated land reclamation projects finds ground for comparison with a seeming time of change in Portugal, as it transitioned away from its reliance on primitive accumulation practices connected to its imperial history and towards an industry not yet developed to the same level of its European counterparts. Seen through the perspective of Boaventura de Sousa Santos, Portugal at the time was a semi-peripheral country relying on an irregular process of industrialization, in which capitalism unevenly combined with non-capitalist forms of production (1985: 867). While this process changed dramatically in the 1990s due to the country's integration into the European Economic Community in 1986, the overall process of economic deregulation, financialization, and an acute process of decentralization pushed by the Economic and Monetary Union since 1999 saw the deepening of the asymmetric relationship between Portugal and other member states (Santos and Reis 2018). With European economic integration, the country developed a financial industry aligned with, and dependent on, the financial centre of the core economies in the bloc, which allowed for the increase of personal debt and access to consumer goods, services, and technology like the telephone, which in the novel works as an index of both shallow economic development and prosperity.

Returning to the parallel with *Faust*, in the German epic the role of magic and technology works both as an index of its society's semi-peripheral position in the world-system of the day and as an index of the tragedy of modern capitalism. As J. M. van der Laan explains in his study of technological fulfilment in *Faust*, in the ruthlessness, embrace of exploitation and disdain for care that Faust exhibits in his drive to achieve the great deed of reclaiming land from the sea to make living space for the very people he has enslaved, technology is far from a positive utopic device; 'technology instead establishes impersonality, totality, domination and subjugation' (2016: 164) because it is inherently connected with productive processes that disregard the wellbeing of those involved in it. In this sense, the Faustian bargain in *As Telefones* happens when this technological medium is relied upon as a way to bridge the gap between mother and daughter, separated due to the economic hardships intrinsically connected with the very material conditions determining the availability of the service to begin with. The tragedy here is, then, the seeming irreparability of the bond between the two women as well as the very loss of a sense of self that the telephone connection would always prevent.

Here, a view of migration in the context of the international division of labour and the longue-durée of capitalism is essential for an appreciation of the depth of *As Telefones*'s critical impact. Speaking of fundamental aspects of life under capitalism that go beyond its expression in terms of racism, the work is capable of eliciting a much stronger decolonial critique than has been conventionally noticed. An important indicator of the Janus-faced expression of Portuguese semi-peripheral condition in the twentieth century, migration made possible by free movement between citizens within the European Union changed the dynamic of migration patterns in the country. With it, Portuguese citizens could emigrate much easier to access the labour markets at the core of Europe and, at the same time, it made Portugal much more attractive to immigrants from various parts of the Portuguese-speaking world (Góis and Marques 2009). This large-scale change in terms of populational movement gave way to a new type of cosmopolitism that the Brazilian critic Silviano Santiago called 'cosmopolitism of the poor'.

In his essay *Cosmopolitismo do pobre* (Cosmopolitism of the poor) (2002) Santiago departs from the analysis of on-screen representations of the identity crisis faced by members of a minoritized Portuguese diaspora in France, forced to migrate from the peripheries to the economic core of Europe in search of better work prospects and living conditions. Turning traditional western ethnocentrism on its head and departing from the postcolonial Brazilian experience as a benchmark for understanding contemporary multiculturalism in Europe, Santiago disrupts the colonial logic by relocating the ethnocentric gaze. Looking at the diasporic composition of the Brazilian population and the impact of the international division of labour on culture, from the dawn of the transatlantic slave trade, he resituates Europe's trouble with multiculturalism caused by migrant labour as part of the same capitalist process. In doing so, he exposes the deep-seated logic of capitalist exploitation that, on one level, approximates the subjective alienation of Franco-Portuguese character in *Viagem ao começo do mundo* (1997) by Manuel Oliveira and the Luso-Angolan Solange, in *As Telefones*. While, in Oliveira's film, the son of a Portuguese immigrant raised in France sees himself devoid of a language to connect with his heritage and extended family, in Pereira de Almeida's book, Solange's separation from her mother deprives her of a concrete sense of physical self. As Solange says repeatedly throughout most of the narrative: *Não conheço o teu corpo, Filomena. Não conheço o meu corpo* (I don't know your body, Filomena. I don't know my own body) (Almeida 2020: 9).

The absence of a physical connection between Solange and Filomena emerges as a condition that marks the 'cosmopolitism of the poor' as the telephone exchanges between them fall short of bridging the intersubjective abyss brought about by their distance across the years. Even though the narrative describes moments of physical encounter between daughter and mother, lived through a few episodes in which the distance is eclipsed during holiday trips of Solange to Luanda or of Filomena to Lisbon – the latter having taken place already in the daughter's adulthood – those are described as moments of awkward estrangement, where the voice of the narrator is brought in as an important device to explain to the reader a process that none of the characters seems to fully apprehend. In one of those passages, Filomena takes a shower in front of an adult Solange and the crushing discomfort caused by the impossibility of the connection between daughter and mother, even in the face of the much desired concreteness of physical presence, is narrated in terms of violence and disappointment: *[Filomena g]ostava de perceber pelo seu olhar se Solange aguentaria a violência de a observar, se aguentaria a visão de seu corpo gasto, memento mori cuja oferta era o seu principal poder sobre ela; perceber que, debaixo da roupa de Filomena, não encontraria aquilo que procurava esmagava [Solange] como quando se vê esfumar uma mistificação que nos assombra* (Filomena would have liked to see, in Solange's eyes, if she could put up with the violence of observing her, if she could put up with the image of her worn out body, *memento mori* whose offer was her main power over Solange; to perceive that, under Filomena's clothes, Solange wouldn't find that what she sought crushed her like when one sees a haunting mystification go up in smoke) (Almeida 2020: 21, emphasis in the original).

Solange's and Filomena's cosmopolitanism of the poor is a condition connected to the very excess of material weight that contraposes their experience with the one traditionally conceived under the guise of cosmopolitanism. As Santiago reminds us [t]odos os artistas e intelectuais da modernidade ocidental, incluindo os marxistas, passaram pela experiência da *madeleine* [de Marcel Proust] (all artists and intellectuals of western modernity, including the Marxist, went through [Marcel Proust's] *madeleine* experience) (2004: 47, emphasis in the original). The resort to the paradigmatic *In Search of Lost Time* (1913–27) by Proust in which sensory experience of an upper-class, middle-aged, man connects present and past allowing him to 'live and enjoy the essence of things, that is to say, entirely outside of time' (Szondi 2006: 13) speaks directly to the weightlessness of an unmarked cosmopolitanism that is a privilege of the wealthy. Proust's hero's ability to find a sensorial connection in the suspension of time based on the recognition between identifiable experiences almost diametrically contraposes Pereira de Almeida's protagonist's complete inability to experience a similar kind of cognition. As *Telefones*'s protagonist is, thus, unable to perceive her mother as much as she is unable to *recognize* herself, crushed by the inescapable historical weight of the underprivileged type of economic migration driving her own cosmopolitan experience. As such, the novel's approach to cosmopolitanism's ability to compress time and bridge experience sheds an important critical light capable of materially situating this phenomenon across the class divide. Starting not with the pleasant taste of a soft madeleine melting in her mouth but with the hard, sharp, and sad image of a *cemitério de cabines telefónicas, à entrada de Lisboa* (cemetery of telephone booths at the entrance of Lisbon) (2020: 9), Pereira de Almeida's cosmopolitan compression of time in late capitalism is marked by the same tone that differentiates Walter Benjamin's revisitation of his childhood experiences to Proust's: 'Proust listens attentively for the echo of the past; Benjamin listens for the first notes of a future which has meanwhile become the past' (Szondi 2006: 13) – a future that, for Solange, is mediated by the telephone as a token of technology's betrayal to live up to its potential to bridge the distance between mother and daughter. This way, speaking of the death of the telephone as known during the protagonist's childhood, itself in a metonymic relation with Solange and her mother explicit in the book's title, the beginning of the narrative speaks of the future death of a bond which has also, meanwhile, become the past.

Time in *As Telefones* is indicated in fragmented and combined ways, as it is visible in the deliberate faltering approach to orientation that leaves many page numbers in the book unprinted (Rendeiro 2022: 52). The narrative thus alternates between the disorienting stream of consciousness and references to easily identifiable milestones in western history. Deployed as the privileged means from which to narrate the relationship between Solange and her mother, the stream of consciousness mixes the retelling of telephone conversations that occurred during the protagonist's childhood with more recent episodes of physical encounters bitterly flavoured by the disappointment of their emotional separation. It situates their relationship with the telephone as device and via the device in the wider narrative of societal change and technological development wherein their tragic disconnection lies: *O século deformou o nosso amor ... A tecnologia cortou-nos o fio ... O telefone é um altere. A chamada, uma tareia. Olho-me ao espelho à tua procura. Dizem-me que somos parecidas de costas. Talvez nunca nos tenhamos visto.* (The century deformed our love. Technology has cut our wire. The telephone is a dumbbell. The call is a beating. I look at myself in the mirror in search of you. They tell me we look alike when seen from the back. Perhaps we have never seen each other) (Almeida 2020: 33). References to world history dotted throughout the book, on the other hand, put their drama alongside important international events, including some specific to the Black diaspora, marking their place in time and with the times. Starting with the opening lines of the story that situate it in a time of technological transition away from the telephone as they knew it, we have references to Alexander Graham Bell and the place of the telephone in Walter Benjamin's childhood scenes in 1900. Further historical references include Mikhail Gorbachev, the deaths of Yasser Arafat, Muammar Kadafi, Saddam Hussein, the World Trade Center attack, the death of Aretha Franklin, the election and retirement of Barack Obama, the election of Donald Trump, the mother of Meghan Markel, and the 2017 Westminster Bridge Attack with a transcription, in English, of a portion of the announcement by Theresa May, the UK Prime Minister at the time. Failing to connect mother and daughter at the physical and emotional level, the telephone allowed them to share a connection with their time: *O telefone através do qual falamos é o nosso elo tangível à história da espécie humana: uma educação simultânea do corpo uma da outra* (The telephone through which we speak is our tangible link to the history of the human species: a simultaneous education of each other's body) (2020: 31–2).

The reference to Walter Benjamin's autobiographical work *Berlin Childhood around 1900* (1950) made in *As Telefones* appears in a section that speaks of Alexander Graham Bell's sketches of the equipment he invented. This two-page long segment in the first half of the story looks at the telephone as a technological advance that jumps from Graham Bell's sketchbook to the triumph and glory of the front rooms of German bourgeois family homes like Benjamin's: *A sua chegada à Alemanha, onde, por volta de 1900, venceu a guerra contra a mobília muda e ultrapassada, na casa onde vivia Walter Benjamin, 'tal como um herói lendário isolado no desfiladeiro da montanha', roubando às antigas relíquias o seu lugar de destaque* (Its arrival in Germany, where, around 1900, it won the war against the silent and obsolete furniture in the house where Walter Benjamin lived, 'like a legendary hero once exposed to die in a mountain gorge', the ancient relics robbed of their prominent place) (2020: 25). The segment, nonetheless, starts by speaking of the telephone's physical and metaphorical weight in a world about to fall apart: *Auscultadores que 'pesavam como alteres'. Foi cem anos antes do começo dos nossos telefonemas intercontinentais, num mundo prestes a ruir* (Receivers that 'were heavy as dumbbells'. It was a hundred years before our intercontinental calls, in a world about to fall apart) (2020: 24). The promising brave new world of technology, which betrayed people like Benjamin by enabling the horror of war; the dumbbell-like weight of the phone crushing the relationship it was supposed to nurture, taking over the human in the prosthetic move that titles the book: *Desde o caderno de Bell até hoje, até o telefone se tornar vício, companhia, segunda pele. E nós, com ele, auscultadores de carne, humanidade telefónica, máquinas de coração na boca, bonecos num caderno em breve antigo* (From Bell's sketches to now, whilst the telefone turned to an addiction, to a second skin. And us, with it, receivers in the flesh, telephonic humanity, machines of heart in their mouth, doll-like figures in a sketchbook) (2020: 25).

Symbolized by the telephone, whose prominence is much larger in the first half of the narrative, the treatment of technology enmeshed in a context of a semi-peripheral Europe is, thus, more in line with Faustian and Benjaminian suspicious and disenchanted views of its liberating potential, than aligned to any technophilic feminist trends in vogue at the American cores of the capitalist world system since the mid-1980s. The odds with a feminist positive view of technology, in line with the work of Donna Haraway originally published in 1985 (2016), are due to the prominent role ascribed to positionality in this narrative, which is itself a product of the inescapable weight of history in the story of physical and emotional separation between this daughter and mother. Rooted in a concrete history of the experience of the international division of labour in the longue durée of capitalism mediated by colonialism, racism, and enslavement that first brought Luanda and Lisbon together, technology in *As Telefones* enables separation rather than inspires any universalist coalitions. As such, the book's treatment of the role of the telephone as a technological device determinant to Solange's own self-recognition in later life echoes Benjamin's *Berlin Childhood around 1900*, which Pereira de Almeida's narrative literally cites. Peter Szondi posits, in the essay 'Hope in the past' that opens the 2006 English translation of *Berlin Childhood*, that in Benjamin's treatment of time in his book '[I]n contrast [with Proust], the future is precisely what it seeks in the past' (2006: 18) but that his search in this book, the manuscripts of which were produced near his death as he fled the Nazi forces, is also 'a quest for the lost future' (2006: 22) in which the author criticized 'the betrayal of utopia that was committed in realizing the idea of technology' (2006: 24). For Benjamin's acute awareness of the intrinsic relation between culture and barbarism, the revisitation of his childhood memories sketched in exile *num mundo prestes a ruir* (in a world about to fall apart) (Almeida 2020: 24) was an opportunity to see the future in a historical background that would never allow it to come into existence. This prompted him to dot 'traces of what was to come' (Szondi 2006: 18) all over his memories, just as we see taking place in *As Telefones*. The cemetery of telephone booths forgotten at the entrance to Lisbon, a trace of a mother-daughter relationship that never was; the misrecognition sustaining the disconnect in the conversations between mother and child, a trace of the later misrecognition of each other and of Solange towards her own body. The telephone is a technological divide, one that takes over their bodies rather than facilitates their physical connection.

Read in such light, the hypercontemporaneity of *As Telefones* has a degree of decolonial potential capable of decoupling the work of Pereira de Almeida from readings concerned solely with her works' ability to speak of the experience of minoritized groups as one of minoritization. Seen in the broader tradition of the European semi-peripheral novel capable of registering the unevenness dividing societies linked in global capitalism since the advent of modernity, *As Telefones* uplifts the perspective of the Black writer to the perspective of the Black woman who writes *in* and *about* the world. As such, the positionality of the Black protagonist in the book speaks as much about the condition of the Afro-European as it speaks about the longue durée of economic migration in the capitalist world-system, inscribing this experience in the same axis of cosmopolitanism of the Proustian madeleine experience or of the poor in Europe's semi-peripheral countries forced to emigrate in search of better economic prospects. Equally, the betrayal of the liberatory promise of technology that distinguishes this Hypercontemporary novel is indebted to the work's conscious embracing of historicity. Located within the structure of feeling of the Afro-European, a critical approach to history rooted in class and racial consciousness is cleverly weaved in a literary representation of intimate intersubjective proportions. As a result, one of the most powerful ways in which *As Telefones* can elicit a decolonial critique is by privileging Black experiences as capable of illuminating critical questions pertaining to realities of capitalist societies at large, way beyond anything pertinent solely to Black or other minoritized experiences, and thus bringing us a little bit closer to a time when we can see the world through a multiplicity of embodied perspectives.

# References

Almeida, D. P. de (2022), 'O Que é Ser uma Escritora Negra Hoje, de Acordo Comigo', *Serrote* 41: 4–21.

Almeida, D. P. de (2020), *As Telefones*, Lisbon: Relógio D'Água Editores.

Arnaut, A. P. (2018), 'Do Pós-Modernismo ao Hipercontrmporâneo: Morfologia(s) do Romance e (Re)figurações da Personagem', *Revista de Estudos Literários* 8: 19–44. Available online: https://doi.org/10.14195/2183-847X_8_1.

Berman, M. (1988), *All That Is Solid Melts into Air*, Baskerville: Penguin Books.

Franco, R. G. (2021), 'A "inseparabilidade" dos Trânsitos na Obra de Djaimilia Pereira de Almeida', *Abril* – NEPA/UFF 13 (27): 109–24. Available online: https://doi.org/10.22409/abriluff.v13i27.50258.

Góis, P. and Marques, J. C. (2009), 'Portugal as a Semi-peripheral Country in the Global Migration System', *International Migration* 47 (3): 21–50.

Haraway, D. J. and Wolfe, C. (2016), 'A Cyborg Manifesto: Science, Technology, and Socialist-Feminism in the Late Twentieth-Century', *Manifestly Haraway*: 3–90. Available online: http://www.jstor.org/stable/10.5749/j.ctt1b7x5f6.4.

Macedo, A. G. (2022), 'Djaimilia Pereira de Almeida, As Telefones. Homenagem ao "Género Literário da Diáspora" e a Reinvenção da Narrativa Poética', in A. G. Macedo, M. Oliveira, M. E. Pereira, J. Passos and L. G. Natalino (eds.), *Mulheres, Artes e Ditadura. Diálogos Interartísticos e Narrativas da Memória*, 17–29, Porto: Edições Húmus.

Mata, I. (2018), 'Uma implosiva geografia exílica', *Público*, December 14, 20189. Available online: https://www.publico.pt/2018/12/14/culturaipsilon/critica/implosiva-geografia-exilica-1854334?fbclid=IwAR3qkbPavIbMhs9AZwoGWNoDSHFxBaRqLWs4CsEc4aFiTwr1mHTCAtbqhF0.

Medeiros, P. de (2020), 'Memórias Pósimperiais: Luuanda, de José Luandino Vieira, e Luanda, Lisboa, Paraíso, de Djaimilia Pereira de Almeida', *Língua-Lugar: Literatura, História, Estudos Culturais* 1 (1): 136–49. Available online: https://doi.org/10.34913/journals/lingua-lugar.2020.e211.

Moretti, F. (2000), 'Conjectures on World Literature', *New Left Review* 1 (1): 54–67.

Rendeiro, M. (2022), 'On How Post-Colonial Fiction Can Contribute to a Discussion of Historical Reparation: An Interpretation of *As Telefones* (2020) by Djaimilia Pereira de Almeida', *Comunicação e Sociedade* 41: 43–59. Available online: http://journals.openedition.org/cs/6353.

Ribeiro, M. C. (2019), 'Luanda, Lisboa, Paraíso?', Buala. Available online: https://www.buala.org/pt/a-ler/luanda-lisboa-paraiso.

Santiago, S. (2004), 'O Cosmopolitismo do Pobre', in S. Santiago (ed.), *O Cosmopolitismo do Pobre: Crítica Literária e Crítica Cultural*, 45–63, Belo Horizonte: Editora da UFMG.

Santos, A. C. and Reis, J. (2018), 'Portugal: Uma Semiperiferia Reconfigurada', *E-cadernos CES* 29: 57–76. Available online: http://journals.openedition.org/eces/3163.

Santos, B. de S. (1985), 'Estado e Sociedade na Semiperiferia do Sistema Mundial: O Caso Português', *Análise Social* XXI (87-88-89): 869–901.

Szondi, P. (2006), 'Hope in the Past: On Walter Benjamin', in Howard Eiland (trans.), *Berlin Childhood Around 1900* by Walter Benjamin, 1–33, Cambridge, London: The Belknap of Harvard University Press.

Van der Laan, J. M. (2016), *Narratives of Technology*, New York: Palgrave Macmillan.

# 11

# Through a Glass Darkly: Violence, Intimacy, and Memory in Dulce Maria Cardoso

Paulo de Medeiros

*Haunting would mark the very existence of Europe.*
Jacques Derrida, Specters of Marx, 3

'No one engaged in thought about history and politics can remain unaware of the enormous role violence has always played in human affairs, and it is at first glance rather surprising that violence has been singled out so seldom for special consideration', thus writes Hannah Arendt at the start of her seminal essay *On Violence* (1969: 8). While fully aware that much had always been written on war, Arendt is critical of the way in which violence has been taken for granted and never really analysed. In the process, as she claims, violence becomes not only trivialized, it is made to seem inevitable. For Arendt such a state of affairs rightly poses a problem, one she attempts to address with her essay. For us, though, the problem, even if not completely changed or annulled, has certainly assumed a different form, proportion, and presence. In presence, because if the twentieth century was an especially violent one, considering two World Wars, all of the wars of independence that marked the end of the colonial era, as late as 1974 in Portugal's case, and a myriad of other conflicts, the twenty-first century seems intent on continuing and expanding it. Even the threat of nuclear Armageddon, which seemed to have eased somewhat with what many thought to be the end of the Cold War and the fall of the Berlin Wall in 1989 is back with a vengeance, except that by now it may even be overshadowed for many by the continuous ecological disasters that our greed and a seemingly blind and savage capitalism has brought about and whose consequences can be felt by us all daily. In proportion because although Europe, and generally speaking, the West, has never stopped being involved in conventional warfare, the conflicts have been staged (until very recently with the invasion of Ukraine by Russia in February 2022) far away and as such, besides occasional flashes in the news, have become more or less invisible to many of us. In form, because besides the spectacular kind of violence that characterizes war, many other forms of violence have come to the fore and, though they were also always there, have become much more visible. One such form of violence that I want to consider in the example of two of Dulce Maria Cardoso's novels, in comparison with other works by J. Coetzee and Ann Enright, is a pervasive, silent form of violence that infiltrates all and everything, that taints us and haunts us. It is thus radically different from the kind of spectacular violence that Arendt and others have mostly analysed, but no less corrosive. And, to paraphrase Derrida, it is the kind of violence that in haunting us all might as well be understood as constitutive of what we both individually and collectively really are.

Dulce Maria Cardoso has emerged as one of the most significant voices of her generation in Portugal. Born in rural Trás-os-Montes in 1964, she was raised initially in Angola, 'returning' to live with her grandparents in 1975 after the April 25th Revolution in Portugal and the subsequent independence of Portugal's African colonies. She has published five novels, two volumes of short narratives, as well as some children's literature and a book collecting her chronicles for the weekly *Visão*. Her work has drawn wide critical acclaim since the beginning and she has received a number of prestigious prizes both in Portugal and internationally, such as The European Union Prize for Literature in 2009 for her novel *Os Meus Sentimentos* (*Violeta among the Stars*). *O Retorno* (The Return), published in 2011 and translated into English in 2016, received the Special Critics' Prize in Portugal and also merited her being awarded a distinction as Chevalier of the Order of Arts and Letters by the French State. Her latest novel, *Eliete* was one of the recipients of the *Oceanos* Prize in 2019 (second place). Even though her novels until now are quite separate from one another (*Eliete*, however, has been announced as the first of a forthcoming trilogy) they share some common interests such as a focus on the experience of women, the banality of life, and the intense violence of it. Indeed, even though my focus will be on violence, it can never be separated from the other two. The violence Dulce Maria Cardoso exposes is not the kind of flashy violence one has become so used to in postmodern textual and filmic narrative, often becoming completely desensitized in the process. Indeed, as opposed to the spectacular violence that marks, say, the films of Quentin Tarantino and that seem to have come to stand for a new normality, Cardoso's novels register and represent a violence that is far more subterranean, under the skin but everywhere; a haunting violence that grabs readers by the throat and never lets go. It is this kind of violence that I want to explore and that, I suggest, might be more marking of the Hypercontemporary.

At one point I also thought that what would demarcate the Hypercontemporary from other modes – among which the postmodern, with which it does share many aspects – would precisely be the extreme, 'hyper', form of spectacular violence that has become so much a part of our daily lives in the twenty-first century. Yet, to pursue such a view to its logical conclusion would lead one rather to embrace, unwittingly as it may be, a kind of nihilism that in itself is no different from the very nihilism that has come to dominate a wide-spread cynical attitude to the present as Wendy Brown exposed, basing herself on Nietzsche as 'a world in which "the highest values devaluate themselves": 'This trivialization and instrumentalization, ubiquitous in commercial, political, and even religious life today, further degrade the value of values, which further abets the nihilism … an unending spiral shaping political culture and subjectivity' (Brown 2019: 161). So, without in any way engaging in a futile contest of denominations, I have come to understand the Hypercontemporary less as a kind of free flow of seemingly groundless and widespread spectacular violence, and more of an insidious, inescapable, and total form of subdued violence, making up in cruelty what it lacks in performativity.

\*\*\*

'*Estão quatro mulheres na sala. Destas mulheres é preciso saber antes de tudo que aqui vieram por causa de um homem que cometeu um crime e que se por acaso se encontrassem na rua não se cumprimentariam* (There are four women in the room. About these women it must be known, before anything else, that they came here because of a man who committed a crime and that if they were to meet by chance on the street they would not greet each other) (Cardoso 2002, 2009). This is the startling opening to *Campo de Sangue* (Field of Blood), Cardoso's first novel, which, even if it still centres around a brutal murder – the crime thus announced from the very beginning – already prepares the way for violence to become less a spectacular event and more of a hidden yet omnipresent, shadowy, condition defining us and our age. Originally, the perpetrator in *Campo de Sangue* could be perceived as suffering from some kind of mental illness. Repeatedly there is reference to a kind of excessive form of love, an obsession, which could be invoked to explain, though not justify, the brutality and seeming randomness of the murder. Indeed, why else would a man be moved to cut open the chest of a young woman to attempt to cut her heart out? *Mas abrir o peito a alguém não é difícil./Difícil é tirar o coração a alguém* (But opening up someone's chest is not difficult./Difficult is to rip the heart out of someone) (Cardoso 2002: 275). Yet, especially reading the novel now, two decades and a few more novels later, one tends to agree with the author's perspective, declared in an interview in 2018, that now such an act no longer appears to us as necessarily indicating a mental condition. Rather, as she says, that kind of 'empty man, nothing more than a simulacrum of himself in the vortex of creating an image for the consumption of others' has become normalized (Cardoso 2018: 1': 03" – 1':39).

Obsession may be said to be one of the key components of Cardoso's writing, which attempts to represent the intensity of feeling – whether the negative intensity of banality and tediousness, or the intensity of pain – that mark her characters. If one were to rely on conventional ways of conceptualizing World Literature one may have reason to hesitate concerning Cardoso whose work, even if widely received and critically acclaimed, has yet to receive the kind of attention and legitimation usually associated with writers who have received greater international accolades or have by now safely entered the list of canonical masters. However, if one were to focus on the multiple ways in which she writes and, I would suggest, through such writing also exposes and resists, the processes through which individuals become dehumanized over and over again, then one can have a firmer grounding towards claiming a place for her texts in that same hallowed list of World Literature works. It is perhaps no coincidence that of all her published work so far, the four novels and two collections of short prose, it was *O Retorno* that first saw translation into English. Its post-imperial concerns, its focus on the plight of the 'retornados' – those who were caught by the events of 1974 and 1975, Portugal's revolution and the subsequent independence of its colonies, and 'returned' to Portugal – and its relentless questioning of both imperial and patriarchal structures make it capable of resonating directly with many people across Europe whose memories or post-memories are still tied up with the various traumas of Europe's colonial past. Even though not every nation has gone through a process of decolonization within recent memory as Portugal, France, and the UK have, to mention but a few, all have dealt in one way or another with the problems of forced large-scale migration, be it from one country to another, fleeing war zones, or even for plain subsistence, so that the question of survival will certainly resonate in many varied ways across the globe.

*Campo de Sangue*, by contrast, would appear more localized, more restricted to the working class and petty bourgeoisie of Lisbon and its surrounding areas, without any claims being made for a tie in with the end of an era, with the final demise of empire, at both Portuguese and European levels. And yet, I would suggest, the way in which that first novel obsessively explores some of the deep anxieties of the urban working class, and the hopes, however dashed, of escaping their reduced circumstances, resonates as much, if not more, across Europe and other parts of the world. Again, what I want to argue is not that one novel or another somehow has a better fit in World Literature, but rather that both novels make clear how a late capitalist world-system operates. *Campo de Sangue*, for instance, presents a stark critique of how we all have become enmeshed in the 'society of spectacle' to use Guy Débord's apt classification. It is not only that television, with its incessant claims at shaping reality through illusion, is shown as both the promise of salvation (to rescue the landlady from forced demolition of her building) and as accessory to murder (as it was the promise to appear on television that lured the woman who was murdered to go to the boarding house). Perhaps more important is the notion that all is but an image, the image that each character has of her or his life, as well as of the lives of others.

The novel is firmly grounded on reality; it is as far from being a postmodern flirtation with aesthetic games as can be. The almost desperate attempts at escaping from the neighbourhood of their childhood, from a dead future or from poverty in general, are exposed in a language that is both powerful and down to earth, obsessive and very direct, and without trace of sentimentality. There is a stark sense of tragedy throughout the novel that both makes it difficult to read through and compels one not to stop. Without being completely allegorical, there is a sense in which the characters function as such. We have the 'four women' in the waiting room, all related in one way or another to the man we come to find out has committed an incomprehensible murder, trying to remove by force a woman's heart. They are discussed as individuals but also function in terms of their different relations to the murderer, as mother, lover, ex-wife, and landlady. The novel is as much about betrayal as it is about survival. The title, by naming the cemetery bought with the thirty silver pieces Judas had first accepted and then, overtaken by remorse, returned, already points to this. And the allusions to diverse forms of betrayal are multiplied throughout the text. One could say that the novel hinges precisely on the dialectic between betrayal and survival. As long as Eva and her ex-husband go on being faithful to their own self-image as lovers they survive; it is only when he betrays that illusion by pursuing another, in the shape of the young girl he saw at the beach, that their lives start to unravel. Yet, their very survival is only possible by betraying who they are, their past, their identities, and in the end, even if Eva tries to survive by hiding further that past and its consequences, its claims on her, one senses that it is but temporary. Reading *Campo de Sangue* is an intense, and painful, exposure to the ways in which human beings can be reduced and dehumanized: *a pobreza é uma doença difícil de curar a partir de certa idade* poverty is an illness that is difficult to cure after a certain age (Cardoso 2002: 129). In the end the reader knows that the male protagonist is shown to us as having become clinically insane. Does that mean he no longer bears any responsibility? Yet, in his insanity, if that is at all accurate and not just a widespread Hypercontemporary condition, he can perhaps still discern key aspects of life as when he observes a spider and the flies that fall prey to its web: *A mosca desiste de lutar. Lentamente. Aceita a derrota. – Luta até ao fim – diz com voz alterada. – Luta* (The fly gives up fighting. Slowly. It accepts defeat. – Fight to the end – he says with a changed voice. – Fight) (Cardoso 2002: 284).

***

One of the unifying threads throughout Cardoso's works is precisely that exhortation to fight, to continue resisting, and not accept the defeat that death brings. This should in no way be construed as a denial of death, nor even as a fear of it, or at least not beyond that normally experienced by most of us. Cardoso's works mercilessly expose the devastation of contemporary Portuguese society and the festering wounds that its fascist and imperialist past left as a sort of damned legacy. But they never play with defeatism, never allow self-pity, and never stop pleading for a better future. A key example of that fundamental attitude to life can be seen in the character of Violeta, the protagonist narrator of *Os Meus Sentimentos* (*Violeta among the Stars*). In this, her second novel, Cardoso both continues the project initiated with *Campo de Sangue*, that is, the ruthless exposure of the sordidness and violence of daily life and goes significantly further. In one point it differs starkly from all the other novels: it is written in what one could designate an extreme stream of consciousness style, running to close to four hundred pages, without a single full stop, not even after its last word, 'inesperadamente' (suddenly; Cardoso 2005: 307) (Cardoso 2021: 396). It is Cardoso's most experimental novel, in terms of its form, and this merits some attention as well in terms of how it relates to the narrative's content. The experimentation with form in which the narrative basically could be seen as one single sentence, one single moment, if we want, directly relates to one moment in which the car Violeta is driving in a storm while intoxicated 'suddenly' overturns. Seen that way, both past and present excessively conflate into that one moment that, instead of offering any closure, remains in suspension, as if infinite. At the end of the novel, we know, or rather, think that we know, that Violeta is dead, that her lifelong endurance of abuse has finally come to an end. And yet, reading through the novel, even though there are clear suggestions of Violeta having died, her 'past' is continuously shown to us as if it were still 'present'. As to the future, even the death of Violeta, what we must understand as her death if we are to remain at the level of realism, is not annulled: in part because that ending, 'suddenly', functions more like a return to the moment just before the accident, in part because Violeta will make a brief appearance in Cardoso's subsequent novel, *O Chão dos Pardais* (The Sparrows' Ground) (2009: 84), her hair soaked even though it was a sunny day, reeking of beer, and explaining the run in her stockings as having been caused by the accident. Sofia, the person in the subway to whom Violeta addresses that explanation not only has no idea to what it might refer, or who Violeta is (or was), nor could she be bothered about it as she herself was undergoing a significant crisis. In this too Cardoso, beyond nodding to her readers who will be aware of the significance of that brief encounter, further pushes the notion of our contemporary lives being like ships passing in the night, without any possibility of communication, much less empathy. As much as both women's lives were marked by endless misery and unfathomable abuse at the hands of various men, they will never know it and will never be able to find support in each other, even though each, in her way, far more than being a victim, is a survivor.

*Os Meus Sentimentos* – literally 'my feelings', though idiomatically also used to express condolences – is a difficult title to translate. Various translators have opted to use the protagonist's name, 'Violeta', whether in conjunction with the stars as in English or angels in both French and Dutch. Initially presented as a riddle, a name that designates both a flower and a colour, it is a doubly ambiguous cypher, that the translations notoriously miss as they cannot reproduce the ambiguity of the original title, nor the bit of suspense that the original text preserves for some time. Furthermore, 'My Feelings' evokes a kind of light, confessional, and sentimental narrative that contrasts with the harshness of the reality the text registers: the father's infidelity, the physical and mental abuse that mark a childhood in fear, later the incest as Violeta chooses her half-brother as partner, the intense and aleatory promiscuity from an early age on, to which would be added the frequent inebriation, and the impossibility of ever breaking out of the vicious circle of degradation and dehumanization.

Perhaps one of the most extreme forms of such dehumanization is at the core of Cardoso's third novel, *O Chão dos Pardais* (The Sparrow's Ground), already mentioned. Without going into any detail, I want to reflect on it briefly. Indeed, were one to choose only one instance of the many in Cardoso's novels, that relentlessly expose human cruelty, the second chapter of *O Chão dos Pardais*, most certainly would be it. In *Violet Among the Stars* the one determining event, the 'sudden' car crash that ends Violeta's life, we assume, is really at the core of the novel and not just at its conclusion – in a sense, one could say that it is in itself the original spring for the narrative, though not its cause. Even though there were no witnesses to that potentially spectacular form of violence, and Cardoso refrains from describing it even from Violeta's perspective (which would have been the only plausible one), it remains indisputably central. However, in *O Chão dos Pardais* the one ostensible act of extreme violence that can be considered spectacular, Júlio's pointing of a gun at Afonso during his birthday party, yet deciding not to execute him, but rather to kill himself, pales in comparison with the extreme violence inherent in the complete dehumanisation of Sofia, Júlio's fiancée, at the hands of Afonso, her employer. Besides taking advantage of his position of power and fortune to exploit Sofia sexually, Afonso crosses a line when he decides to offer her to one of the hotel's employees, Nate Garza, by forcing him to choose between possessing Sofia or taking a considerable sum of money. Indeed, not only Sofia but also the hotel employee both are rendered into objects by Afonso, even if the humiliation of the man is not as complete as that of Sofia. By deciding to take the money after some agonizing deliberation, only to renounce it when Sofia reminds him that it will be highly suspect for him to have come into such a large amount of cash, Nate has not in fact decided to do the honourable thing, as he has simply acted selfishly, first out of greed and second out of fear.

Afonso does indeed cross a line but his utter reification of Sofia in that episode is not that different from all of the times in which he also would buy her or destroy the lives of others, just more excessive. Indeed, what Cardoso relentlessly exposes, in all her novels, is not so much individual cruelty as systemic oppression, an oppression that runs so deep it leaves nothing and no one untouched. In a sense *O Chão dos Pardais* is arguably the one novel in which Cardoso most intensely makes us see the degradation of our age, mired in simulacra, addicted to spectacle, and rotten to the core of its neoliberal, savage capitalist existence. Afonso and his equally empty wife represent a certain kind of class violence that in reducing everyone to a sub-human level shows its own inhumanity. But those like Júlio, representative of a large majority who spend their lives trying to advance themselves, when not emulating their oppressors, might be different only in degree. After all, Júlio not only is unable to understand Sofia, let alone express solidarity with her or accept that in spite of it all, she did love him, but also his decision to first kill Afonso is simply an expression of the same patriarchal logic that sees women primarily, if not exclusively, as possessions. By choosing to run in parallel with the main narrative the reactions to the death of Princess Diana in 1997, Cardoso further reinforces the idea not only of the banality of the everyday but also how we crave, to fill that same banality the spectacular, even the tragic, as Diana's death not only burst a certain kind of bubble, as in the fairy tale title of the first chapter, 'princesses never die. They get married and live happily ever after', it also provided millions the world over with an opportunity to grieve vicariously, feeling a pain, which because it was not theirs, could better fill the general emptiness of their lives.

*\*\*\**

Another key concern in all of Cardoso's narratives is memory. Or to be more specific, traumatic memory and the way in which it both forms many of the characters and haunts them, how it forms them through that very haunting. In *Spectres of Marx* Jacques Derrida suggests that '[H]aunting would mark the very existence of Europe' (Derrida 1984: 3). Dulce Maria Cardoso, in her writing, further explores that notion as she asks us to look at Portugal, as a polity and in terms of its individual citizens, as hopelessly haunted. Granted, not everyone appears to suffer from the past. Characters such as Afonso, for instance, would appear oblivious to the devastation they create around them. If anything, they can be said to enjoy it. The same could be said, even if in a minor scale, of Violeta's father, who had been an informer for the P.I.D.E., the secret police in the fascist regime. In the words of Violeta, *o mundo tem fim, da crueldade é que não se lhe conhece o fim* (Cardoso 2005: 302) (the world has an end, but human cruelty is endless (Cardoso 2021: 389). Yet, even those characters, seemingly unaffected by the violence they enjoy, could be said to be incapable of escaping its net, caught as much in their role as perpetrators. Not that Cardoso elicits any pity for them obviously. But it is never a question of pity, or even of morality in general. Rather, what Cardoso does is expose the systemic violence at the base of society and how the often-extreme violence of the past, even if no longer visible today, goes on conditioning who we are, how we act, feel, and think.

To simply refer to a past of violence, whether for Europe in general, or even specifically for Portugal, whose long history could be said to be an endless list of abject cruelties from its struggle for territory in the thirteenth century, the early period of the nation's formation, to its subsequent export of violence all over the world as it embarked on its imperialist 'destiny', to the more recent fascist past, all forty-eight years of it, the longest lasting dictatorship in Europe, to its desperate attempt to hold on to its remaining colonies in Africa, the latter two only ending in 1974 with the 25th of April revolution and the immediate decolonization. Rather, Cardoso focuses her attention crucially on three inseparable elements of the past: the long night of fascism that, among other consequences, stifled development in Portugal and kept the great majority of its population at an abject level of poverty and dependency. Both the revolution as well as decolonization, or at least the way it happened, that caused close to a half million people to leave Africa and have to seek new lives in Portugal in a very short period of time, without any suitable living conditions, can be said to be then the immediate, necessary, and even inevitable, consequences. Cardoso's narrative explores how these traumatic events still fully condition and determine life for all Portuguese, whether old or new. And, even as she upholds the imperative to remember – her fiction could well be termed another form of witnessing – Cardoso also explores the other side of memory, the way in which people would like to forget it all, which in a sense is also a way of forgetting not only why things are as they are, but more fundamentally who we are.

The question of why one novel gets translated and another does not is a vexed one, and any possible answer is usually a mixture of contingency and personal taste. Even without wanting to engage in any kind of speculation as to why *O Retorno* was the first of Cardoso's novels to make into English, it can be noted that as it deals with the dissolution of Europe's last empire and the consequences of the forced dislocation of huge numbers of people, it obviously speaks to an audience beyond the strict confines of Portugal or the Portuguese language. Although by no means the first novel to reflect on Portugal's post-imperial condition, Cardoso's novel is one of the first to focus on the question of the 'retornados', the people who were forced to migrate to Portugal from the former African colonies immediately after they gained independence. A novel that just preceded it, Isabel Figueiredo's *Caderno de Memórias Coloniais* (2010)

(*Notebook of Colonial Memories* 2015) is an obvious point of comparison and Ana Cristina Mendes (2017) has done so in some detail, drawing on various theorists from Derrida to Mignolo, Wallerstein, and Boaventura de Sousa Santos, highlighting their condition as post-imperial narratives and the importance that memory has in both. Furthermore, one could also reflect on how Cardoso's novel directly engages what arguably can be seen as the two most important novels to thematize the end of empire and the bloody colonial wars that Portugal engaged in from 1961 to 1974: António Lobo Antunes *Os Cus de Judas*, which has the distinction of having already been translated twice into English (1979 *South of Nowhere* 1983; *The Land at the End of the World* 2011) and Lídia Jorge's *A Costa dos Murmúrios* (1988 (*The Murmuring Coast* 1995)). Both novels are among the most important texts of contemporary Portuguese literature and both are relentless reckonings with the utter violence wreaked by the fascist regime. In both, memory takes centre stage. One point, though, that separates them – and Figueiredo's novel – from *The Return* is the inescapability of the literal extreme violence of war scenarios. Cardoso's novel, however, never presents us with that type of violence directly. It is there and it is all-determining and all-encompassing, but in the background.

In many respects Cardoso's novel has more affinities to Lídia Jorge's than to any of the other two. For one, in both novels we can sense a clear attempt at engaging in a dialogue with those that have preceded them. Antunes's novel, essentially a long monologue from a soldier returned from Africa directed to a woman who never says a word during an entire night in some Lisbon bar, published in 1979 did not really have any antecedent – the colonial war issues were still, and continued for over two decades to be, a kind of unspoken taboo – except his own earlier version of the same narrative, published as *Memória de Elefante* ((1979) Elephant's Memory). Lídia Jorge's novel, in many ways, is an answer to that male monologue that explores the same traumatic consciousness but from the perspective of a woman, and already at a time distance, so that her novel is simultaneously a reflection on both History and memory. Cardoso's novel engages them both in as much as it not only is a work of memory, several decades after the original trauma, the war and the 'expulsion' from what passed for normal life in the colonies, but also, navigating the gender divide in a novel and successful way as the protagonist of her novel is an adolescent boy who thus better serves to expose the problems and dangers inherent in a traditional, strongly patriarchal society, but who does so from the vantage position of someone who, not yet quite grown-up, has not yet come to fully assume the most toxic aspects of masculinity, a man-child still somewhat innocent, yet already inescapably immersed in the skewered values of his society and time.

Pursuing this line of analysis would undoubtedly be fruitful. However, what interests me now is rather to place *The Return* in a different, international context. To do so, my suggestion is to pair it with J. M. Coetzee's *Foe* (1986), a novel which has received much deserved critical attention even if perhaps not quite matching the author's later novel, *Disgrace* (1999). I would like to focus on two related issues: on the one hand, the question of how violence is registered and represented; on the other, the post-imperial and postcolonial positionality of both Coetzee and Cardoso. There is nothing in *Foe* that is not steeped in violence and various forms of cruelty. The one crucial act of violence that, although not at the origin of the narrative (that would be the start of modern imperialism with the Portuguese 'discoveries', and the novel duly opens with Susan Barton shipwrecked after leaving Brazil where she had gone looking for her missing daughter), can be said to constitute its crux, the cutting of Friday's tongue, is itself absent from the narrative. When, how, and why it happened remain lost in the mist of the past. *Foe*, besides being an extremely powerful, original, narrative, is also a forceful dialogue with tradition, and most obviously, with Daniel Defoe's *Robinson Crusoe*.

The importance of Coetzee's rewriting of Defoe, starting with the exposure of Defoe's original surname, Foe, before he adorned it with 'De', cannot be underscored enough. Take for instance the epigraph Coetzee chose for his Nobel Lecture, taken from *Robinson Crusoe*: '*But to return to my new companion. I was greatly delighted with him, and made it my business to teach him everything that was proper to make him useful, handy, and helpful; but especially to make him speak, and understand me when I spoke; and he was the aptest scholar there ever was*' (Coetzee 2003). What Coetzee does in *Foe*, then, is a total inversion. Instead of the fable of the European civilizing mission, still now sometimes invoked to claim the 'benefits' of colonialism, we have the brutal annihilation of any possibility for the 'native', Friday as his 'master' had named him so as to better objectify him, to speak, much less enter into any kind of dialogue. Thus, when Coetzee gives us a 'Friday' whose tongue has been cut, and who thus has been deprived of a voice, he fully exposes the inhuman cruelty at the base of any such consolatory myths of civilization. Coetzee's Friday is utterly silent and yet his silence is most eloquent at the novel's very conclusion when Friday has descended to the depth of a subgerged wreck: 'His mouth opens. From inside him comes a slow stream, without breath, without interruption. It flows up through his body and out upon me ... Soft and cold, dark and unending, it beats against my eyelids, against the skin of my face' (Coetzee 1986: 157).

The conclusion to Cardoso's *The Return* has an equally powerful allegory for a conclusion, though it is rather different. Instead of showing us a stream of blood issuing from the drowned man, covering the narrator's face and spreading 'northward and southward to the ends of the earth' (Coetzee 1986: 157), Cardoso presents us with the image of Rui, the narrator, looking upwards to the sky, watching a seemingly silent jet go by and affirming his existence as well as his will to continue resisting, by stressing that even though he is still on the move, he was there; which in the 10th anniversary hardback Portuguese edition is underscored as the last words, *Eu estive aqui* (I was here Cardoso 2016: 267; Cardoso 2021: 276); are printed twice, first appearing in typographical characters, and then as if handwritten. Besides the starkness of both images, there is one other point they have in common, and that I wish to stress – silence. Friday obviously could not speak even before drowning and the blood that emanates from his mouth underwater is a silent flow. But Rui too, even though he can speak, watches the jet in silence, imagining what he might have said, what he might still come to say to God, so as to affirm himself in spite of all the violent transitoriness he has experienced in his brief life. The silence of both stands at once for the voicelessness of those whom colonialism has annihilated, and I would suggest, is most eloquent in giving them a voice, a form of witnessing even beyond death, or beyond the violence of uprooting and exile.

***

Both Coetzee's and Cardoso's novels are haunted and haunting narratives. In both, the ghosts, though different, have one common denominator: colonial violence. Both narratives also, in their different mode, serve both as a damning witness and as a forceful answer to those ghosts of the past. As Faulkner so poignantly said in *Requiem for a Nun*, 'The past is never dead. It's not even past' (Faulkner 1950: 85). In her most recent novel, *Eliete*, Dulce Maria Cardoso still takes up Portugal's troubled colonial past as that past is still very evident in all sorts of ways. But she also reflects extensively on how, paired with colonialism and the violence inflicted in the colonies to the populations which were only euphemistically and very partially considered 'Portuguese' in spite of all the regime's rhetoric of the multiplicity of nations that made Portugal, fascism still casts a long shadow over the lives of the Portuguese, even if soon the commemorations of fifty years of democracy will be celebrated in April 2024. As the narrator, Eliete herself, thinks as an unvoiced answer to the provocation Duarte throws at her before leaving the house to imagine that the dictator, Salazar, was her grandfather: *Sim, o Salazar é o meu avô e o Eder é o jardineiro lá de casa* (Yes, Salazar is my grandfather and Eder is the house gardener) (Cardoso 2018: 244). Referring to Eder, the Black footballer who would score the decisive goal for Portugal at a European championship, as the house gardener, which is how Eliete's demented grandmother 'recognised him' when she watched him on television, is but one of many biting ironic remarks as Cardoso thus exposes how many Portuguese – and not just of an older generation – think about the multi-ethnic polity Portugal has become.

*Eliete* deploys both memory as well as postmemory in order to continue witnessing and exposing the systemic violence at the base of contemporary Portuguese society. The grandmother's fading memory will not disappear as Eliete survives to carry it forward even though, of course, capable of reflecting on it very differently. As one of the neurologists examining the grandmother observes: *Somos a nossa memória … e quando lhe perdemos o acesso, mergulhamos num vazio inimaginável, … podemos dizer sem exagero que se assiste à construção do nada* (We are our memory … and when we lose access to it, we dive into an unimaginable void, … we can say without exaggeration, that we watch the construction of nothingness) (Cardoso 2018: 244–5). At the same time, *Eliete* makes us contemplate the void that our lives have become in great part, in our ultra-individualistic society dominated by the constant interaction via a multiplicity of screens and other specular forms such as social media, which constitute yet another form of haunting. As I have had occasion to remark previously, 'the first literal mention of ghosts occurs late in the narrative and refers not to those ghosts of the past I have just mentioned but rather to the ghosts of the present, the virtual lives the family has come to embrace:

> Quando estávamos juntos, passara a ser habitual que as miúdas e o Jorge consultassem o telemóvel, a Internet, o Facebook, o Instagram, que trocassem mensagens enquanto eu estava a falar com eles … Acabei por me calar, e a nossa vivência familiar passou a incluir os fantasmas a que cada um deles tinha acesso e com quem muitas vezes pareciam dar-se melhor ou entreter-se melhor do que comigo.
>
> (When we were together it started being usual that the girls and Jorge would consult their smart phones, the Internet, Facebook, Instagram, that they

would exchange messages while I was talking with them ... I ended up holding my tongue, and our family life started to include the ghosts each one of them had access to and with whom often it seemed they could get along better, or entertain themselves better, than with me.)'

(Cardoso 2018: 171, cited in Medeiros 2020: 9)

The novel's conclusion, as stark as that of *The Return*, is a simple, but stunning sentence: Não te vais apagar agora, pois não, Eliete? (You are not going to extinguish yourself now, are you Eliete?) (Cardoso 2018: 285) that comes right after the transcription of an (imaginary) letter by Salazar to a 'beloved son', Eliete finds hidden inside the base of a statue of the Sacred Heart that belonged to her grandmother. Eliete is, like Rui, or Violeta, and other characters in Cardoso's novels, a figure of resistance. Eliete even adapts herself so as to turn the same social media that was the visible instrument of how her family life and her identity had been plunged into a void, into a tool to fight back and regain a sense of who she was. But that letter makes inescapably clear how, all the Portuguese, in their daily, mundane, banality, are still in the grip of the haunting inheritance of the fascist past. That sentence is similar to Rui's imagined declaration of his own presence in the world in as much as it does represent a sign of resistance against all odds. But it has now become a question, a plea even, to avoid erasure and in that it can be said to have become an even starker call to our attention not to let that happen. The violence of fascism and colonialism might be ever more remote as *Eliete* shows, yet its grip is getting stronger and can perhaps only be countered by the renewed call for witnessing, for keeping memory present. It is significant that the title given to this, the first part of an announced trilogy is precisely, 'normal life', as it is the normalization of violence and cruelty that makes our time, in its very banality, so dangerous. The Hypercontemporary is the timespace of a haunted modernity.

# References

Antunes, A. L. (1979a), *Memória de Elefante* [(Elephant's Memory), Lisbon: Vega.
Antunes, A. L. (1979b; 1988), *Os Cus de Judas*, Lisbon: Vega; Dom Quixote.
Antunes, A. L. (2011), *The Land at the End of the World*, London, New York: W. W. Norton & Co.
Arendt, H. (1969), *On Violence*, Sand Diego, New York, London: Harcourt Brace Jovanovich.

Brown, Wendy (2019), *In the Ruins of Neoliberalism: The Rise of Antidemocratic Politics in the West*, New York: Columbia University Press.
Cardoso, D. M. (2002), *Campo de Sangue* [(Field of Blood), Lisbon: ASA.
Cardoso, D. M. (2005), *Os Meus Sentimentos*, Lisbon: ASA.
Cardoso, D. M. (2009), *O Chão dos Pardais* (The Sparrow's Ground), Lisbon: ASA.
Cardoso, D. M. (2011; 2021), *O Retorno*, Lisbon: Tinta-da-china.
Cardoso, D. M. (2016), *The Return*, London: MacLehose Press.
Cardoso, D. M. (2018), *Eliete, A Vida Normal* (Eliete or Normal Life), Lisbon: Tinta-da-china.
Cardoso, D. M. (2021), *Violet Among the Stars*, London: MacLehose Press.
Coetzee, J. M. (1986: 2010), *Foe*, London: Penguin.
Coetzee, J. M. (1999), *Disgrace*, London: Secker & Warburg.
Coetzee, J. M. (2003), 'His Man', Nobel Lecture. Available online: https://www.nobelprize.org/prizes/literature/2003/coetzee/lecture/.
Débord, G. (1967), *La société du spectacle*, Paris: Buhet – Chastel.
Defoe, D. ([1719] 2007), *Robinson Crusoe*, Oxford: Oxford University Press.
Derrida, J. (1984), *Specters of Marx: The State of the Debt, the Work of Mourning and the New International*, London: Routledge.
Faulkner, W. ([1950] 2015), *Requiem for a Nun*, London: Vintage.
Figueiredo, I. (2010), *Caderno de Memórias Coloniais*.
Figueiredo, I. (2015), *Notebook of Colonial Memories*, Dartmouth, Mass.: University of Massachusetts Dartmouth.
Jorge, L. (1988), *A Costa dos Murmúrios*, Lisboa: Dom Quixote.
Jorge, L. (1995), *The Murmuring Coast*, Minneapolis: University of Minnesota Press.
Medeiros, P. de (2020) 'Caring for the Sacred Heart: Eliete, memory, and (im)possible returns, or a politics of banality', *Portuguese Studies* 36 (1): 32–48.
Mendes, A. C. (2017) 'Remembering and fictionalizing inhospitable Europe: The experience of Portuguese retornados in Dulce Maria Cardoso's *The Return* and Isabela Figueiredo's *Notebook of Colonial Memories*', *Journal of Postcolonial Writing* 53 (6): 729–42.

# Index

absence 20, 25, 30, 34, 59, 67, 73, 91, 102, 149
abstract art 52
abulia 73
abuse 163
acceleration 31, 33–4, 90
Adolfo, Ricardo *Depois de morrer aconteceram-me muitas coisas* 57–70
adoptive witness 102, 110
Africa and African 60, 101–7, 133, 143–4, 146, 158, 166–7
Agamben, Giorgio 1–2, 5, 87–9, 91, 93, 98
Alighieri, Dante *The Divine Comedy* 37, 75–6
allegorical 20, 81, 161
allegory 131, 169
alternate worlds 43, 55
Amaral, Ana Luísa 90, 98
anagnorisis 77
anamorphosis 23–5, 34
Andrade, Cláudia 3–4, 71–83
André, Marie-Odille 57
Angola 48, 103, 142, 144, 148, 158
anti-hero 11, 73
archaic 2
Arena, Joaquim 102
Arendt, Hannah *On Violence* 157–8, 171
Aristophanes *The Frogs* 75
armed conflict 101, 103
Arnaut, Ana Paula 26, 38, 43–4, 48, 50, 55, 74, 83, 91, 96, 98, 130, 138, 144–5, 154
Augé, Marc 64–6, 68, 70
autobiographical pact 115, 117
autobiography 23, 115, 117–19
autofiction 116–25, 132

Badiou, Alain 1, 5
Bal, Mieke 128
Barrento, João 33, 38, 74, 83

Baudelaire, Charles *The Painter of Modern Life* 90–9, 98
Bauman, Zygmunt 66–7, 70, 98, 118, 125; *Liquid Modernity* 66
Bértholo, Joana 2, 5, 9–22
betrayal 146, 150, 153, 161
blood 95, 97, 110, 167, 169
book 10–21, 30, 32, 35, 38, 41–2, 44, 48, 50
Booth, Wayne 127–30, 136, 138
borders 3, 58, 65, 69, 109, 124, 130, 144
Botelho, Abel 4, 96, 98
boundaries 9, 10, 34, 68, 97
Boym, Svetlana 34, 38
Brady, Mathew B. 48, 53
Britain 59
Broch, Hermann, *The Death of Virgil* 37
Brown, Wend 159, 172
Bulgakow, Mikhail *The Master and Margarita* 75

Calvino, Italo, *Il castelo dei destini incrociati* 45
Campos, Álvaro de 26
Cancela, Helder Gomes 94–8
capitalist 33, 38, 145–8, 152–5, 161, 165
Cardoso, Dulce Maria 2–4, 43, 102, 157–172
Carmelo, Luís 3–5, 41–55, 144
Carvalho, Ana Margarida de 3, 96–8
Carvalho, Mário de 87
castaways 97
cathartic
  descent 76
  function 102–3
  process 77
  situation 110
centre 58, 60, 62, 69, 119, 147, 167
change 2, 17, 31, 34, 38, 41, 45, 48, 67, 74, 80, 82, 92, 106, 117, 123, 128, 130–31, 133, 135, 137, 147–50, 157, 162, 171

chaos 36, 95, 133, 138
Chatman, Seymor 128, 138–9.
Chul-Han, Byung
  *The Expulsion of the Other* 123
cinema and cinematograph 53
Cláudio, Mário 2–3, 23–39, 118
Coetzee, J. M., *Foe* 4, 158, 168–9, 172
colonial
  debacle 103
  memory 101–3, 105, 109
  past 110
  system 105
  trauma 105
  war 101–3, 106–13
colonialism 102, 104, 112–13, 141, 143, 152, 168–9, 171
Colonna, Vincent *L'autofiction* 119, 125
concealment 25
constellation 26, 37, 123
contemporaneity 88–9, 91, 94, 124, 145
contemporary 1–2, 5, 21, 33–4, 37–8, 57–8, 63–4, 66, 74, 87–91, 93–4, 98, 101–2, 110, 129, 133, 139, 142, 146, 148, 162–3, 167, 170
Cortázar, Julio *Rayuela*,51
cosmic imagery 23, 35
cosmopolitanism 57, 149–50, 153
COVID-19 115, 142
creative euphoria 77
crisis 31, 33, 39, 58, 115, 131, 148, 163
cruelty 97, 159, 164–5, 168, 171
cybercapitalism 34

Dante *The Divine Comedy* 37, 75–6
dark and war tourism 60–1, 64
darkness 1–2, 37, 88–9, 91–3
death 24, 27, 29–30, 35, 37, 54, 63, 66, 71–3, 75, 77–8, 81, 83, 90, 121, 131, 134, 150–2, 162–3, 165, 170
decadence 54, 132
decaying 33
deception 42
decolonization 101, 160, 166
deconstructing 118
Deconstruction 4, 38, 131
defamiliarization 138
dehumanization 131, 160, 162, 164
DeLillo, Don *Point Omega* 53
democratic transition 33

denarration,134
Derrida, Jacques *Specters of Marx* 157–8, 165, 167, 172
deterritorialization 131
digital viii, 11, 17–19, 32, 117
disconnected images 31
discontinuity 89
disorientation 44, 150
distance 62, 77, 88–90, 93, 95, 104, 108, 110, 123–4, 135, 145–6, 149–50, 167
Doubrowsky, Serge *Fils* 117–18
dyssynchrony 88
dystopia 57–61, 69

Eaglestone, Robert *Routledge Companion to Twenty-First Century Literary Fiction* 93–4, 98
elsewhere 3, 57–69
empire 103, 117–18, 141, 143, 161, 166–7
entropy 43, 54, 92, 96
epistemological urgency 96
*Estado Novo* 102–03
Ételain, Jeanne 63
Europe 64, 68, 70, 102, 104, 112, 132, 141, 144, 145–8, 152–3, 157–8, 160–1, 165–6, 168, 170, 172
European Union 33
expansion 52, 58
experience, ownership of 102, 104–08, 110
experimental 12–13, 55, 162

fado music 53
fake news 131
Faria, Paulo 3, 101–13
fascist 161, 165–7, 171
Faulkner, William *Requiem for a Nun* 169
fictional autobiography 23, 115
Figueiredo, Isabela 102, 171
foreigners 58, 60–61, 64, 68, 76
fractures 131
fragmentation 4, 38, 48, 117
Friedman, Norman 128

game 11–12, 14, 16–17, 25, 44, 52, 54–5, 73, 116, 161
generational trauma 102
Genette, Gérard 128–30, 138

genre subversion 43
geography 3, 63, 65, 69
ghosts 78, 169–71
Gilliam, Terry 82
global reader 57
globalized world 2–3, 58, 60, 92
globalization 33–4, 43, 69, 131, 144, 146
Great War 101
Greek mythology 11, 75, 78
Gusdorf, Georges 117

haunted modernity 171
haunting 149, 157–9, 165, 169–170
hermaphrodite 50
Hirsch, Marianne 28, 30, 39, 103–05, 110, 113
historicity 37–9, 153
historiography 124
Homer
    *The Odyssey* 75
*homo fictus* 120
Horace 82
horror 101, 112, 131, 146, 152
Hugo, Victor *The Last Day of a Condemned Man* 75
human bestialization 97
humour 82–3
Huyssen, Andreas 33–4, 39
hybrid dimension 9
hybrid narrative 3, 10, 12, 14, 22, 50
hyperconsumption 61
hyperfictional hypothesis 9–22

identity 3, 11, 14, 58, 64–9, 74, 90, 95, 115–118, 121–5, 131, 143, 148, 171
identity erasing 131
illegal immigration 58, 61, 66–7
image 5, 17, 20, 23–4, 27, 29–31, 34–5, 48, 51, 53, 58, 60–4, 68, 75–6, 78–9, 101, 105–6, 108–9, 113, 116–18, 120–2, 134, 138, 149, 150, 160–61, 169
imagology 58
imperial 144, 147, 162, 166, 168
incommunicability 58, 66
inconsistency 13, 88
insubordination of art 47
intercultural 58

intermedial 2–3, 5, 7, 9–10, 13, 23, 26, 29–30, 34, 39, 50, 52, 55, 144
interstitial space 102, 111
intertextuality 2–3, 7, 23, 26, 29–30, 39, 42–3, 52, 72, 74, 112, 135
irony 38, 58, 72, 77, 82
Iser, Wolfgang 46, 55
Ivo Cruz, Mafalda 3–4, 127–139

Jorge, Lídia *A Costa dos Murmúrios* 2, 89, 167, 172
Judaeo-Christian tradition 75

Kieslowski, Krzysztof *Blue* 53
Knausgård, Karl Ove 111

labyrinths 37, 41, 43–4, 47, 53, 66, 80–1
Lejeune, Philippe *Le Pacte Autobiographique* 117–18, 126
Lipovetsky, Gilles 61, 70, 90, 98
literary translation 111–12, 163
Lobo Antunes, António, 2, 103–04, 107, 110, 129, 144, 167; *Os Cus de Judas*, 103, 113, 167
Loss 11, 31, 35, 42, 45, 143, 148
Lubbock, Pierce 128

machine simulation 18, 32
Mãe, Valter Hugo 3, 96, 115, 118–20, 123, 125–26, 144
Manguel, Alberto 51
Mann, Thomas *Death in Venice*, 75
Marceneiro, Alfredo 153
marginal condition 60
Martens, David 25, 39
mass tourism 58
materiality 5, 14, 18, 145
mediated testimony 104, 106
melancholy 77
mémoire de l'écriture 135
memory
    borrowed 102
    childhood 115–17, 120–3, 131, 134, 137, 150, 153
    familiar 7, 104–5, 137
    sites 101
metafictional 4, 11–12, 16, 21, 52
metamedial 9–10, 19
metamorphic novel 41–2, 50

Michel, Frank *Désirs d'ailleurs* 68, 70
migration 4, 58–59, 62, 65, 141, 146, 148, 150, 153–4, 160
modern 1–4, 11, 31–6, 38, 118, 128, 139, 146, 168
Modernism 38, 117
modernity 4, 36, 39, 64, 66, 90–1, 141, 149, 153, 171
moral collapse 103
Moura, Jean-Marc 58–9, 61–2, 70
Mozambique 101–2, 104
multimodal 9, 12, 19–21, 37, 94
multisemiotic texts 19
mutation 45, 106, 109

narrative 3–4, 9–25, 27–30, 39, 41–5, 49–56, 72, 74–5. 81–2, 84, 91, 94–5, 105–07, 109–12, 115–17, 119–25, 127–39, 141–6, 149–51, 155, 158, 162–70
   archaeology 131
   non-linear 133
   sedimentation 41
   typology 127
neoliberal 165, 172
neonaturalist 95–6
Nietzsche, Friedrich 41, 45–6, 88, 159; *Untimely Meditations* 88
nihilism 159
non-mimetic 129
non-place 63–70, 89
nostalgia 2, 23, 27, 30, 34, 38, 82, 143
novel of objects 11, 20

O'Gorman, Daniel *Routledge Companion to Twenty-First Century Literary Fiction* 93–8
obsession 34, 77, 159–160
onomastics 59
ontological 36, 77, 138
otherness 3, 58–9, 65, 69

page as surface 9, 18, 21
paradigm 2, 4, 10–11, 20, 95, 103, 107, 118, 145, 149
paratextual 14–17, 116
Patinir, Joachim *Charon Crossing the Styx* 72
patriarchal 160, 165, 168

*pentirsi* 135
Perec, George *La Vie, mode d'emploi* 42
Pereira de Almeida, Djaimilia 4, 102, 141–54
performative 10, 21
periphery 58, 60, 62
Perrault, Charles *Little Thumbling* 28
perspective 29, 34, 39, 42, 52, 58–62, 68–9, 82, 96, 101, 120, 123–4, 127, 132–33, 137–9, 147, 153, 160, 164, 167
Pessoa, Fernando 1, 39, 61, 87–8, 96–9
petty bourgeoisie 161
Phelan, James 128, 135–7, 139
photographs 19, 29, 105, 118
photography 39, 53, 141
pictographic elements 9, 19
Pindar 75
Pirandello, Luigi *Sei personaggi in cerca d'autore* 49
Pires, José Cardoso *O Delfim* 43
Plato *The Banquet* 12; *The Republic* 75
platonic 13, 24, 35–7
Portela, Patrícia 2, 5, 9–22
Portugal 23, 26, 33, 43, 50–1, 58, 64, 65, 67–9, 96, 103, 106, 110, 122, 132, 146–8, 154–5, 157–8, 160, 165–7, 169–70
post-colonial 33, 102–103, 143, 154
postcolonial 104, 148, 168, 172
post-digital 19
post-imperial 33, 146, 160, 167–8
post-post-modern 2
postmemorial literature 3
postmemory 30, 39, 101–13
postmodern, postodernist 37–8, 43–4, 48–50, 55, 89, 125, 138, 158–9, 161
postmodernism 37–8, 43, 56, 89, 96
precariousness 3, 32, 35, 58–9
prefixes 89–90
prejudices 59, 69
presence 10, 19, 25, 30, 34, 50, 62, 82, 104, 106, 111–12, 149, 157, 171
Prince, Gerald 128, 130, 139
private archives 105
pseudonym 25, 39
purification 105
Pythagorean 24, 35–6

Queirós, Eça de 124, 126
Queneau, Raymond, *Exercises de style* 45

Ramalho, Maria Irene 26
reading as archaeology 44
Real, Miguel 57–8, 96
realism 3, 37–8, 84, 92, 163
realist aesthetics 124
recursive memories 44–50
recycled paper 18
reflection 5, 10, 12–13, 21, 23–4, 27–8, 32, 34, 57–8, 63, 69, 73, 78, 103, 118–19, 121, 167
repetition 18, 48–9, 53, 133–6
resistance 2–3, 34, 71, 80, 92, 171
revelation 25, 32, 79, 120
revolution of 25 April 1974 (Carnation Revolution) 122, 158, 160, 166
rhizomatic 43–5
Ribeiro, Margarida Calafate 102–103, 141, 154; and Ribeiro, António 104–5, 110–13
Richardson, Brian 128–30, 134, 136, 138–9
Riço Direitinho, José 96, 98
Ricoeur, Paul 128, 133, 136, 138–9
Rifaterre, Michel 74, 84
*roman à clef* 120
Romanticism 38, 92, 117
Rosa, Guimarães *The Third Bank of the River* 75
ruinophilia 23
ruins 25, 27, 30, 34, 60, 172

Sadokierski, Zoë 19, 22
Samosata, Luciano de 75
Saramago, José 2; *The Year of the Death of Ricardo Reis* 90, 99; *Blindness* 96; *Diálogos com José Saramago* 119, 126
Sarlo, Beatriz 112–13
Savater, Fernando *Charon Is Waiting* 75
Schoenberg, Arnold *Verklärte Nacht* 53
secrets 118, 120
self-projection 25
self-reflexivity 5, 7, 9, 12, 45–50
semi-peripheral 4, 141, 146–8, 152–4

semiotic channels 53
Sena, Jorge de 89, 99
shipwreck 72, 83, 97, 168
silence 72, 77, 80, 102, 112, 128, 168–9
simulacra 165
slave 97, 133; slavery 146; slave ship, 97; enslaved 147, 152
social media 19, 170–1
Sollers, Philippe 74, 84
'sons of the war' 105
Spitzer, Leo 30, 39
*Stella Matutina* 27
Stephan, Matthias 43, 56
stereotypes 58–69
structure of enunciation 23–4
suicide 68, 72–3
survival 1, 22, 49, 160–2
symbolic heir 105
systemic oppression 164

Tavares, Gonçalo M. 84, 96
taxonomy 89
Taylor-Collins, Nicholas, *Reading Hypercontemporary Literature and the Book Prize Shortlists* 92–3, 99
Taylor, Charles 36
technology 4, 22, 32, 41, 43, 141–55
tedium 73
telepresent 69
terrorism 58
testimonial work 102–5
theory of literature 127, 129, 130
thought maze 10
time 1–5, 14, 24–7, 30–4, 36–7, 42–3, 45, 49, 51–2, 54–5, 58, 62–4, 66–7, 71–3, 75, 77, 80–2, 87–91, 94, 96–8, 104, 106, 115, 117–18, 120, 124, 133, 139, 146–7, 149–53, 167–8, 171; time-space 4–5, 14, 24, 33–34, 136–7, 145
tolerance 58
Tolstoy, Leo *The Death of Ivan Ilyich* 75
totalizing present 32
tour guide 76
tragedy 146–8, 161
traumatic 29, 101–4, 110, 112, 165–7

travel backwards 71
truth 82, 84, 90, 93, 95, 110, 115–19, 123–5, 134
typography 9–10, 12, 19–20

unreliable narrator 128, 136
utopia 60–3, 65, 69, 146, 153

videogame language 11, 14
Vieira Amaral, Bruno 102
Vieira Júnior, Itamar 96
violence 2–4, 48, 60, 68, 92, 94–8, 103, 106–11, 122, 131–32, 149, 157–71
Virgil, *Aeneid* 73, 75
Virilio, Paul 69–70

visual 9–10, 13–14, 18–21
Voltaire 82

war 3, 18, 60–1, 63, 68, 94, 101–13, 117, 132, 142–4, 151–3, 157–8, 167; war tourism 61
witnessing 110, 166, 169–71
Woolf, Virginia, *The Voyage Out* 75
working class 59, 161
World War 117
world-system 33, 141, 144–7, 153, 161

Zink, Rui 3, 58; *O Destino Turístico* 57, 60–5, 69–70; *Depois de morreraconteceram-me muitas coisas* 57
zone 61–70, 160

www.ingramcontent.com/pod-product-compliance
Lightning Source LLC
Chambersburg PA
CBHW050327020526
44117CB00031B/1996